# Arise

## MY LOVE

"ARISE! SHINE! FOR THE GLORY OF
THE LORD IS UPON YOU."
ISAIAH 60:1

365 DAILY DEVOTIONS

CHRISTY SAWYER

*Presented To:*

---

*From:*

---

*Date:*

---

# ACKNOWLEDGMENTS

To my family – thank you for pushing me to finish this project, and ignoring me every time I said, "Why in the world didn't I just write 52 weeks worth instead of 365 days???"

To "The Mighty Five" the best ministry team anywhere on the planet – thank you for always holding up my arms when they get weak.

To my River Dwellers family – thank you for loving me, but mostly thank you for putting your faith to action! You are His arms and legs and feet!

To Jonathan – thank you for reading every single word of this and correcting my errors. (You finally got your chance!)

# FOREWORD

*I*t has been amazing to see the rise of the effectiveness of Christy Sawyer's ministry, evidenced by packed-out Bible studies she has taught and sold-out retreats she has led. And now God is using her through the printed page with this helpful and anointed book, "Arise, My Love." These devotionals you hold in your hand will become indelibly imprinted in your very soul in these pressure-driven days, in which we all eagerly seek spiritual sanctuary for our souls. Christy – wife, mother and fabulous lover of Christ and His Church – is terrifically anointed in making the Word come alive and vitally relevant in everyday life. I believe this book will quickly become one of the most cherished ones you have, and that you will read it over and over and even secure more copies to give to and bless your friends. I write this as Christy's pastor and friend – and fan!

Dan Betzer
Senior Pastor
First Assembly of God
Fort Myers, Florida

# INTRODUCTION

## ARE YOU READY TO ARISE AND SHINE?

*I* am so excited to be sharing this moment in time with you, and I do not believe it is by accident that you are holding this book in your hand. Even though there is a beautiful girl on the front cover (my beautiful daughter, Jenna), this book is intended for both men and women. Whether you purchased *Arise, My Love* or it was given to you, I believe that the words in this book are for you.

I want you to know that I have been praying for you from the moment I began this project. I've prayed that your life will be changed by the words inside these pages. I've prayed that you will be encouraged and challenged. But more than anything, I've prayed (and believe) that these simple, little devotions will bring you closer to the Lover of your soul, Jesus Christ.

May you arise and shine this year!

All my love,


Christy

# Get Ready

*"Twenty years from now you will be more disappointed*
*by the things that you didn't do than by the ones you did do."*
*– Mark Twain*

*Then Joshua issued instructions to the leaders of Israel to tell the people*
*to "get ready" to cross the Jordan River. (paraphrased - Joshua 1)*

I believe with this new year, God is about to take you across a threshold into something new.

With Joshua and all through Scripture, God gives His people a promise. Then He gives them the opportunity to choose whether or not they are going to walk *into* that promise or not. Growing up, I was a fairly well behaved child. Although there were moments where my will got me into some trouble. My dad would give me *choices* like, "If you don't ____, then you can't ____." I missed out on some opportunities to say the least. My father had a plan for me. But my behavior and my will kept me out of the plan that my father had for me. I made a choice to not go where my father had prepared for me to go, because I wanted to do what I wanted to do, not what he wanted me to do. Now that didn't stop me from being my father's daughter. It didn't change my father's feelings for me. It just changed the plan that my father had for me.

Beginning this New Year, your Father has a great plan for you. If you will grab hold of it and agree, "I'm ready to go all in, holding nothing back" doors will open for you this year that you never thought possible. Obedience always equals blessing. Obedience always equals breakthrough. God says, "I led you here and I have bigger plans for you than you could ever hope, think, or imagine."

Get ready!

# Get Up!

*"God is looking for people to use, and if you can get usable,*
*He will wear you out. The most dangerous prayer you*
*can pray is this: 'Use me.'" – Rick Warren*

*Then I heard the voice of the Lord saying, "Whom shall I send? And*
*who will go for us?" And I said, "Here am I. Send me!" (Isaiah 6:8)*

*I* have had bouts of depression throughout my adult life. Things can get very dark and seem very bleak. This is a place where the enemy loves to get us. When all we can see is ourselves and our circumstances, our outlook can get grim. This then leads to a cycle of self-pity, guilt, shame, and hopelessness.

I learned, a long time ago, that one of the best ways to combat this darkness, was to get to work for the Lord. I became desperate and cried out to Him for help. I thought He would baby me and say, "Poor thing. Bless your little heart." But instead, He said, "Get out of bed. Get dressed. Brush your teeth. And go feed My sheep."

It's really hard to feel sorry for yourself when you're serving someone else. Where are you today? Are you in the light or are you fighting some shadows? Trust me on this: "Come out of darkness and into His marvelous light!" Get out of bed. Get dressed. Brush your teeth. And go feed His sheep.

## JANUARY 3

# Here I Am Lord!

*"Use me, God. Show me how to take who I am, who I want to be,*
*and what I can do, and use it for a purpose greater than myself."*
*— Martin Luther King Jr.*

*...Who has saved us and called us to be a holy calling, not because*
*of our works but because of His own purpose and grace, which He*
*gave us in Christ Jesus before the ages began... (2 Timothy 1:9)*

*I*n this world, we are all about self-promotion. And with the ease of promoting ourselves on social media, it can sometimes become a full-time job.

My youngest daughter Jenna played volleyball all through middle school and high school. She would get frustrated sometimes because she wouldn't get the playing time that other girls did. My advice to her was, "just always be *available*." So many want the spotlight, and if they don't get it, they just quit or move on to another "spotlight" opportunity. Jenna found that because she made herself available, she eventually got to play.

God isn't looking for ability. He's looking for availability. We don't have to work hard to be noticed. When He calls us, He promotes us. We don't have to knock down doors. He opens them for us.

Just say to Him today, "Here I am Lord. Use me. I may not be the smartest, the fastest, the most talented, the most eloquent, or the most attractive. But I'm available, Lord. Use me for Your glory." Then, be ready to be used!

))

# He's Wild

*"There is something else I am after, out here in the wild.*
*I am searching for an even more elusive prey…something*
*that can only be found through the help of wilderness. I am*
*looking for my heart." – John Eldredge (Wild At Heart)*

*Deep calls to deep in the roar of your waterfalls; all your*
*waves and breakers have swept over me. (Psalm 42:7)*

*I*'m a waterfall chaser, and I've learned that the same power and might that draws me to waterfalls, also draws me to Jesus.

Growing up, my perception of Jesus was that of a wimp: quiet, mild-mannered, with hands folded. This image contradicted what I read in Scripture. I mean, how is this guy going to save the world? Jesus is anything but a wimp. He's dangerous. He's wild. He will stop at *nothing* to get to us. There's something deep within me that runs after *that* Jesus.

The "Sunday School" Jesus just won't do. Deep in my bones there is agony. I ache and I thirst for this Man who is so wild and so dangerous that He fought the world and won…for me…and for you.

☙

# It's Gotta Go!

*The secret of spiritual success is a hunger that persists…*
*It is an awful condition to be satisfied with one's spiritual attainments…*
*God was and is looking for hungry, thirsty people. – Smith Wigglesworth*

*And Peter remembered the word of Jesus who had said to him,*
*"Before the rooster crows, you will deny Me three times."*
*So he went out and wept bitterly. (Matthew 26:75)*

My family and I went on a hike recently. I've hiked my entire adult life and I love it! When I take people, I always advise them to take everything out of their backpack that is NOT absolutely necessary. Otherwise, the hike is miserable. The question is always, "Is it beneficial?" If so, great! If not, it's gotta go!

What if we looked within ourselves and said, "Everything must go that is no longer beneficial or profitable"? What if you looked at your bitterness and said, "Bitterness, you have to go because you're taking up space where my peace could be?" Or, what if you looked at your misery and said, "You have to go because you're taking up space where my purpose could be." Or, what if you looked at your depression and said, "You have to go because you're taking up space where my joy should be"?

Peter had to get rid of his fear and his denial so that he could make space to become the rock upon which Christ would build His church on.

What has to go in your life? Where do you need to make some space?

Father, remove from us anything that is not beneficial. Help us to make space for the things that are.

# A Sure Thing

*"Fasting helps express, deepens, confirms the resolution*
*that we are ready to sacrifice anything, even ourselves,*
*to attain what we seek for the kingdom of God."*
*— Andrew Murray*

*So I turned to the Lord God and pleaded with*
*Him in prayer and fasting. (Daniel 9:3)*

*D*aniel was in a mess. His people refused to obey God and now curses and judgments were pouring down on them because of their sin. Daniel was out of options. He was pleading to the Lord on their behalf. There was nothing in his human strength that would move this mountain that he and his people faced. Daniel was desperate. Are there mountains in your life that just won't budge? You've tried everything and nothing seems to change. Maybe the mountain is there of your own doing. Maybe you are living with the consequences of a decision or choice you made long ago. Maybe you have a child who's lost or going in the wrong direction. Maybe you are in a marriage where you can't even find a tiny spark of hope left. Maybe there's a habit that you've tried to kick over and over, but it keeps calling your name and you can't seem to break the cycle. Maybe God has been calling you higher. You know He has an assignment for you, but you can't seem to figure out the next move. Daniel was desperate, so he humbled himself and turned to the Lord God with prayer and fasting. Fasting is a sure way of humbling yourself.

Are you desperate today? May I suggest that you humble yourself, push the plate away and call on the Lord your God?

# Just Getting Started

*"Our quitting point is God's beginning point."*
*– Woodrow Kroll*

*And the One seated on the throne said, "Behold, I make*
*all things new." Then He said, "Write this down, for these*
*words are faithful and true." (Revelation 21:5)*

*I* love that this is the last chapter, of the last book, of the Bible. Everything that has happened so far has been amazing and awesome. And then God says, "But I'm going to do something brand new!" God loves new. It's the theme of the very first miracle that Jesus performs. Jesus turns water into wine. But not just any water. He tells the servants to take some water out of the pots and take it to the governor of the feast. Jesus could have snapped his fingers and everyone would have a glass of wine in their hands. But He doesn't do that. He takes the old water pitchers containing the dirty water used to wash off the guests' feet, and says, "Take some of *that* water…the nasty, unusable, gross water…that nobody would ever think of using…take it through the judgment process, through the governor of the feast, and I'll turn that old into something new." Jesus can take the grubby and unusable and make it new!

It doesn't matter how last year ended for you. It doesn't matter how your whole life-story reads. You may feel like you are in the last chapter, but God says, "Excellent! Even now and especially now, I make all things new! Write this down, for these words are faithful and true!"

## JANUARY 8

# Soar

*"You cannot fly like an eagle with the wings of a wren."*
*– William Henry Hudson*

*But those who wait on the Lord shall renew their strength;*
*they shall mount up with wings like eagles, they shall run*
*and not be weary, they shall walk and not faint.*
*(Isaiah 40:31)*

Eagles are born with big and heavy wings. Did you know that they are able to soar without actually flapping those wings? They have to learn how to do this in order to conserve energy. They will die if too much energy is spent flapping their wings during flight rather than soaring without flapping their wings. They have to learn to wait for wind thermals to come up on them. A wind thermal is a big gust of wind. Sometimes eagles will wait for a wind thermal for days. In Isaiah 40:31, God is comparing us to the eagle. Our wings represent our faith in God. The wind thermals represent the Holy Spirit. This thought brings another verse to mind: "Not by might, nor by power, but by My Spirit," says the Lord (Zechariah 4:6). God is telling us that things will only get accomplished by the power of the Holy Spirit, and not by our own power. Just like the eagle has to learn to soar without flapping its wings, we have to learn to fly on the Holy Spirit in our lives.

Are you flapping your wings when you should instead wait on the wind of the Holy Spirit? God made you to soar, not to flap!

# Sing A New Song!

*"It is never too late to be what you might have been."*
*– George Eliot*

*Sing a new song to the Lord! Let the whole*
*earth sing to the Lord! (Psalm 96:1)*

*D*o you ever get a song in your head and you can't stop humming it? Scripture says it's time to sing a new song. And my concern is that many of us coming into a new year are singing an old song. Fighting the same old battles. Dealing with the same old stuff. And doing it the same old way. God is calling you to do it a new way this year. Even small things can make big differences. What if you jumped in and started serving at your church? What if you "tested" God with tithing this year? I wonder, if you would resolve to just do the basic things for one year… get connected and stay connected to each other, give, serve, stay in the Word, how much better would you end this year than you did last year? What if you would quit trying to figure it all out yourself? What if you let a Holy God, the One Who knows you, the One Who created you, the One Who knows every intricate detail of your life have some input? I believe that God wants to do, and is doing, something amazing. Get that old tune out of your head! It's time to sing a new song!

Lord, we're tired of doing things our way. Put a new song in us today!

# If My People…

*"Let God have your life; He can do more with
it than you can." – Dwight L. Moody*

*If My people, who are called by My name, will humble
themselves and pray and seek My face and turn from their
wicked ways, then I will hear from heaven, and I will forgive
their sin and will heal their land. (2 Chronicles 7:14)*

"If My people will pray and seek My face…" We get the praying part. And through praying, we seek His face. But what about the "humbling ourselves" part? How do we do that? There was a man in the Old Testament named Ezra. He and his people had been exiled to Babylonia. When the exile was over, the king made a decree to send Ezra back to Jerusalem. This was good news except that Ezra was afraid to make this trip without government protection. He could have asked the king for protection, but he was ashamed to do that because he had boasted to the king, "The hand of our God is for good upon all that seek Him, and the power of His wrath is against all that forsake Him." After declaring that, how is he going to say, "…but just in case, could you send some bodyguards with me?" So, in the book of Ezra, he makes a decision. "There…I proclaimed a fast, so that we might humble ourselves before our God and ask Him for a safe journey for us and our children." Besides praying, Ezra knew they needed to humble themselves before God.

Do you need help today? Have you tried everything else? Try fasting with prayer. Fasting will bring you into a deeper and more powerful relationship with the Lord.

꩜

# The Hand Of The Lord

*"Wherever you are going, God has already been there
and paved the way for you." – Anonymous*

*The hand of the Lord came upon me and brought me
out in the Spirit of the Lord…(Ezekiel 37:1)*

*I*t's a powerful thing when the hand of the Lord comes upon you and
you get in sync with the Holy Spirit to do something. When the
hand of the Lord is upon you, you do what others cannot do. You will
be more effective than someone who tries to do it without the hand of
the Lord. The hand of the Lord provides protection. The hand of the
Lord will hold you up. When the hand of the Lord is upon you, no one
can take it off of you. The devil can't touch you. Jabez, another man in
scripture prayed the same prayer. He prayed, "Let Your hand be upon
me." Maybe like me, you have many prayer requests. You may have
need of many things in your life. But more important than praying for
things, your prayer needs to be, "Oh God, let Your hand be upon me!"

Friend, will you pray that today? Let's pray that the hand of the Lord
be upon us and that He would reveal to us what His hand is on us to do.

Lord, more than things, we pray that Your hand be upon us today.
We want to be effective in all that we do. Lead us, Holy Spirit.

JANUARY 12

# Dare To Believe

*"Create the highest, grandest vision possible for your life,
because you become what you believe." – Oprah Winfrey*

*"Blessed is she who believed, for there will be a fulfillment of
those things which were told her from the Lord." (Luke 1:45)*

*W*hat if we dared to believe God could do anything in, and through, us? God speaks promises to us all. What if we really believed? The Word says that if we dare to believe Him, we'll be blessed. Consider Mary, an ordinary young woman living a quiet little life in Nazareth. While going about her very average daily routine, suddenly, the angel Gabriel steps from Heaven right in front of her and says something outrageous. And then Mary does something equally outrageous. She believes! Simple? Not really. It may be simple to believe that God speaks promises, but believing God's promises are actually for *us* is sometimes the hardest part. Believing is daring to take your eyes off your circumstances and keeping them fixed on Jesus. What if we're making it all up? Our faith can feel like shaking legs and trembling voices. But if you dare to believe, scripture says you'll "be blessed among women." Has God spoken promises to your heart and perhaps you're wondering, "How in the world can it come to pass?" Your heart soaks in the promise but can't comprehend the "how." Maybe you are in an impossible situation. The verse says, "There WILL be a fulfillment of those things which were told her from the Lord." But, before that happens, you have to dare to believe.

Will you do that today, child of God? Will you dare to believe that He will do it?

## JANUARY 13

# Keep Going!

*"Courage is not having the strength to go on; it is going on when you don't have the strength." – Theodore Roosevelt*

*Whatever you ask in My name this I will do, that the Father may be glorified in the Son. If you ask Me anything in My name, I will do it. (John 14:13-14)*

*I*'ve been given the highest compliment of being an influencer. But let me tell you who has the most influence of all. The person who has the greatest hope has the greatest influence. Hope leaves the door open for God to fight for us in our circumstances. Without hope, your faith diminishes. Hope brings boldness and confidence in God. As you use this weapon called hope, it allows you to pray with faith and receive God's grace even when you make a mess. Hope empowers you to believe and pray into the deliverance of impossible situations.

Are you facing an impossible situation? Sometimes the mountain in front of you can paralyze you and you don't know which way to turn. But let me encourage you to keep moving. Just keep taking the next step. Keep your eyes fixed on the One Who will guide your next move, even when it feels like the eleventh hour! What do you need? Ask Him! Do you feel like you don't even have the strength to take the next step? He is your strength! Your weaknesses will be made strong in Him!

# There Is Hope

*"Our greatest weakness lies in giving up. The most certain
way to succeed is always to try just one more time."*
*– Thomas A. Edison*

*And you will feel secure, because there is hope; you will look
around and take your rest in security. You will lie down and
none will make you afraid; many will court your favor.*
*(Job 11:18-19)*

Isn't it so much easier to believe that God can do things in and
through other people? He wants you to know today, that He can do
anything in and through you! Even in the midst of your most baffling,
uncomfortable and unlikely situations. You are not reading this by
accident. God ordained this moment. He is calling you to rise and take
your rightful positions. God wants to birth supernatural things through
you. He wants you to believe his beautiful, staggering, and sometimes,
scandalous promises. Even when you feel you're at your worst. When
you choose to believe Him, He is honored. When you choose to hope
in Him, He is glorified. And then His promises begin to unfold.

What promises are you holding on to? What is the miracle that you
need today? What do you need that is so big that there's no way it can
be accomplished apart from Him? My friend, God loves impossible
situations!

Lord, we believe You! We are ready to rise and take our rightful
positions! We choose to place our hope in You today.

# His Hand

*"Start where you are. Use what you have. Do what you can." – Arthur Ashe*

*Now when they had gone through Phrygia and the region of Galatia, they were forbidden by the Holy Spirit to preach the word in Asia... (Acts 16:6)*

*I*n other words, God said, "I'm withdrawing My hand." Paul and Timothy wanted to preach the gospel in Asia. But God didn't want them to do that. I'm so glad that we not only have a God who opens doors, but we have a God who closes doors. Paul wanted to preach everywhere! But he was forbidden to go by the Holy Spirit. It's crucial to have the hand of the Lord on you, and it's just as important to understand that the hand of the Lord is on you to do a specific thing. If you get caught up in trying to do everything, it becomes a distraction from the thing that the hand of the Lord is upon you to do. And that will lead to frustration, lack of peace, competition, jealousy, and dissatisfaction. Beloved, God is a master orchestrator! He says, "If you do the thing that My hand is upon you to do, you will do it very well and it will prosper." If you try to do everything, you'll miss your one thing.

What is God's hand upon you to do? If you don't know, ask Him. If you do know, begin to say "no" to distractions and put your focus on the *one* thing.

God, remove any and all distractions from us today. Show us what Your hand is upon us to do.

## JANUARY 16

# I Can't Wait!

*"Do not be fooled by its commonplace appearance. Like so many things, it is not what's outside, but what's inside that counts." – Aladdin*

*Dear friends, we are God's children now, and what we will be has not yet been revealed. (1 John 3:2)*

The devil is not concerned with what you used to be. And he's not too bothered by what you are now. But he is terrorized by what you can be. He is not afraid of your yesterday, but he's scared to death of your tomorrow. He's terrified by what "has not yet been revealed." I love 1 John 3:2 because it tells us that our best is yet to come! Your biggest victories and your biggest miracles are *not* behind you! Maybe you feel as if your best is behind you. Or maybe you think you've went past your prime. Maybe you think you will coast for the rest of this journey. But I have news for you from the Lord! "Your eyes have not seen, and your ears have not heard, and your mind cannot take in what God has prepared for those who love Him" (1 Corinthians 2:9).

Do you love Him? Then that promise is for you! You have to keep going! Pray for a spirit of expectation! The best is still yet to come! You serve a God that is greater than your faith. You serve a God that is greater than your prayer life!

God, we enter in to this day with our hands wide open and standing on tiptoe!

# Speak To These Dry Bones!

*"It is not our part to master all the tides of the world, but
to do what is in us for the succor of those years wherein we
are set, uprooting the evil in the fields that we know, so that
those who live after may have clean earth to till."*
*– Gandalf (Return of the King)*

*He asked me, "Son of man, can these bones live?" Then He
said to me, "Prophesy to these bones and say to them, 'Dry
bones, hear the word of the Lord!'" (Ezekiel 37:3-4)*

I love the fact that God asked Ezekiel a question. He asked the prophet, "Can these bones live?" And Ezekiel gave Him a brilliant, political response, "Lord, only You know. I don't want to take a stand either way." Then the Lord said, "Prophesy! Speak to these bones! Ezekiel, speak! Because you serve the God of the impossible!" Nothing happens in the Spirit world until you open your mouth and you speak life. Speak life into your dreams. Speak life into your calling. Speak life into a God-encounter. Speak life into your children. Speak life into your children's future. Speak life into your marriage. Speak life into your body. Speak life into the low places. Speak life into the dry bones. You don't speak complaints. You don't speak disappointments. You speak life! And when you begin to speak life, then things begin to live because the power of life is in your tongue.

God is looking for life-speakers. Are you available to be a life-speaker? Are you willing to go into the impossible low places of people's lives and speak life? Are you willing to say, "In the name of Jesus, you are coming out of this valley of dry bones"?

꩜

## JANUARY 18

# God Likes Math Problems

*"We want to avoid suffering, death, sin, ashes. But we live in a world crushed and broken and torn, a world God Himself visited to redeem. We received His poured-out life and being allowed the high privilege of suffering with Him, may then pour ourselves out for others." – Elizabeth Elliot*

*"We have here only five loaves of bread and two fish,"*
*they answered. "Bring them here to me," He said.*
*(Matthew 14:17-18)*

God likes math. Let me show you. If you read about the very familiar story of Jesus feeding the five thousand (not including women and children), it says that Jesus *took* the loaves and the fishes. That means He subtracted from the boy who had them. Then He *blessed* the loaves and fish, He added His blessings to it. Then He *broke* the bread and the fish. That's called division. Then He *distributed* the bread and the fish. That's multiplication. So, He subtracted, He added, He divided, and He multiplied. And then, He had a remainder left over! Twelve baskets were left over! That is the Christian life. God *takes* you out of darkness. He *adds* His blessing on you. Then He *breaks* you. Then He *distributes* you. The problem is often we want to stop at the "addition" part. We like that He took us out of the darkness, and we love that He adds His blessing on us. But of course He never stops there. He means to break you, so He can multiply you, and send you out.

Here we are Lord. Use us today.

☽

## JANUARY 19

# Overcomers

*"Forgiveness is not always easy. At times, it feels more painful than the wound we suffered, to forgive the one that inflicted it. And yet, there is no peace without forgiveness."*
– Marianne Williamson

*For whatever is born of God overcomes the world. And this is the victory that has overcome the world – our faith.*
*(1 John 5:4)*

Jesus didn't die on the cross to give us the ability to cope. He died on the cross to give us the ability to conquer and to overcome. There is no enemy, no situation that you cannot overcome because of the work on the cross. This includes unforgiveness. Jesus died on the cross so that you can overcome unforgiveness. We've all been hurt by someone. It may be minor things or it may be devastating things. I've had my share of both, and I know what it is to just cope but not overcome. The Lord never keeps you or me from the ability to forgive. We have to do it daily, even if we don't mean it. There will come a moment when you *will* mean it, and that's when you become an overcomer. That is when you will live victoriously.

Are you just coping today? Or are you conquering? Is there someone that you need to forgive? Ask the Lord to help you. You are more than a conqueror!

# Wounds Bring Opportunity

*"Our infirmities become the black velvet on which the diamond of God's love glitters all the more brightly."*
*– Charles Spurgeon*

*Peter, Satan has desired to sift you like wheat… but I have prayed for you that your faith should not fail. So, when you have been healed you may strengthen your brothers.*
*(Luke 22:31-32)*

Jesus was warning Peter that the devil would do everything he could to silence his voice on the day of Pentecost. The devil *would* wound Peter. And Jesus told him that *when* he was healed, not if he was healed, to then go find his brothers to strengthen them. We all get attacked by the enemy. But Jesus always heals our wounds. And when you are healed of your wounds, it will open up the opportunity for you to help someone else. Prayer makes a difference. Jesus said to Peter, "I'm praying for you. I'm praying that the wounds that the enemy is going to hit you with, do not destroy your faith." Healing *will* come. Restoration *will* come. Don't give up! Jesus is interceding on your behalf.

Are you being attacked today? Think on this: Jesus, right now, right this moment is praying for you! He wants to heal you and restore you because He wants you to strengthen someone else.

Lord, intercede for us today. Increase our faith. Heal and restore us. And use us for Your will and glory.

# Come On In, Jesus!

*"Jesus, take the wheel... Take it from my hands...*
*'Cause I can't do this on my own... I'm letting go."*
*– Carrie Underwood (lyrics – Jesus, Take the Wheel)*

*To as many as received Him, He gave them the power. (John 1:12)*

To as many as invited Him in, He gave them power to become sons and daughters of God. Do you need answers to prayer today? Then you must invite Jesus in! You must *receive* Him. It's tempting to try and run the show yourself! It's tempting to say, "Jesus, I don't really want you running my WHOLE life, but I do need you to do this one thing for me." You can't use Jesus. You have to invite Him into every part of your life. You have to let Him take over everything. When you do that, then it's fitting and proper to say, "Let's talk business now, Jesus. You have to help me! I've invited you in, now please help me!" Whenever and wherever Jesus is invited, He comes. If you don't invite Him in, He won't come in.

The Bible says that when we invite Him in, when we receive Him, He gives us power. I don't know about you, but I could use some power today. Will you receive Him? Will you invite Him in?

Jesus, we thank you that all it takes is our invitation and You come. Whenever and wherever and however we need You, You always come where You're invited. Thank you.

JANUARY 22

# Indeed

*"God bestows His blessings without discrimination."*
*– F.F. Bruce*

*"…Oh, that You would bless me indeed…"*
*(1 Chronicles 4:10)*

The word "indeed" lets us know that this is a serious prayer. This is not a casual prayer. There are situations in our lives that require more than casual prayers. Jabez says, "Bless me, indeed." In other words, "If You don't intervene in my situation," "If you don't reverse this thing that I've been facing for so long," "I'm throwing myself on Your mercy and I'm asking for You to bless me *indeed*." Jabez didn't want his life to keep going the way it was going. He wanted an impartation of supernatural favor. Notice that Jabez isn't very specific. He says, "Bless me indeed." He leaves it open. Because when you're in enough pain, you'll take anything that God gives you. When you're desperate, you're not very particular. Because anything that God does is better than the situation that you're in.

Do you need an "indeed" kind of blessing today? You can pray that prayer right now:

Lord I come to you today, and in my pain, would You bless me, indeed?

# Deep Wounds, Deep Healing

*"Our scars are a witness to the world. They are part of our story.*
*Healed wounds are symbols that God has restored us." – Louie Giglio*

*The thief comes only to steal and kill and destroy.*
*(John 10:10)*

The devil does not fight fair. He will not give up until he wounds or kills you. He will attack you in one area of your life and then another area of your life. It's problem after problem and issue after issue. He'll come at you and if he can't wound you, he'll attack your family. If he can't get to your family, he will attack your business. His goal is to steal, kill and destroy you. He wants to steal your worship, kill your joy and your dreams. He wants to wound you and your marriage and your family. The definition of a mortal or deadly wound: "a very severe injury, always a form of penetration, which leads directly to the death of the victim. Death need not be instantaneous but follows soon after." But where you have deep wounds, the Healer has deep healing. The Bible says in Isaiah 30:26, "The moon will shine like the sun, and the sunlight will be seven times brighter, like the light of seven full days, when the Lord binds up the bruises of His people and heals the wounds that were inflicted."

Are your wounds deep, my friend? God's healing is deeper.

Lord, protect us from the attacks of the enemy. We pray that you bind up our bruises and heal the wounds that we carry today.

JANUARY 24

# Blindfolded

*"To one who has faith, no explanation is necessary. To one without faith, no explanation is possible."*
*– Thomas Aquinas*

*For we live by faith and not by sight. (2 Corinthians 5:7)*

When Paul said, "We live by faith and not by sight," he was in the middle of telling about some of the trials and tribulations he had went through. And the message for you is that regardless of the trials or what your situation "looks like," you must walk by faith and not by what you see. The gifts and the blessings of the cross are only accomplished by faith. The sacrifice and the blessing of the cross come to you by believing what God said about what happened on the cross. Jesus sent the Holy Spirit. And with the gift of the Holy Spirit you received all power to live, all power to defeat hell, all power to escape temptation, and all power to break habits and addictions. What activates that power in your life? Trying? Doing? Gritting your teeth and plugging through life? Nope. Faith activates that power in your life. The power of God operating in your life can only come from you believing Him and having faith that He's going to do what He says He's going to do. Do you believe it? Do you believe that He's working all things together for your good?

Maybe your prayer sounds like this: "Lord, I'm tired of trying to solve all these problems. I believe that You will work it all out for me. I choose this day to trust You."

## JANUARY 25

# Enlarge

*"You must go forward on your knees." – Hudson Taylor*

*"Enlarge the place of your tent, stretch your tent curtains wide, don't hold back; lengthen your cords, strengthen your stakes." (Isaiah 54:2)*

The definition of stretch is "to be made, or be capable of being made, longer or wider or bigger, without tearing or breaking." God was telling Israel long ago, and He is telling you today, that regardless of how it looks right now, He is calling you to enlarge and to stretch. Any time something is to be birthed, or produced, or delivered, or brought forth, extra room is required. If extra room is required, stretching will be necessary. I'm so thankful that scripture proves over and over that your background, your gender, or your highest level of education, is irrelevant. Your Father isn't looking for the most gifted, the most talented, the most educated, the most popular, the best looking, the most charismatic, or the most eloquent. He's just looking for ordinary people who are willing to let Him take their pain and use it any way He wishes.

Are you available for Him to enlarge the place of your tent? What holds you back? He needs more room to do in you, and for you, and through you, what He wants to do.

Lord, we make ourselves available to you today. Stretch us and use us.

JANUARY 26

# Remember!

*"God's work done in God's way will never lack
God's supplies." – Hudson Taylor*

*"And do you not remember? When I broke the five loaves for
the five thousand, how many baskets full of fragments did
you take up? … How is it you do not understand?"
(Mark 8:18, 21)*

Jesus and the disciples are on the boat and the disciples realize they only have one loaf of bread. And even though they've been exposed to who Jesus is, and even though they've been exposed to the new information about His power, they are troubled by what they *did not know*. They've seen the miracles, but they haven't changed their way of thinking. They're still thinking the way they did before they met Jesus. Sometimes we try to use our old routines and our old thinking in our new seasons. Jesus is frustrated in this text. His frustration has nothing to do with the bread they are discussing. His frustration is that, even though the disciples are in a new season, their thoughts haven't changed to reflect that. Their thinking hasn't changed, even though their situation has changed. I believe the hardest thing to change about myself is my mind! How you look at people or how you perceive money… it doesn't matter whether you have five dollars or five hundred thousand dollars, if your mind hasn't changed, then you will spend five hundred thousand dollars and be broke as if it was five dollars.

Do you need to change your thinking today? Jesus says, "Do you not remember what I've done for you so far? Do you not understand that I will do it again?"

## JANUARY 27

# Your Speech Betrays You

*"If you can't fly, then run, if you can't run, then walk, if you can't walk, then crawl, but whatever you do, you have to keep moving forward." – Martin Luther King Jr.*

*And a little later those who stood by came up and said to Peter, "Surely you also are one of them, for your speech betrays you." (Matthew 26:73)*

*I*f you hear me speak, my accent is a *fairly* neutral one. But if you listen very closely, and especially when I get tired, you will hear traces of my "hill country" roots. My speech gives me away. Even though I'm no longer in the hills, they are firmly ingrained in me from my childhood in the mountains.

In this text, they said to Peter, "There's something about the way that you're speaking that let us know that you were once with Jesus Christ of Galilee." Even though Peter wasn't with Jesus anymore, THAT which had been AROUND him, had ended up getting IN him.

You may feel like you are far away from Jesus today. But I remind you that Jesus is in you still. You may be limping today, but you dragged yourself into the presence of God to read this devotional. You may have said that it's over, but your speech is betraying you. I can tell that you've walked with Jesus.

The plans that He has for you are still on. Keep moving.

# He Knows

*"I have a great need for Christ; I have a great
Christ for my need." – Charles Spurgeon*

*Therefore, since we have a great high priest Who has ascended into
heaven, Jesus the Son of God, let us hold firmly to the faith we profess.
For we do not have a high priest Who is unable to empathize with
our weaknesses, but we have One Who has been tempted in every
way, just as we are – yet He did not sin. (Hebrews 4:14-15)*

*A*s High Priest, Jesus is representing you to God, the Father, even right
now as you are reading this. He is praying for you *now*. Because He
came and lived on earth, He understands every human condition that
we go through. He was tempted. He was assaulted. He cried. He was
rejected. He was hated. You don't have a High Priest, an intercessor up
in heaven Who says, "You failed again. You messed up again." Instead
You have a High Priest Who knows what the battle is like when Satan
attacks you. And so, my friend, Jesus knows. He knows everything.
There is nothing hidden. There is no ache or pain that your heart goes
through, that He doesn't understand. He knows if your family has turned
against you. He knows if you're attacked by fear and anxiety. He knows
everything. And He's not mad at you. He loves you.

You are not alone. There is nothing that you are going through today
that He doesn't understand. He is praying for you right now!

JANUARY 29

# Victory Over Fear

*"I'm not afraid of the devil. He can't handle the
One to whom I'm joined." – A. W. Tozer*

*It happened after this that the people...came to battle against
Jehoshaphat... And Jehoshaphat feared, and set himself to seek the Lord...
(2 Chronicles 20:1-3)*

*H*ave you ever been gripped by fear? I know I have. But I know that if I'm ever going to fulfill the assignment that the Lord has for my life, I have no choice but to overcome fear. God tells us not to fear 365 times in His Word. Once for every day of the year! God never meant for fear to hold you back or hold you down. You have to get up, even if your knees are knocking. You have to use your gifts, even if your hands are trembling. You have to speak out and speak up, even if your voice is shaking.

God has given Jehoshaphat an assignment. And yet, he finds himself in a very troubling situation. "And Jehoshaphat feared," Please notice there's a comma after the word fear and not a period. The comma means that the story doesn't stop with Jehoshaphat being afraid. Jehoshaphat did something about his fear. He "set himself to seek the Lord..." And that is how we get victory over our fear. Set yourself to seek the Lord.

What fear do you need to overcome today? What fear is keeping you from becoming everything that Jesus wants you to become?

## JANUARY 30

# Are You Not The God…?

*"Our God is not an impotent God with one arm; but as he is
slow to anger, so is he great in power." – Abraham Wright*

*Then Jehoshaphat stood…in the house of the Lord…and said, "O Lord
God of our fathers, are You not God in Heaven, and do You not rule over
all the kingdoms of the nations, and in Your hand is there not power and
might, so that no one is able to withstand You? Are You not our God,
who drove out the inhabitants of this land before Your people Israel…?"
(2 Chronicles 20:5-7)*

Jehoshaphat and his people were surrounded on all sides by trouble.
He was afraid. But scripture says that, "He set himself to seek the
Lord." He called his people to fast and to pray. When they prayed,
they prayed a prayer that not only reminded God of Who HE was, it
reminded THEM of who God was. Today, you may feel surrounded
on every side. You may need to pray, "God, You're the God of Heaven.
You're the one who rules over all the kingdoms and the nations of the
world. And God, in Your hand is there not power and might, so that NO
ONE is able to withstand You? Are You not the God who delivered me
last time? Are You not the God who healed me before? Are You not the
God who rescued me from the pit? Are You not the God who changed
me from who and what I once was? Are You not the God of who and
what I am becoming?

Besides reminding God of Who He is, perhaps you need to remind
yourself of Who He is.

# This Battle Is Not Yours

*"There's nothing more calming in difficult moments*
*than knowing there's someone fighting with you."*
*– Mother Teresa*

*"Listen, all you of Judah and you inhabitants of Jerusalem!*
*Do not be afraid or dismayed because of this great*
*multitude, for the battle is not yours...but God's."*
*(2 Chronicles 20:15)*

*A*re you in a battle today? Is your time consumed with fighting to survive this crisis? Is your energy depleted because this thing is sucking every ounce of life out of you? My friend, there are times when God expects us to participate in the action. And then there are other seasons when we don't have to do anything. When you are at a place where there is absolutely nothing you can do about it, when there's nothing you can do to change it, that's when God says, "I've got this one. This battle is not yours. It's Mine."

"You will not need to fight in this battle" (v. 17). You won't have to argue anymore. You won't have to defend. You won't have to make any phone calls. God says, "I've got this one."

Read this verse again. Out loud. And this time put your name in the blank. "Listen..._____! Do not be afraid or dismayed because of this great multitude, for the battle is not yours...but God's." Now, sit back and enjoy your coffee.

### FEBRUARY 1

# What's Your Problem?

*"Problems are not stop signs…they are guidelines."*
*– Robert Schuller*

*When the wine ran out, the mother of Jesus said to*
*Him, "They have no wine." (John 2:3)*

Mary, the mother of Jesus, tells Him in one sentence the thing that started a miracle. "They have no more wine." Five words. She didn't even say, "Would you please do something?" She just told Him what the problem was. It wasn't Mary's wedding. Why would she care if they ran out of wine? In those days, two thousand years ago, if you hosted a wedding and you ran out of wine, that was a disaster. That was a social disaster. Mary didn't beg or plead with Jesus. She just told Him the need.

What problem are you facing today? Whatever it is, just tell Jesus what you need. Rather than telling everyone at work or all your friends and family, just tell Jesus. That's how all the miracles happened in the Bible. Jesus said to the blind man, "What do you want Me to do?" And the man simply told him the problem, "I want to see." That's it. That's all it took to move God to help him. Mary told Jesus what the problem was. And then a miracle took place.

Jesus, I lift my friend to You today. You know the problems they may be facing. I thank you that all we have to do is bring it all to You, the Problem Solver.

# And They Felt No Shame

*"The most terrifying thing is to accept oneself completely."*
*– Carl Jung*

*Adam and his wife were both naked, and*
*they felt no shame. (Genesis 2:25)*

God wanted you to know that, before you get to the chapter of "the fall," that He made you to feel no shame. Our world piles shame on us. From television, to social media, to the magazines in the grocery story aisle…we can think we are doing pretty good, until we see how well the world says we should be doing. But God says, "I'm taking you right back to the beginning, because I need you to know that I made you to be enough. In fact, Me in you, is MORE than enough." Perhaps along the way, someone told you that you were not enough, that you're not worthy, but your worth is not defined by what you've done or what you haven't done. Your worth is defined by what Jesus did two thousand years ago at Calvary. You are more than enough. You were worth dying for.

Do you believe that? If you feel shame, that does not come from your Father in Heaven. That comes from your accuser who wants nothing more than to destroy you. Your enemy will stop at nothing to prevent you from realizing who you are. Who are you? You are a child of God who was worth dying for. He died so that you would feel no shame.

Father, remind us today that we are more than enough and that feelings of shame do not come from You.

# What And Who You Believe

*"Bring your sins, and He will bear them away into the wilderness of forgetfulness, and you will never see them again." – Dwight L. Moody*

*…They knew no shame. (Genesis 2:25)*

Shame can destroy you. Shame can cause you to run *from* God and not *to* God. Shame can cause you to lie to yourself and to others. Shame can lead to addictions. Shame causes destructive patterns of behavior to develop. Shame can lead to an endless cycle of seeking the approval of others.

What and who you believe will affect your entire life. What and who you believe can affect your children's entire lives. If we don't arrest the lies that we believe now, it can affect generation after generation. You can choose this day, "I'm not going to keep passing on the dysfunctions of the generations before me. Just because THIS has always been in my family, doesn't mean it's always going to be in my family. It stops with me! I *choose* to leave a great legacy for the next generation."

Let's get back to what God intended for us, that we live a shame-free life and that we flourish. There is no need for you to hide from your Father. It is time to become all that He has intended for you to be so that you can do what He has called you to do. Today, will you be a light in the middle of the darkness as you were called to be?

FEBRUARY 4

# Did God Really Say…?

*"To secure one's freedom the Christian must experience God's light which is God's truth."* – Watchman Nee

*Now the serpent was more crafty than any of the wild animals the Lord God had made. He said to the woman, "Did God really say…?" (Genesis 3:1)*

*A*nd herein lies the root of everything. If you don't know what God really says, then you will believe what the enemy says. If you don't know the truth, you'll believe the lies. Adam and Eve blew it, and they ran away from God. They covered themselves with fig leaves and tried to hide. And that's what we do when we blow it. That's what we do when we feel unworthy. We run *from* God instead of running *to* God.

My friend, the only way for us to know what God really said, is to stay in His Word and talk with Him. The enemy will use anything and everything to undermine what God is doing in your life. If you don't know that God is a good God, then you'll believe that He is a mean God and wants to punish you. If you don't *know* He is good, then you'll believe the lie. And so, you have to know what God said so that when the devil says, "Did God really say…?", you'll know how to counteract the enemy.

Have you believed a lie that has enabled you to end up far removed from what God has for your life? If so, then I encourage you to get in His Word and let Him tell you what He really says about you.

# Afar Off

*"The next best thing to being wise oneself is to live
in a circle of those who are." – C.S. Lewis*

*Now it happened as He went to Jerusalem that He passed through the
midst of Samaria and Galilee. Then as He entered a certain village, there
met Him ten men who were lepers, who stood afar off. (Luke 17:11-12)*

I wonder how many people you know who, because of whatever drama they have in their lives, don't feel connected to anything good or life-giving. They feel like they don't belong and find themselves standing "afar off." You may have friends or family or coworkers who go to church. But they don't "belong." They haven't connected to a life-source. Maybe that's you.

I want to tell you something that's mind-blowing! God loves people who are "afar off." God is especially fond of the outcasts. These ten lepers were standing "afar off."

Maybe someone comes to mind when you read this. May I encourage you to reach out to that person today and just tell them that you are thinking about them? Or maybe you feel "afar off" and like an outcast. God wants to remind you that you're not. My friend, may I encourage you to press in a little bit more, hold on to Jesus a little bit tighter, and let Him be your life-source.

Jesus, we cling to You today and ask that You quiet the voice who whispers that we don't belong.

# Open Your Mouth!

*"There is hope for the helpless, rest for the weary, and love for the broken heart. And there is grace and forgiveness, mercy and healing, He'll meet you wherever you are. Cry out to Jesus. Cry out to Jesus." – Third Day (Cry out to Jesus)*

*…They lifted up their voices and said, "Jesus, Master, have mercy on us." (Luke 17:13)*

*W*hen you want to get someone's attention, sometimes you have to open your mouth! One of the dilemmas in our churches is that we want to pray to God conservatively. But there come moments in your life when you must open up your mouth and cry out to God! When the pain gets so intense and the drama overtakes you… when the situation cuts your legs out from underneath you, you must lift up your voice and cry out, "Jesus! Have mercy on me!" The ten lepers were in a desperate situation. They had major health issues. They were rejected. They were outcasts. They weren't living. And so, when they saw Him, they cried out to Jesus. So many of us cry out to people when we are desperate. But people can NEVER take the place of Jesus. Jesus is the only one who can transform your life. He is the one who can, and WILL, deliver you.

Do you need to lift up your voice and cry out to Jesus? Or maybe there's someone in your life who needs you to stand in the gap for them today and cry out to Jesus on their behalf. "Jesus, Master, have mercy on us!"

FEBRUARY 7

# Mercy

*"There is not a flower that opens, not a seed that falls into*
*the ground, and not an ear of wheat that nods on the end of*
*its stalk in the wind that does not preach and proclaim the*
*greatness and the mercy of God to the whole world."*
*– Thomas Merton*

*"…Have mercy on us!" (Luke 17:13)*

I wonder if we realize how much we need the mercy of God? Mercy is when God gives you what you don't deserve. Mercy is what woke you up this morning. Mercy is what you get instead of condemnation. Mercy is what you get instead of judgment. I am so thankful that I serve a God who doesn't give me what I deserve. I deserve punishment. I deserve rejection. I deserve Hell. I am so thankful for His mercy! And He not only gives us mercy, the Bible says that He gives us *tender mercies.* And he doesn't give us hand-me-down mercies either! The Bible and the old hymn says, "Morning by morning NEW mercies I see." Every single day we get a fresh batch of mercy! Sometimes you just need to look behind you and proclaim, "Surely goodness and MERCY shall follow me all the days of my life!"

Today, will you take a moment and thank God that He gives you what you don't deserve.

"Have mercy on us!" And He does. Enjoy your fresh batch of brand new mercy all day long! No need to save it up, you'll get a whole new batch tomorrow!

# He Sees You

*"God loves each of us as if there were only one of us."*
*– Augustine*

*So, when He saw them… (Luke 17:14)*

*I*n Luke 17, we read the story of the ten lepers. One of the most striking verses is verse 14. The lepers were desperate, and they cried out to Jesus. The Bible says that Jesus "saw them."

Just those words…that's enough to make me fizzy on the inside! Even when you feel rejected, even when you feel like an outcast, even when you are sick, even when you are in an impossible situation, it's good to know that if you cry out to Him, *He will see you.* If you feel lonely or unloved today, my friend, He says to you, "If you will cry out to Me, I will see you. I don't care how low you've fallen. I will see you. I don't care how bound you are to those bad habits. I will see you. I don't care what the doctor says. I will see you. I don't care what is or isn't in your bank account. I will see you. I don't care what they said about you. I'll see you. I don't care what they did to you. I'll see you. I don't care how impossible the situation seems. I'll see you. I don't care how dark it is where you are. I can see in the dark. I don't care if you're hung over. I'll see you. If you'll cry out to Me. I'll see you."

He sees you today. If you, like the lepers, will cry out to Jesus, He will see you.

# Deep Calls Unto Deep

*"From birth, man carries the weight of gravity on his shoulders. He is bolted to earth. But man has only to sink beneath the surface and he is free."*
*– Jacques Yves Cousteau*

*Deep calls unto deep at the voice of Your waterfalls; all your waves and billows have gone over me. (Psalm 42:7)*

*D*id you know that in lakes or in rivers, trash always washes to the shallow, the edges? If you're in the shallow, you're still in the water, but it's dirty. You're in the river, but just up to your ankles. And that's where many Christians live…only as deep as the edge of "the river." They are in church, but they're so entangled with the trash of this world, it washes up on them every day of their lives. They refuse to move out into the deep where it's pure and life giving. It's in the deep where there's a frequency between the depths of God's heart and the depths of our souls. If you just play around the edges or the shallows of the "river" in the church and spiritually, you may love the church, but you'll have no love for the Lord. You may be busy in the church, but you'll not yearn for Jesus. Did you know that if you live in the shallows long enough, and if you go without communicating with God on His frequency long enough, you'll actually grow complacent with staying right where you are? My friend, there is no safer place to be than in the deepest part of "the river" with the water over your head. It's pure in the deep. You can hear Him in the deep. You have the Spirit's power in the deep. God's Word comes alive in the deep. God calls you to the deep today.

# A Few Good Men

*"It's easier to be a man when you're surrounded by men."*
*– Cory Griffin*

*"Don't pray for easier lives, pray to be stronger men."*
*– J. F. Kennedy*

*"How can I," he said, "unless someone explains it to me?" (Acts 8:31)*

*I*n a generation where more than 1 in 4 children grow up without a father, it's easy to understand why so many men do not understand their identity in Christ. And with no example for them, how can they, and what can be done? And with no example, how can they? So, what to do…? I was discussing this with my 23-year-old son, Cory. I asked him this question: "How important is it for men to have community with other men?" And he answered, "Mom, I believe it's critical, and frankly, I think it's even more important than women having community with other women." He reminded me of a Christian fraternity he met with a few hours a week all four years he was in college. For him, it was an oasis and a place where he, and others, shared their lives. All of them were striving to become better and courageous men with high moral standards.

We all need community. We all need to know that we aren't the only ones going through what we're going through. We need each other. Who needs you today?

# Blessed Is She Who Believed

*"We are all faced with a series of great opportunities*
*brilliantly disguised as impossible situations."*
*– Chuck Swindoll*

*"Blessed is she who believed, for there will be a fulfillment of*
*those things which were told her from the Lord." (Luke 1:45)*

"Blessed is she who believed…" Blessed are you if you believe that God will do what He said He would do. Mary believed. It looked impossible because it WAS impossible. But the verse says, "*Blessed* is she who believed, for *there will be* a fulfillment of those things which were told her from the Lord."

No matter what you are going through today, child of God, you must say, "I know it looks impossible and I know I will have to fight, but I believe what God said is true and *it will* come to pass." It doesn't matter how impossible it looks. *It will come to pass.*

How do we believe? Stay deep in His word. Talk to Him frequently. Ask Him to help you. Surround yourself with godly people whom God has made the impossible, possible in their lives. All of these things will increase your faith.

Blessed are *you* who believe, for *there will be* a fulfillment of those things which were told *you* from the Lord!

# Surprised?

*"The enemy will not see you vanish into God's company
without an effort to reclaim you." – C.S. Lewis*

*"Beloved, do not think it strange concerning the fiery trial which is to
try you, as though some strange thing happened to you." (1 Peter 4:12)*

Why do we think it strange or act surprised when a "fiery trial" comes our way? Our obstacles and issues shouldn't be strange to us. We want to believe that because we are His, it will be smooth sailing in this Christian walk. But, *because* you're His, all Hell *will* come against you. Hell doesn't rest or take a vacation. The devil is relentless. You may get tired and weary, but Satan doesn't. He will come at you again and again and again. But that should not be strange. That shouldn't be unusual. Jesus told us to expect it. "But greater is He that is in me, than He that is in the world." You are in a fight and you have to fight the right fight, in the right way. As elementary as this may sound, the only way to fight this good fight of faith is through prayer. But you will never win a battle without a prayer life. Prayer is the most formidable thing in which you'll ever engage. Your Father, Who is in Heaven, knows what you have need of, when you have need of it, before you even ask. You can ask anything. You can ask anything at any time, AND GOD WILL HEAR! And He always answers!

What is coming against you today, beloved? God reminds you that He is in you and He is greater than any obstacle. Tell Him about it. He already knows, but He awaits you to initiate the conversation. Tell Him.

FEBRUARY 13

# This Is A Fight!

*"There's nothing more calming in difficult moments
than knowing there's someone fighting with you."*
*— Mother Teresa*

*"I have told you these things, so that in me you may
have peace. In this world you will have trouble. But take
heart! I have overcome the world." (John 16:33)*

You can't fight this good fight of faith without prayer and you can't fight this fight without the Word. You have to know what the Bible says! The Word is food! If you don't eat food, you get weak and you wither. If you don't eat the Word, your spirit gets weak and withers. You can't fight this good fight of faith without prayer and without the Word…OR, without the church. We need each other. I need you and you need me. How do you think God answers prayers? He answers prayers through His people. When you are sitting in church, you are sitting beside His hands and His feet. You are sitting beside His voice. You are sitting beside His embrace. And, child of God, do you not know that YOU are the answer to someone's prayer? "I have a relationship with God, why do I need the church?" God uses the church, you and me, to minister to one another. Our coming together is a vital part of fighting this fight. You cannot be strong alone. We are the army of the Lord! I don't know what you battle today. But I know that the battle is won with prayer, the Word, and surrounding yourself with His people. "But take heart! I have overcome the world!"

# FEBRUARY 14

# "Do You Believe That I Love You?"

*"Though our feelings come and go, God's love for us does not." – C.S. Lewis*

*He emptied Himself... (Philippians 2:7)*

Jesus cried His heart out. He let Himself be nailed to a cross with His blood poured out. Why would He do that? To show us that He loves us. Jesus chose the cross as the demonstrative sign of His absolute love for you and for me. He died in our place! His is a love that didn't count death as too high a price. Can you see how crazy it is to ever imagine that Christianity has anything to do with what *we do* for God? Do you think that Jesus "emptied" Himself merely to make nicer men and women with higher standards and better morals? The gospel is absurd, and the life of Jesus meaningless, unless we know that He lived, died, and rose again with but one purpose in mind. He did this that we would know the love of God and share the love of God. He spilled His blood that we would be made new and filled with His peace, His joy, His goodness, and His extravagant love.

Maybe you didn't receive the love from your parents that a child should receive. Maybe even today, you feel like love is nowhere to be found. Jesus spreads His nail-scarred hands as far as the east is from the west and says, "I love you THIS much!"

Bask in His extravagant love today.

# Faith Requires Action

*"Faith sees the invisible, believes the unbelievable, and receives the impossible." – Corrie Ten Boom*

*So you see, it isn't enough just to have faith. You must also do good to prove that you have it. Faith that doesn't show itself by good works is no faith at all – it is dead and useless. (James 2:17)*

*D*o you have faith? Do you have great faith or truly the faith of a mustard seed? How do we increase our faith? Faith requires action sometimes. Are you lonely? Step out and be a friend to someone else who is lonely. Are you sick in your body? Pray for someone else who is sick in his or her body. Are you struggling financially? Check your giving. God says to test Him on these things. All of these actions activate, and increase, your faith. God responds to faith. God delights in crazy faith.

Where else in your life are you struggling with faith? If you examine it, you'll probably find that it's in an area where God wants you to take a step forward into a place in which you can't see what's in front of you. Remember, when the Israelites had to step out into the Jordan before the waters parted? I'm sure the thought crossed their minds, "Will He really do it? Or will we be swept away?" Faith requires action. So step out, even if your knees are knocking. Speak up, even if your voice is shaking. Reach out, even if your hands are trembling.

## FEBRUARY 16

# No Greater Love

*"God is love. He didn't need us. But He wanted us. And that is the most amazing thing." – Rick Warren*

*For God so loved the world that He gave His only begotten Son, that whoever believes in Him shall not perish but have everlasting life. (John 3:16)*

Imagine that Jesus walked right up to you today, pulled up a chair, and looked you in the eye and said, "I know everything you've ever done. I know every skeleton in your closet. I know every moment of sin, shame, and dishonesty. I know that your faith is shallow and that your prayer life is feeble. Nothing is hidden from My eyes. And My Word to you today is this: I dare you to trust that I love you as you are right in this moment and not as you should be. Because you're never going to be as you should be." How would you respond?

One of the single, biggest mistakes that we fall into is an attitude or mindset that says, "If I change…" or "When I change, THEN God will love me." Or, "If I try a little harder or run a little faster or work a little longer, THEN God will love me." If you think you have to earn His love, you have it backwards. He says, "You don't have to change for Me to love you. I love you and then you want to change." You don't have to change, grow or get better for Him to love you. You are so intensely, passionately, unconditionally loved that it makes you WANT to change and to grow and to get better.

He can't stop loving you. He won't stop loving you. You'll find no greater love than this.

# Unrestricted Love

*"The wild, unrestricted love of God is not simply an inspiring idea. When it imposes itself on mind and heart with the stark reality of ontological truth, it determines why and at what time you get up in the morning, how you pass your evenings, how you spend your weekends, what you read, and who you hang with; it affects what breaks your heart, what amazes you, and what makes your heart happy." – Brennan Manning*

*"May you experience the love of Christ, though it is too great to understand fully. Then you will be made complete with all the fullness of life and power that comes from God." (Ephesians 3:19)*

When you reflect on the unrestricted love of God, it's good to read the stories of people in scripture. It's full of people just like us with the same struggles and hang-ups that we have. There was Peter, the "rock", who couldn't keep his mouth shut if he tried. There was Zacchaeus, the runt, who was also a cheat. There were prostitutes and thieves. There were James and John who were "mama's boys". What about Thomas who was bullheaded and doubt-filled his whole life? There was Martha, the worrier and complainer. And who could forget Saul, the Christian-killer? But Jesus loved them all. He forgave them all. He affirmed them all. He enabled them all. And Jesus challenged them all to live in the fullness of Him. That same Jesus, who was the same yesterday in Galilee, is the same right where you are this very moment.

Will you let go of any false perceptions of who He is and openly surrender to the God who loves you as you are?

# Furious Love

*"What comes to our minds when we think about God is
the most important thing about us." – A. W. Tozer*

*"Here I am! I stand at the door and knock. If anyone
hears my voice and opens the door, I will come in and eat
with him, and he with me." (Revelation 3:20)*

*Y*ou're only going to be as big as your own concept of God. Rather
than us being made in His image, we like to make Him into our
image. We make Him to be as fussy, rude, narrow-minded, legalistic,
judgmental, and unforgiving as we are. Honestly, the God of so many
Christians that I meet is a god that is too small for me! Because their god
is not the god of the Word and he is not the God Who loves us as we
are and not as we should be. The most radical demand of the Christian
faith is at this moment, in your brokenness, with your shallow faith to
allow yourself to be the object of the vast delight of the risen Jesus. He
says to you today, "No matter what happens in your life, no matter if
you fall and when you fall, no matter if you walk away from Me, *I can't
walk away from you."* If you don't believe that, no matter how young or
old you are, no matter how long you've been saved, or even if you serve
in ministry, you are not living the abundant life that He's called you
to live. And I would bet my life that is why you are reading this at this
very moment. He is calling you by name, not to scold, fuss or frighten,
but to make you aware, with new depth and greater dimension of His
relentless tenderness and of His passionate and pursuing, healing, and
reconciling "furious love."

# What If?

*"The gospel is good news of mercy to the undeserving. The symbol of the religion of Jesus is the cross, not the scales."*
*– John Stott*

*Jesus fixed his gaze upon the man, with tender love…*
*(Mark 10:21)*

What if you opened your front door and Jesus stood before you, looking you straight in the eye? What would the look on His face say to you in that moment? What is Jesus' face saying to you in this moment? Is He saying, "I am sick and tired of your broken promises, your un-kept resolutions, all of your false starts and your hypocrisy?" If Jesus could say only one word to you right now, would the word be, "REPENT"? Or…would He ask, "Do you know what a joy it is to live in your heart?" "Do you know how proud I am of you? After I chose you, you freely chose Me? Do you know the only time you break My heart? When you refuse to accept that every repented sin of your past is not only forgiven, it's so entirely forgotten that I can't even remember what it was! Do you know that I've loved you from before you were even born? And no matter what you've done or will do, I can't stop loving you."

What is Jesus saying to you right now? If it's negative, it's not Jesus who's talking to you.

## FEBRUARY 20

# It's Okay To Not Be Okay

*"Keep your face to the sunshine and you cannot*
*see a shadow." – Helen Keller*

*God met me more than halfway. He freed me from my*
*anxious fears. Look at Him; give Him your warmest smile.*
*Never hide your feelings from Him. (Psalm 34:4-5)*

Sometimes we say we're fine and we're not fine at all. Sometimes we look fine on the outside, but on the inside we're a wreck. In Psalms, David writes, "When I was desperate, I called out, and God got me out of a tight spot." We need to quit faking "fine." God gives us an open invitation to be gut-level honest with Him. When we silence our pain, we rob ourselves of the opportunity to be healed. We cope in whatever way we've learned. We escape. We keep busy. We keep stuffing our "not okay," deeper and deeper. God's people find wholeness by bringing their brokenness to Him. David says of God, "Never hide your feelings from Him." In other words, whatever it is, maybe it's grief, maybe it's rage. Whatever it is, your Father can handle it.

Today, my friend, He will meet you more than halfway. He will free you from your anxious fears. Tell Him.

# Honesty

*"In Sunday worship, as in every dimension of our existence,*
*many of us pretend to believe we are sinners. Consequently, all*
*we can do is pretend to believe we have been forgiven."*
*– Brennan Manning*

*"Be anxious for nothing, but in everything by prayer*
*and supplication, with thanksgiving, let your requests*
*be made known to God." (Philippians 4:6)*

*W*e can often find ourselves bringing *some* concerns before God, but keeping others close to our chests. Perhaps we are wary of what God will call us to do or maybe we're just too ashamed of something that we have done. My friend, God's loving-kindness and forgiveness are boundless. Being honest with Him opens up the floodgate for you to receive His grace in greater abundance. It's wonderful that you've trusted Him with *"that"* thing, but He wants you to give Him the rest of your concerns too. He has endless grace for those *other* situations.

Is there something that is causing you anxiety? Your Father wants you to be anxious for nothing! Practice Philippians 4:6 today. Tell Him what's keeping you up at night and causing your nerves to be frayed. Ask Him to work in that situation on your behalf. And before you see an answer to that prayer, go ahead and thank Him in advance for taking care of it!

# I Need You. You Need Me.

*"You can't stay in your corner of the Forest waiting for others
to come to you. You have to go to them sometimes."*
*— Winnie-the-Pooh*

*"Therefore, confess your sins to one another and pray for
one another, so that you may be healed. The urgent request
of a righteous person is very powerful in its effect."*
*(James 5:16)*

No one should walk alone. God tells us to help carry one another's burdens. But instead, we often hide. We strive for perfection and efficiency. We cry into our pillows silently. We put on masks that protect us from revealing our weaknesses. We change who we are around different people because we long to be worthy, approved of, loved, and accepted. When we don't reveal our shortcomings, hide our weakness, and cover up our failures, we keep ourselves from feeling true love. We lie to the outside world because being honest makes us vulnerable and we risk getting hurt. And this armor we wear makes those lies more believable, not only to the onlookers, but to us.

Developing honesty and realness in your relationships is also a way to break down the barriers of pretending. To do this, you need to be real with yourself and others. When you can do that, your relationships will deepen and become enriched. As Paul said, "I am the chief sinner!" We all fail! You are not alone! When you try to cover it up, you miss out on the grace that God freely and abundantly gives to accept your failings. You don't have to creatively explain them.

You don't have to walk alone! And you don't have to hide! We ALL have fallen!

Father, surround us with godly men and women.

# Wherever You Go…

*"Maybe the paths that you each shall tread are already
laid before your feet, though you do not see them."*
*– J.R.R. Tolkien (The Fellowship of the Ring)*

*Be strong and of good courage, do not fear nor be afraid
of them; for the Lord your God, He is the One Who goes
with you. He will not leave you nor forsake you."*
*(Deuteronomy 31:6-8)*

Where are you right now in your life? Wherever it is, God is there. "He is the One Who goes with you." Wherever you go, He goes. He won't leave you. You can't make Him mad enough to leave you. There's no offense that will cause Him to leave you. You can't insult Him enough to leave you. The lower you fall, the lower He goes to pick you up, or to just sit with you on the asphalt. The Lord will not leave you. The Lord will not forsake you. He is the One Who goes before you. You're never discovering new territory. You're not a pioneer in the situation in which you find yourself. God was already there, in that situation. Wherever you go, God goes with you. When you get in your car, God will get in your car with you. When you go to sleep tonight, God will watch over you. Wherever you find yourself, He's already there.

Lord, we thank You for Your presence. You never leave us, even when we mess up.

# FEBRUARY 24

# I See Your Roots

*"Even the smallest person can change the course of the future." – J.R.R Tolkien (The Fellowship of the Ring)*

*This is a record of the ancestors of Jesus the Messiah, a descendant of David and of Abraham. (Matthew 1:1)*

Be honest. Are there parts of the Bible you skip over? Like Leviticus or Numbers? What about genealogy? What's the point anyway? Genealogy was important so that lineage could be shown. If you were a Hebrew, a genealogy would show that you had true Jewish heritage. Ancestry was important. Roots were *very* important. Before Matthew starts telling us about one of the most important events in the Bible, Jesus' birth, He first gives us a genealogical record of Jesus. What is incredible in this genealogy is that Matthew mentions four women. It's odd because women would never normally be included in a genealogical record. It was only men who counted. I think the Holy Spirit made sure this was in scripture so that all of us would see that no matter our sex, our race, or our background, He has a purpose for us. He came to lift us out of whatever ditch we ever find ourselves in. And He says, "If I can use a prostitute in the lineage of Jesus, I can use you too. I have plans for you. I have great plans for you. I have plans for a future and plans to prosper you. I see your roots. I gave them to you. They will be used for your good and My glory."

My friend, don't ever listen to the lie that you are insignificant. Don't ever listen to the lie that God can't and won't use you because of your past.

FEBRUARY 25

# The Secret Place

*"When you neglect the secret place, He's not disappointed
in you, He's disappointed for you." – Bob Sorge*

*"But when you pray, go away by yourself, shut the door behind
you, and pray to your Father in private. Then your Father,
Who sees everything, will reward you." (Matthew 6:6)*

*A* more literal translation of Matthew 6:6 is, "Shut the door behind you and pray to your Father in secret. Then your Father, Who sees in secret, will reward you." What's interesting is that it's in secret where the devil almost always makes his first attack. It's in secret where you're tempted most. When asked what defines character in a Christian, D.L. Moody replied, "Character is what you do in secret." It's in secret where the devil gets his foothold. But it's also in secret where God wants us to get the victory. It's in secret where the devil is lurking. It's in secret where you pray, so you beat him in the secret place. What does that look like? You're lying in bed one night and you have some thoughts… and they're not good ones. You're in secret. That's when you have to call out to God and get your mind, and your heart, and your voice on Him. That's when you pray. That's when you worship. That's when the devil takes a beating. In secret, if you pray, you will beat Satan.

My friend, I hope you are taking the time to "shut the door behind you and pray to your Father in private."

# No Babbling

*"God does almost nothing unless someone prays."*
*– Martin Luther*

*"When you pray, don't babble on and on as other religions do.*
*They think their prayers are answered merely by repeating their*
*words again and again. Don't be like them, for your Father knows*
*exactly what you need even before you ask him!" (Matthew 6:7)*

When we talk to Him, God isn't interested in religious tones or flowery words. He just wants you to talk to Him. You don't have to go on and on and on and say it again and again and again! Saying it over and over is not going to cause God to say, "Alright. I can't take it anymore. Here. Take what you need." We can take comfort knowing He's just one sentence away. Sometimes, He's just one word away. "Jesus!" "But I've sinned a lot! So, I must say a lot because it will somehow atone." No! Nothing atones for your sin but the blood of Jesus. Real talk, real prayer causes things to happen. Don't think you need to pray like someone else. God made you who you are. Be who He made you to be. How are you going to talk to God acting like someone else? Since He made you, I think He's going to figure out the truth.

How about it? Just be you today. You may have no words – you may only have one word. "Jesus." And that's all you need.

# It's Okay To Change Your Mind

*"Once you replace negative thoughts with positive ones,
you'll start having positive results." – Willie Nelson*

*And do not be conformed to this world, but be transformed
by the renewing of your mind, that you may prove what is
that good, and acceptable, and perfect will of God.*
*(Romans 12:2)*

*I* believe this year will be a year of change and supernatural growth. I believe that you are in a new season. And the most important thing you can do in a new season is to change your mind. The way you are thinking now is not going to work for who you are becoming. You have to be willing to surrender your thoughts. You have to be willing to surrender your patterns. Don't you know that you are becoming clay again on the potter's wheel? Something is happening and you can't just rely upon the thoughts you've had before. You have to be willing to change your mind. You can't think like everybody else. You can't think like the people with whom you work. Maybe that worked for you in the past. But you're not in the past anymore, so that thinking won't work for you now. God is asking you to change your mind.

Has God thrown a situation at you to see if you *have* changed your mind? "Do not be conformed to this world, but be transformed by the renewing of your mind…" This is critical for who you are becoming!

## FEBRUARY 28

# Insurance

*"For you who wonder if you've played too long to change, take courage from Jacob's legacy. No man is too bad for God. To transform a riverboat gambler into a man of faith would be no easy task. But for God, it was all in a night's work." – Max Lucado*

*And do not be conformed to this world, but be transformed by the renewing of your mind, that you may prove what is that good and acceptable and perfect will of God.*
*(Romans 12:2)*

Why should you try to live your life within the perfect will of God? Because there's insurance connected to that. Because there are resources connected to that. Because there is provision connected to that. Renewing my mind changes my perspective. Renewing my mind helps me to lay hold of the promises of God. Renewing my mind clears the fog when making important decisions. It is critical that we renew our minds! A lot of times our mind reflects the environment we were raised in. We can't always rely on that environment to really be a reflection of the best version of who we can and were meant to be. And in some environments, there are some belief systems that can hinder you from really laying hold of the identity, and the vision of who God calls you to be.

Are you lacking resources? Are you lacking provision? Do you need some insurance? All this is available when you renew your mind "that you may prove what is that good and acceptable and perfect will of God."

## MARCH 1

# Restraining Order

*"A God wise enough to create me and the world I live in is
wise enough to watch out for me." – Philip Yancey*

*"Oh, that You would bless me indeed…and that You would
keep me from harm so that I will be free from pain."
(1 Chronicles 4:10)*

*W*hy would Jabez pray to be kept from evil or harm and for blessings in the same prayer? Because the more that God blesses you, the more Satan sees you. Success is a greater opportunity for failure. The higher you go, the further down you fall. Blessings can dull our senses for our dependency on God. Jabez is basically asking God to put a restraining order on the devil. Child of God, the only way you know you're in the battle is that you're being attacked. If the devil isn't messing with you, it's because he's not worried about you. If he's not coming after you it's because he knows you're not a threat to his program. But, if he's messing with you all day, every day, it's because your name spells "trouble" for him. So Jabez says, "Lord, as You bless me, as You expand my borders, and as Your presence goes with me, keep the enemy off my back. Keep the enemy from detouring me from where You have me headed."

Are you being attacked today? Depend on God today. Ask Him to bless you and keep you from harm today.

## MARCH 2

# Do You Not Remember?

*"We will remember. We will remember. We will*
*remember, the works of Your hands."*
*– Tommy Walker (lyrics – We Will Remember)*

*Jesus asked them: "Why are you talking about having no bread?*
*Do you still not see or understand? ... And don't you remember?*
*When I broke the five loaves for the five thousand, how many*
*basketfuls of pieces did you pick up?" (Mark 8:18-19)*

What we see here is Jesus with His disciples and two totally different perspectives on what that one loaf of bread means. For the disciples, that one loaf represents lack. It represents a shortcoming. It represents not measuring up. That one loaf represents running out before they're finished. But to Jesus, that one loaf represents something that the disciples should have seen from the time that they saw what can happen when you have a loaf of bread and Jesus in the same place! Jesus had fed four thousand with seven loaves of bread and five thousand with five loaves of bread. The disciples had one loaf, and there were only thirteen of them! That's why He reminds them: "Do you not remember? Do you not remember what I did with the loaves of bread before?"

My friend, do *you* not remember? Sometimes we look at our one loaf of bread with the wrong mindset. I believe God says to you today, "That one thing that you have is enough for me to bless it, break it and multiply it."

## MARCH 3

# No Condemnation

*"One of these days, some simple soul will pick up the
book of God, read it, and believe it. Then the rest of
us will be embarrassed." – Leonard Ravenhill*

*Dear friends, if our hearts do not condemn us, we have confidence
before God and receive from Him anything we ask, because we keep
His commands and do what pleases Him. (1 John 3:21-22)*

But, what if your heart *does* condemn you? What if you judge yourself
unworthy? I believe there are countless people in the body of Christ
who do *not* get answers to prayer and do not receive the goodness of God
in their lives because they don't feel like they're worthy of it. If you judge
yourself unworthy, you are judging Jesus to be unworthy …unworthy
to be your Redeemer, unworthy to be your Savior. My friend, if you will
ever get the focus off yourself and fix your eyes on Jesus, blessing will
begin pouring out on you… not based on "performance," but based on
the Lamb that is worthy. Miracles and healing will happen because Jesus
bought them with His stripes and His blood. Revelation refers to Jesus
when it speaks of the "new song" – "Worthy is the Lamb!" But, some of
us here on Earth are still singing the old song, "I'm so unworthy", and
we call it "humility." Just remember, humility is not putting yourself
down. Humility is lifting Jesus up.

What about you? Is your heart condemning you? Jesus paid the
highest price that there would be no condemnation!

MARCH 4

# I Believe

*"I'm amazed, that You love me..."*
*– Carol Cymbala (I'm Amazed)*

*The one that Jesus loved dearly was reclining against*
*Him, his head on His shoulder. (John 13:23)*

If Jesus asks you on Judgment Day, "Did you believe that I loved you?" What would you say? I think Jesus is very concerned with the answer to that question. "Did you believe that I loved you? That I desired you? That I waited for you, day-after-day? That I longed to hear the sound of your voice?" Some of us are going to have to answer, "No, I didn't. I never really believed it." It's only when we sit where no one else will sit, and lean on the very breast of Jesus, that we will ever understand the depth and the intensity of God's love. My kids know that I love them, and it's not just because I gave birth to them. They know that I love them because of the time we've spent together, and the closeness we've shared. Knowing the depth and intensity of my love would be impossible to believe if they refused to be near and spend time with me. Likewise, it is impossible to believe the love of Jesus if we don't get to know Him or neglect to spend time in His presence.

Do you believe that He loves you? If there is any doubt at all, lean on Him today and spend some time with Him.

Jesus, we choose to "recline against You" with our head on Your shoulder. We will bask in Your love for us today.

# Resist

*"Prayer is putting oneself in the hands of God."*
*– Mother Theresa*

*Cast all your anxiety on Him because He cares for you. Be*
*alert and of sober mind. … The devil prowls around like a*
*roaring lion looking for someone to devour. Resist him…*
*(1 Peter 5:7-9)*

The enemy is prowling around like a roaring lion, looking for someone he can eat alive. He's looking for a family he can tear apart. He's looking for a future that he can ruin before it even gets started. The devil is busy. The devil is active. I heard a preacher once say, "The birthmark of a believer is a bull's-eye." But let me tell you what else has "marked" you since you were born again: "Surely goodness and mercy will follow you *all the days of your life!*" We are born again into a living hope. But we are also born again into an eternal struggle. The day you give your life to Christ, a battle begins. You'd think that after Peter tells us about this roaring lion that he would tell us to "RUN!" But he doesn't tell us to "run." Instead he tells us to "resist." Earlier in the text, Peter says, "Humble yourselves, therefore, under God's mighty hand." Peter is speaking to those who are under the attack of the enemy…anxiety and depression, disappointment, and failure. To those who have hit rock bottom and don't know what's next…Peter says to every believer, "You've got the upper hand." The hand of God is mighty. The hand of God is strong. And no matter how it looks or how it feels, the hand of God is over your life. You can resist the enemy because the hand of God is over your life!

# In His Grip

*"What are you doing right now that requires faith?"*
*– Francis Chan*

*But when he saw the wind, he was afraid and beginning*
*to sink, cried out, "Lord, save me!" (Matthew 14:30)*

Sometimes, it's when you're right on the verge of something…you know the story. Peter is out on the sea. He's trying to make his way toward Jesus. He's just about to reach him when he begins to sink. He's sinking, but he's not sunk. He's going down, but he's not out. The lion is prowling, but he has not prevailed. And in the next verse it says, "*Immediately,* Jesus reached out His hand and caught him. 'You of little faith, why did you doubt?'" What's important to note is that Jesus is *not* walking towards Peter. Peter is walking towards Jesus. When Jesus sees Peter falling and hears him crying, He reaches out His hand and Peter is *close enough* for Jesus to reach. The problem for some of us, is not that we're sinking. It's that we won't stay close enough for God to get us in His grip.

Let me encourage today. Even if you're in a storm, if you will get close to Jesus, He will reach out His hand and keep you in His grip.

Jesus, there are storms brewing all around us. We draw near to You and thank You for keeping us in the grip of Your hand.

☙

# His Way

*"The beginning of anxiety is the end of faith, and the*
*beginning of true faith, is the end of anxiety."*
*– George Mueller*

*Cast all your anxiety (and depression, fears, frustrations, negative*
*thoughts, guilt, loneliness) on Him because He cares for you. (1 Peter 5:7)*

Peter fell asleep in the Garden of Gethsemane while he was supposed to be watching Jesus' back. Later, he tells the church to be alert, which translates into "be prayerful." Peter knew the enemy eats Christians who sleep in times of battle. The devil doesn't like it one bit that you're moving forward in your relationship with God and away from anxiety and depression. The good news about anxiety and depression is that when you're desperate enough, they will drive you to seek God. The verse says, "Cast all your anxiety, (depression)…" Peter was a fisherman, so I picture him casting the nets from one side of the boat to the other, just because Jesus told him to. Sometimes the anxiety in our life is a result of our unwillingness to be obedient. Maybe Jesus, like he did with Peter, is telling you to cast your net on the other side. It's time to do it His way now. "We fished all night and caught nothing," Peter said. "I've been trying to do this my way. I've been trying to handle it on my own."

Is there something that is causing you to have anxiety today? What is the Holy Spirit saying about it? Maybe today is the day to do it His way. "Cast it all on Him because He cares about you."

## MARCH 8

# Joy

*"Joy is not the absence of suffering. It is the
presence of God." – Robert Schuller*

*Fight the good fight of faith, lay hold of eternal life, to
which you were also called, and have confessed the good
confession in the presence of many witnesses.
(1 Timothy 6:12)*

When Paul says to "fight the good fight of faith" he's talking to the children of God. He's not telling them to fight to stay saved. He's telling them to fight for the joy that comes with their salvation. Their salvation is an eternal gift from God. He's telling them to remember that, with that salvation, we've been promised that we can draw water from the well of salvation with joy. We can have joy. I want it. Don't you? This one thing I know: Satan seeks to destroy my faith and my joy. He can't destroy my soul. He can't destroy me. So, his effort is spent to destroy my faith.

When was the last time that you felt real joy? The enemy will attack you on all sides hoping to diminish your faith. If your faith can be diminished, then your joy becomes non-existent. Paul says to fight the good fight of faith. How do you do that? Remember what the Lord has done for you so far. Get in His Word and consume every verse about faith and about joy. No matter what your circumstances are today, God still has joy for you.

# Still Rejoicing?

*"Joy is the serious business of Heaven." – C.S. Lewis*

*For this reason, when I could no longer endure it, I sent*
*to know your faith, lest by some means the tempter had*
*tempted you, and our labor might be in vain.*
*(1 Thessalonians 3:5)*

Paul wasn't saying, "I couldn't wait any longer, I had to find out if you were still saved." That is never the issue, my friends. He wanted to know if they were still rejoicing in their salvation. He said, "I couldn't put it off any longer. After all we've taught you, we walked away and left you in God's hands. But I had to know, because I know that when Satan comes, he comes to destroy your faith." Why does the devil want to destroy your faith? Because faith and joy go together. If you don't have any faith, you won't have any joy. But, if you have faith in God, there is joy beyond description. And it's not so much a joy that is on the outside. It's a deep, abiding, and powerful current of joy in your soul that makes no sense to the world. Paul's concern was that after he left them and they began to deal with life and all the powers of darkness that come against believers, that their faith would be whittled down to the point where they couldn't rejoice anymore.

Have you ever been there? Whether through attacks from the enemy or just all that life throws at you, your faith gets whittled down to nothing? Rejoicing is non-existent. Paul says, "Fight the good fight of faith!"

## MARCH 10

# You Are Not Alone

*"Christ literally walked in our shoes and entered
into our affliction." – Tim Keller*

*For God is working in you, giving you the desire and the
power to do what pleases Him. (Philippians 2:13)*

In other words, you are not doing this by yourself. You are not
walking this walk alone. You are not fighting this fight alone. There
is Someone inside of you who is strengthening you for the day. This
Someone, Who is your Savior, has already decided that He's going to
give you the power, hunger, and thirst for righteousness. He gives it to
you. All you have to do is "fight this good fight of faith." That's just
keeping your eyes on Jesus! You don't have to figure out anything else.
You just keep your eyes on Jesus. Even when everything is raging around
you, you keep your eyes on Jesus. It's a good fight of faith. Jesus came
to carry your burdens. However, I have found my struggle is not really
in carrying a burden. My struggle is letting my burden be carried for
me by somebody else. So, every day I have to fight this good fight that
says, "Here it is, Jesus."

Have you felt that the outcome of your situation is dependent upon
you? It isn't! You're not alone! Jesus reaches out His arms to you today
to carry your burden for you. All you have to do is hand it to Him and
say, "Here it is, Jesus."

# Come To Me

*"Simply put, if you want Bible results, you have to live by Bible principles." – Brian Houston*

*Come to Me, all you who labor and are heavy-laden, and I will give you rest. My yoke is easy, and My burden is light. (Matthew 11:28-30)*

*I*n the old days, they never put two strong oxen in the same yoke because they tend to compete. They fight against each other. They want to pull in opposite directions. Jesus is saying to us, "If this is going to work, you'll need to get in My yoke. But I'm the strong One. I'm the One Who knows where we're going." Have you ever noticed how burdens can suck the life right out of you? How they can make life seem hopeless? And then our thoughts can go something like: "Well, this is just my lot in life. I'm getting what I deserve." With this thinking, we are missing the point! Jesus died on the cross so you would NOT be burdened. The requirement of God to keep the law had never been kept by any human being, so Jesus kept it for you. And died in your place. And rose again so that now, there should be no burden that breaks your back. He is your burden-bearer and He delights in carrying them. No weight is too heavy for Him.

How heavy is your burden today? I believe that if you will find the strength to raise your hands to Him and say, "Here it is, Lord, take it," I believe He will. And I believe that He will fill you with joy unspeakable.

# Down In The Dumps

*"Our infirmities become the black velvet on which the
diamond of God's love glitters all the more brightly."*
*– Charles Spurgeon*

*Why are you down in the dumps, dear soul? Why are you
crying the blues? Fix my eyes on God – soon I'll be praising
again. He puts a smile on my face. He's my God.*
*(Psalm 42:5)*

Florida is famous for its sinkholes. The ground just opens up and swallows homes and people. How does this happen? It happens gradually. Over time, the foundation has been compromised by acidic rainwater and there comes a day when the surface layer will just give away. There's not enough solid stuff left underneath to support what's left of the loose stuff above, and then the whole thing collapses. Depression and sinkholes have a lot in common. Depression can feel like it comes on suddenly when it's usually the result of a much longer process…over time. Inner resources are slowly depleted until, one day, there's nothing left. It feels like the world caves in and darkness rules.

Be careful to take care of yourself today. Do you need to rest? Do you need to hydrate? Do you need some time with a friend? You have to be careful not to let your inner resources be depleted.

Do you ever feel "down in the dumps"? Psalm 42:5 tells you to "fix your eyes on God" and "*soon*" He'll put a smile on your face, and you will be praising again.

# I Will Yet Praise Him

*"Whatever troubles are weighing you down are not chains.*
*They are featherweight when compared to the glory yet*
*to come. With a sweep of a prayer and the praise of a*
*child's heart, God can strip away any cobweb."*
*— Joni Eareckson Tada*

*Why, my soul, are you downcast? Why so disturbed*
*within me? Put your hope in God, for I will yet praise*
*Him, my Savior and my God." (Psalm 42:11)*

The Christian faith is not about pretending everything is great all the time. The Christian faith is not about never seeing a cloud in the sky. The Christian faith is about a God Who shows up in the middle of the storm and asks us to choose to believe Him, and to believe *in* Him. He asks us to trust in Him even though the winds and the waves seem to overtake us. And, by trusting Him anyway, praising Him anyway, and believing Him anyway, it's actually possible to go through seasons of sadness or depression but still live a life of incredible faith.

Are you downcast today? No matter how it looks, God promises if you will put your hope in Him, choose to believe Him and trust Him anyway, your faith will increase. He will never leave you. He will get you through to the other side of this.

## MARCH 14

# He Picks You!

*"The truth, even though I cannot feel it right now, is that I am the chosen child of God, precious in God's eyes, called the beloved from all eternity and held safe in an everlasting embrace… We must dare to opt consciously for our chosenness and not allow our emotions, feelings, or passions to seduce us into self-rejection."*
*– Henri J.M. Nouwen*

*…He Himself has said, "I will never leave you nor forsake you." So we may boldly say: "The Lord is my helper; I will not fear. What can man do to me?" (Hebrews 13:5-6)*

This verse means that Jesus will never physically reject you, nor will He ever turn His heart away from you. God has promised all of us that there will never be a moment in all of eternity that He will ever reject us. This is a promise in Ephesians 1:5-6: "…having predestined us to adoption as sons by Jesus Christ to Himself, according to the good pleasure of His will, to the praise of the glory of His grace, by which He made us accepted in the Beloved." You are a part of God's family. You've been adopted. You are a member of the most secure family that has ever, or will ever exist.

Have you ever felt rejected? People may have rejected you, but God never has and never will. You belong to Him. There's nothing that you can ever do to change that. He picks you!

# Desperate

*"Desperate prayers are the most powerful prayers."*
*– Leonard Ravenhill*

*The Lord is close to the brokenhearted and saves those*
*who are crushed in spirit. (Psalm 34:18)*

The Lord doesn't want us to hide our troubles. He isn't pleased when we cover things up. Someone asks how you're doing and you say, "Oh, I'm fine. I'm doing great." When, in truth, you're falling apart on the inside. Do you not realize that He works through people? He sends people to be Him to you. He is fond of desperate people because He is close to the brokenhearted, and He wants you to draw closer to Him. He uses your circumstances to bring you closer to Him. If you are desperate today, cry out to God. Great faith is characterized by desperation. Great faith is characterized by persistence. It's always too soon to quit! We tend to be persistent about everything else that has no spiritual significance, but when it comes to spiritual things, we cave! Great faith fights through obstacles. Great faith fights through setbacks. God always honors persistent and desperate prayer.

Whatever you're facing today, Jesus can touch it. Jesus can fix it. Jesus can go to wherever that situation is. He is still in the healing business. He's still in the restoration business. "He is close to the brokenhearted and saves the crushed in spirit."

# Divine Exchange

*"If the Spirit of God detects anything in you that is wrong,*
*He does not ask you to put it right; He asks you to accept the*
*light, and He will put it right." – Oswald Chambers*

*For God took the sinless Christ and poured into Him our sins. Then,*
*in exchange, He poured God's goodness into us. (2 Corinthians 5:21)*

"Father, is there any other way? Will You take this cup from Me?" The answer was "no." When the answer was no, Jesus didn't continue praying for it to pass from Him. He went on praying for God to help Him in drinking it. He went on praying that He would be able to fulfill His assignment of death in exchange for our lives! There was no other way than the cross. Jesus, the Lamb, would have the reward of His suffering. "For the joy that was set before Him, He endured the cross." (Hebrews 12:2) I have had the joy of visiting Israel multiple times. I sat in the dungeon where they believe Jesus was held before His crucifixion. I was overcome with emotion and I remember whispering, "What were You thinking about when You were down here?" I heard, as clear as my spirit could hear, "I was thinking about You."

My friend, you and I have been given a Divine exchange. He took every sin from our past, our present, and our future upon Himself, and in exchange, poured God's goodness into us. No matter what this day brings you, you have every reason to worship and praise Him all-the-day long!

# We Need Each Other

*"Christ has no body now on Earth but yours."*
*— Teresa of Avila*

*I look to the right and see; for there is no one who regards me; there*
*is no escape for me, and no one cares for my soul. (Psalm 142:4)*

In this text, David is sitting among four hundred men in a cave. He's looking at these men and thinking: "I'm sitting in a crowded place and no one is giving me a passing thought. No one really knows who I am, or what I'm thinking, or what I'm struggling with. Though they may see me on the outside, they have no idea what's happening on the inside. I'm surrounded by a bunch of people and not feeling any connection to them at all." Not only did this happen thousands of years ago, in a cave, to a man after God's own heart, it can happen to us, in our own church. You can look to the right and to the left and think, "Even though we're in church singing and worshipping together, no one has any idea what's going on in my life." Just like David and his men, you're all pursuing the same thing, but oftentimes, still feeling disconnected. Can I tell you just how valuable the body of Christ is to our lives? For us not to be connected is a tragedy. We need each other. Maybe you feel like David did. Maybe you don't feel connected to anyone. May I encourage you today that, perhaps, God is calling you to make the first move? Who can you reach out to and connect with today?

## MARCH 18

# Which Part Are You?

*"The object of love is to serve, not to win."*
*– Woodrow Wilson*

*Just as there are many parts to our bodies, so it is with*
*Christ's body. We are all parts of it, and it takes every*
*one of us to make it complete. (Romans 12:4-5)*

*y*ou are important to the body of Christ. Every gift that God has given you is crucial. From being kind to the person who sits next to you in church on Sunday, to giving someone a ride, to visiting someone who is in the hospital. Everyone is important to Jesus and to the body of Christ. Don't sell yourself short. You have a place. Hudson Taylor, one of the greatest missionaries to China that ever lived, was speaking in Scotland and a one-legged schoolteacher came up to him and offered himself to be used in China. Taylor asked, "With only one leg, why do you think of going as a missionary?" And this was the one-legged schoolteacher's response: "I don't see those with two legs going, so one leg is better than no legs." God uses one-legged schoolteachers, and if you are breathing today, God has something for you to do as well.

What is it, my friend? One of the greatest joys of life is serving our Father and the Body of Christ. And, the Body of Christ is not complete without you.

# We Go Together

*"Some Christians try to go to Heaven alone, in solitude.*
*But believers are not compared to bears or lions or other*
*animals that wander alone. Those who belong to Christ are*
*sheep in this respect - that they love to get together. Sheep go*
*in flocks, and so do God's people." – Charles Spurgeon*

*He who separates himself seeks his own desires and he*
*quarrels against all sound wisdom. (Proverbs 18:1)*

He who separates himself *seeks* his own desire. One of Satan's greatest goals is to isolate us - to get you away from everyone else and make you think you are the only one who struggles. It's a tactic that's as old as time. He did this with Eve. He isolated her from her own husband. He got her alone and started whispering lies. There's something powerful when a group of believers in Christ are unified and come together. But the enemy would try to keep you secluded and make you think that no one needs you or no one cares about you. And, you can come up with all sorts of excuses: "I'm not relational. I'm too shy. I don't make friends easily. I'm an introvert." Excuses! Isolation is really a form of selfishness. "He who separates (or isolates) himself seeks his own desires…"

We are all part of the body of Christ. We all have a contribution to make to the family of God. The enemy does not want you to make your contribution. Shut him down today! You are needed in the Body of Christ!

# Wisdom

*"Men are not prisoners of fate, but only prisoners of their own minds." – Franklin D. Roosevelt*

*Where there is no guidance the people fall, but in abundance of counselors there is victory. (Proverbs 11:14)*

We need to surround ourselves with other believers. There is wisdom in a multitude of counselors. But you lose a stream of wisdom when you isolate yourself. When you live isolated, you end up counseling yourself. You talk to yourself. Next to Jesus, Solomon was the wisest man who ever lived; and even he says, "You get smarter when you surround yourself with wise people." It's very dangerous to make decisions without wise counsel in your life. Alienation elevates you, and you begin to think you have all the answers and begin to lose the voice of sound wisdom.

Are you feeling isolated today? God wants to put someone in your life who can help you, walk with you, share with you, and speak truth and life to you. Ask Him to send someone. Find a good church, if you don't have one already, and I believe He will have new friends waiting for you.

MARCH 21

# Faith

*"Faith is believing in something when common sense tells you not to." – Valentine Davies (Miracle On 34ᵗʰ Street)*

*Then Jesus said to her, "Woman, you have great faith! Your request is granted." (Matthew 15:21-28)*

This woman is pestering Jesus. And she won't stop. Her daughter's life is on the line. "Lord…have mercy on me!" Jesus ignored her. This time, she kneels before Him, "Lord, help me!" He answers her, but not the answer any of us are expecting. He had just made it clear earlier that He was there to save the children of Israel. Since this woman was not a Jew, Jesus says to her, "It is not right to take the children's bread and toss it to the dogs." What?? Did He just call her a dog? (This was common language for Jews in that day.) I'm guessing that most of us would have given up at this point. Not this woman. She was desperate. She wasn't moving. There was no obstacle that was going to get in the way of her receiving a blessing from the Healer. And so, she replies to Jesus, "Yes, it is, Lord. Even the dogs eat crumbs that fall from their master's table." I would have loved to have seen the look on Jesus' face at that moment. At her comment, Jesus said to her, "Woman, you have great faith! Your request is granted."

What about you? Are you desperate for an answer today? He is "close to the brokenhearted and saves those who are crushed in spirit." (Psalm 34:18)

# Arise! Shine!

*"There is no one who is insignificant in the purpose of God." – Alistair Begg*

*"Arise, shine, for your light has come, and the glory of the Lord rises upon you." (Isaiah 60:1)*

I grew up in a small, country church where my grandfather was the pastor. It took forty minutes, one way, on mountainous, single lane roads, in rain, sleet or snow, with the obnoxious combination of my dad's Old Spice, my mom's Miss Breck hairspray, and my grandmother's rose toilette, all swirling around our Ford LTD…to get to church. (Did I mention that I get carsick?) Church was on Wednesday nights, Saturday nights, Sunday mornings and Sunday nights. There was no schedule to evening services. In other words, you NEVER knew when you would get out of there. As a child, I really dreaded going to church. It was always fine once I was there. The music was great, the services were exciting, but the trip! There was only one person who, if I fixed my thoughts on him, could get me through it - Mr. Henry Wykle. Mr. Wykle would always be outside the church doors when we got there. He would smile at me, shake my hand, reach into his pocket, and hand me either a piece of gum or a fireball candy. That fireball would last me all throughout most church services. I used to think that Mr. Wykle came just for me, that I was the only one he was there to see.

Isn't that just like Jesus? Do you realize the impact you have on others? Like Mr. Wykle, today let's "Arise, shine and let the glory of the Lord rise upon us!"

# Vision

*"A man without a vision is a man without a future. A
man without a future will always return to his past."*
*— P.K. Bernard*

*Where there is no vision, the people are unrestrained, but
happy is he who keeps the law. (Proverbs 29:18)*

*I* wear contact lenses. Without them, I'm legally blind. On a recent trip, I had a contact lens emergency. I had no spares and I had no glasses…and I was alone. While I waited until my optometrist's office opened, I decided to try to go to breakfast in my hotel…with no vision. After bumping into people, spilling milk all over the counter, and "losing" my table when I went to get more coffee, fasting breakfast would have been a better choice. Then, after a 45-minute van ride (the hotel was nice enough to have an employee to drive the blind woman), and a splitting headache, I finally had my vision restored. What a difference two little pieces of plastic made! I was so grateful; I could have cried for joy! Losing your vision spiritually can be even more disastrous. Losing your vision is painful, it's frustrating, it's messy, it hurts other people, and it keeps you in the dark. God has a plan and a purpose for your life. Walking in that purpose requires obedience and the power of the Holy Spirit – VISION!

If you feel like your life has become blurry, get back in the Word and ask the Holy Spirit to put you back on your path and to light the way so you get your vision back.

# What's Your Story?

*"The Bible makes it clear that every time that there is a story of faith, it is completely original. God's creative genius is endless." – Eugene H. Peterson*

*It has seemed good to me to show the signs and wonders that the Most High God has done for me. (Daniel 4:2)*

*I*'ll never forget the night when a female pastor began telling the congregation "her story." I sat there stunned and amazed at all that she had been through. But mostly, I was moved by how honest she was about the mistakes she had made in her life. A pastor?? Are you kidding me?

I was raised in the church. My grandfather was a pastor. Yet, I had never been touched so deeply in a church service. For the first time in my life, I began to have hope that somehow God *could* use me. And not only that, He had planned to use me all along.

We all have a story. One of our greatest callings is to tell people of God's goodness in our lives. Do you realize that God wants to intersect your life with someone else *just* so you can tell them what God has done for you? Your biggest secrets could be the very key that will unlock someone else's prison.

Your truth will truly set someone else free. Will you tell it?

# One Loaf

*"There is nothing impossible with God. All the impossibility is with us when we measure God by the limitations of our unbelief." – Smith Wigglesworth*

*The disciples had forgotten to bring bread, except for one loaf they had with them in the boat. (Mark 8:14)*

Earlier in Mark 8, the disciples had just seen Jesus break seven loaves of bread and feed four thousand people. And yet, they're on the boat, they only have one loaf, and they're upset and afraid. They're worried they won't have enough to outlast or withstand the duration of their journey. "I only have one loaf of bread." I only have one idea. I only have one seemingly dead-end job. I only have one pitiful amount of money in my bank account. And I'm afraid my one job, my one idea won't be enough to withstand the journey that's ahead of me.

Do you know what it's like to only have one loaf of bread? One true friend… One source of income… When you look ahead, there are so many obstacles, so many days that you have to get through. And you only have one loaf of bread. Today I encourage you to go back and remember what Jesus can do with just one loaf!

# Change Your Diet

*"Insanity: Doing the same thing over and over again and expecting different results." – Albert Einstein*

*Every moving thing that lives shall be food for you. I have given you all things, even as the green herbs.*
*(Genesis 9:3-4)*

Sometimes God wants to change our diets. In order to do that, our appetites must change. You have to be willing to change relationships. You have to be willing to no longer need validation like you have in the past. When God takes you higher, you must be willing to change your diet by letting Him change what you crave in your appetites. You need to cry out:

*"God, I want to be so empty that all I'm filled with is Your Spirit."*

*"God, change my cravings so that bitterness doesn't make me happy anymore. Change my appetite so that unforgiveness doesn't satisfy me anymore. Change my hunger so that I can start blessing the people who have hurt me."*

# Jesus Needed To Go There

*"The unbelieving world should see our testimony lived out
daily because it just may point them to the Savior."*
— *Billy Graham*

*Jesus left Judea and departed again to Galilee. But He
NEEDED to go through Samaria. (John 4:4)*

Geographically, the easiest and quickest way to get to Galilee from Judea was to go due north right through Samaria. However, because Jews hated Samaritans so much, most would take the longer route to avoid going through Samaritan territory. So why did Jesus "need to" go through Samaria when the Jews didn't go there at all? Jesus "*needed*" to go through Samaria because He had a divine appointment with a downcast woman. Jesus needed to meet with this woman because He first wanted to change her life so that then her life could change the lives of others.

Perhaps, like the Samaritan woman, you feel downcast and life has been tough. I want to encourage and remind you that your past and your mistakes may be the very things that God wants to use to set another free. An entire city was saved *only* because of the testimony of the Samaritan woman.

I invite you to fill in the blanks: "Jesus *needed* to go through (<u>your town)</u> because He had a divine appointment with (<u>your name)</u>."

# Be With Me

*"God can't give us peace and happiness apart from Himself
because there is no such thing." – C.S. Lewis*

*"Oh that You would bless me indeed…that
Your hand would be with me…"*
*(1 Chronicles 4:10)*

J abez prayed that the Lord's hand would be with him. In other words, "I don't want your blessing unless I can have You." "I don't want You to just give me more stuff." "I don't want You to bless my business." "I don't want You to enlarge my ministry if You're not going to be with me." God wants to bless you, "indeed," but He wants to do so much more than that. He doesn't want you to become comfortable with "the blessing" so that you no longer seek or need the "Blesser." Just like Moses said, "If You don't go with me, I won't go."

Think about last year. Begin to thank God for all the blessings of last year. But would you pray that His hand would be with you? Having the One who gives the blessings is way more important than any blessing that any of us could ever receive!

Oh, that You would bless us indeed, Lord. But more than the blessings, we want You.

# The Least Of These

*"Self-righteousness is difficult to recognize as sin because
we picked it up in such a respectable place, in the company
of Christians sitting in a church pew, singing hymns
and reading the Bible, working "in Jesus' name. "*
*– Eugene H. Peterson*

*Who can say, "I have cleansed my heart, I am
pure from my sin?" (Proverbs 20:9)*

My oldest daughter, Ashley, had an opportunity a few years ago to visit a Muslim family in their home. She called me afterwards and said, "Mom, I've never been with a group of people who were so genuine, generous and kind." I immediately felt defensive, but I let her continue. Her observation was that most Christians she had ever been around acted one way at church, but then acted completely different once they left the property. She said, "They raise their hands during worship, but turn up their nose at the person in front of them who looks like they are hung over from a long night at the bar." I wanted to defend. I wanted to argue. But I couldn't. I had to come to terms with what she said. I knew she wasn't the only person in the world who feels that way.

Let's not forget who Jesus hung out with. Let's never lose sight of the truth that we are all the "least of these." We've all, like sheep, gone astray.

Like me, do you need to ask forgiveness for a spirit of self-righteousness today? Nothing should keep us from showing the love of Jesus.

# Woe To You

*"Legalism is concerned simply with external conformity
and is blind to internal motivation." – R.C. Sproul*

*Jesus replied, "And you experts in the law, woe to you, because you
load people down with burdens they can hardly carry, and you
yourselves will not lift one finger to help them." (Luke 11:46)*

My son recently told me of a spirited debate he had with one of
his college friends. The six-hour conversation had to do with
communion. His friend insisted that if communion was not done exactly
the "right way," then the grace of God could not be received. The "right
way" meant down to the type of candle that was burned, the words that
were spoken, the person who administered the communion, and so on
and so on. I am not disrespecting any denominations or cultures, but
Jesus warned us about these things. I told my son the testimony of a
lady that I know. She was unable to leave her house because of an illness.
She was watching a church service via streaming. The Holy Spirit told
her to take communion with the people in the church service that she
was watching. She didn't have the juice or the wafers, or the pastor, but
she grabbed what she did have and followed along anyway. Was her
communion void because it was done differently?

Let's be careful not to "load people down with burdens." Jesus has
unending grace, mercy and healing for all of us. I believe Jesus was well
pleased by the lady's personal and private communion service. Jesus was
more interested in what was in her heart than what was in her cup. And
Jesus is most interested in your heart as well.

## MARCH 31

# Two Are Better Than One

*"It is one of the blessings of old friends that you can afford
to be stupid with them." – Ralph Waldo Emerson*

*Two are better than one because they have a good return for their labor;
if either of them falls down, one can help the other up. But pity anyone
who falls and has no one to help them up. (Ecclesiastes 4:9-10)*

Isolation is dangerous. If you're in isolation, there's no one to help you when you need it. Who do you have to pray for you…to confide in…to give you strength…to lift you up? Who can you call in a tragedy? The Body of Christ is meant to include you and to include me. One of the best ways to combat loneliness and depression is to serve someone else. Jesus uses us to help each other. We all fall down. It's so much easier to get back up when a hand comes down to where you are and helps you up. We need each other. We need to know that we are not alone. Isolation makes us think that we are the only person wrestling with a particular sin, problem, difficulty, or addiction. We need someone who can tell us that they've been where we've been. "You can, and you will, make it; because I made it." But when you isolate yourself, you miss the words of encouragement. When you isolate yourself, you stagnate your growth. You can't grow without the Body of Christ. Let's surround ourselves with godly people and come out of the darkness into His marvelous light!

Father send us good, Godly, transparent friends.

# Don't Be A Fool!

*"A wise man may look ridiculous in the company of fools."*
*– Thomas Fuller*

*"Do not forsake wisdom, and she will protect you; love her, and*
*she will watch over you. Wisdom is supreme; therefore, get wisdom.*
*Though it cost all you have, get understanding." (Proverbs 4:6-7)*

April Fool's Day…I admit it. I love it. I'm one of those people you would hate on April Fool's Day. I've convinced people that I was in jail. I've convinced my husband that my engagement ring was missing. The list is endless. I know. I'm bad.

We have an enemy who would also like every day to be "Fool's Day." He will spend much time studying you and figuring out your "triggers", and whispering lies in your ear in order to "fool" you. He wants to fool you about who you are. He wants to fool you about "Whose" you are. He wants to fool you about your future, your marriage, and your children. You need truth and wisdom to combat these lies!

How do you get wisdom? *Desire* wisdom with everything within you. *Study* and know the Word of the Lord. Like Solomon, *pray* for wisdom. But first and foremost, to get wisdom "Come to Jesus", in Whom all the treasures of wisdom are hidden.

Father, we ask You for wisdom today. Please guide us in every decision, conversation and encounter.

# Do You Believe That I Love You?

*"Define yourself radically as one beloved by God. This
is the true self. Every other identity is illusion."*
*– Brennan Manning (Abba's Child)*

*And He said to them, "Cast the net on the right-hand side of the boat
and you will find a catch." So they cast, and then they were not able to
haul it in because of the great number of fish. Therefore, that disciple
whom Jesus loved said to Peter, "It is the Lord." (John 21:4-7)*

Some are always wondering what in the world is the matter... at home,
on their job, and in the church. But "the disciple whom Jesus loves"
knows that God is doing something. He can see the hand of God at
work where others only see pain and grief. John had been close enough
to Jesus to recognize His whisper; surely he would recognize His shout!
If we can't recognize His whisper or His shout, we probably won't notice
Him passing through. What would it mean if you came to a place where
you saw your primary identity in life as "the one whom Jesus loves?"
I've been labeled a good number of things: abandoned, rejected, not
good enough, unclean, and unworthy for ministry. But when I ask my
Father who He says I am, He tells me I am His. He tells me, "You are
the one I love." I believe it. Will you believe it? You are the one that
Jesus loves. Even with all the wrong turns you've made in your past; the
mistakes, the moments of selfishness, dishonesty, and degraded love...
Jesus really loves you.

# Don't Give Up!

*"Endurance is not just the ability to bear a hard thing,
but to turn it into glory." – Philip Yancey*

*And let us run with perseverance the race marked out for us, fixing our
eyes on Jesus, the pioneer and perfecter of faith. (Hebrews 12:1-2)*

This morning I hiked to the top of a mountain with an elevation of 4,000 feet. That shouldn't be difficult for a mountain girl, but this mountain girl has been living in the flat lands of Florida for the past five years. Not to mention, the grade was quite steep. Hence the sign that said, "WARNING! VERY STEEP GRADE…HAZARDOUS EDGE." Understandably, I was huffing and puffing a bit and had to stop quite a few times. There were moments when I thought about turning back. My knees were crying. My back was aching. But I had heard about the overlook at the top. I hadn't seen it. But, I'd heard testimonies of those who had lived to see it and tell the story.

So, when it got tough, when it got steep and rocky, I focused on the road right in front of me. One step at a time, one foot in front of the other, but *always* keeping my thoughts on "the prize."

Life can get really painful at times. Sometimes, it can feel like a perpetual uphill battle. Sometimes, you may want to just give up the race. But, you must "run with perseverance" this race that has been marked out just for you by keeping your eyes fixed on the One Who is cheering you on!

# I've Got The Joy, Joy, Joy, Joy…

*"If you have no joy, there's a leak in your Christianity somewhere." – Billy Sunday*

*You make known to me the path of life; in your presence there is fullness of joy; at your right hand are pleasures forevermore. (Psalm 16:11)*

As I write this, I'm on a mini-sabbatical in the mountains. What I hear right now are the waters of a gentle brook and a lovely voice humming and singing bits and pieces of songs. The voice belongs to one of the housekeepers at the retreat center at which I'm staying. Hearing Sheila (of course I had to go find her and introduce myself) really caught my attention. How does she have so much joy cleaning my toilet and making my bed? Simple: Joy is a choice. The Bible tells us that in His presence there is *fullness* of joy. I don't have to leave Him in the Bible that's sitting on my bedside table. I certainly don't have to leave Him at church on Sunday. I can take Him with me to my retreat in the mountains, and I can take Him to work with me on Monday. I am certain that Sheila takes Him everywhere she goes.

What about you? Have you lost your joy? In spite of your current circumstances, there is a simple solution. *Get in His presence.* You can have a fifteen-minute sabbatical yourself this morning. Shut everything else out. Turn your praise and worship music on, get in His Word, and just talk to Him.

# One Thing I Do Know

*""Never underestimate the impact that your mere existence*
*can have on another human being." – Fred Rogers*

*He replied, "Whether he is a sinner or not, I don't know. One*
*thing I do know. I was blind but now I see." (John 9:25)*

I have had many spirited-conversations about Jesus with non-believers and believers alike. I recently spoke to a group of young men and women. Included in this group were a few non-believers. They were poised and ready to argue the existence of God and the gospel of Jesus Christ. I've also had conversations with believers who do not believe that Jesus does the same things today as He did in biblical times. I have never claimed to be a theologian. But I do consider myself above-average Bible literate. But more than that, I have my story. And that is the pattern for sharing our faith: "Here is my story." "This is who I was – blind, helpless and hopeless in my sin. Then I met Jesus, and this is how my life changed."

It's difficult for people to argue with a person's story. This newly sighted man in John 9 was not secondhand faith but the result of a direct encounter with Jesus.

"One thing I do know…" Do you know? Have you had an encounter with Jesus? If your answer is yes, then there is your pattern for sharing your faith. "Here is my story."

# A True Believer

*"Where I found truth, there found I my God,*
*Who is truth itself." – Augustine*

*"Yet you are looking for a way to kill me, because you*
*have no room for my word." (John 8:37)*

*H*ave you ever fought so hard on an issue that the focus was more on being right than on the actual issue? It's exhausting. It causes conflict in your heart and leads to stress and anxiety. It also leaves no room for peace or actual truth.

One mark of a true believer is that Jesus' words live within him or her. God's Word either changes a person's heart or causes internal conflict. Earlier in John 8, Jesus said in verses 31 and 32, "If you hold to my teaching, you are really my disciples. Then you will know the truth and the truth will set you free."

So many solutions to so many issues is surrender. Surrendering to Jesus, surrendering our right to be right, surrendering our hearts to be changed by God's Word.

Have you made room for His Word? And is His Word what is coming from your heart? If you need freedom today, just surrender to Him and then "you will know the truth and the truth will set you free."

# If You Don't Finish Your Assignment, Someone Else Will

*"Whenever God calls us to a task, He will equip us and enable us to complete that task." – Michael Youssef*

*And they cast their lots, and the lot fell on Matthias. And he was numbered with the eleven apostles. (Acts 1:26)*

According to Revelation, there are twelve foundations in heaven. On each of these twelve foundations, a name of each of the twelve apostles is written on them. One of those foundations had Judas' name on it, but it had to be scratched out. And Matthias' name has instead been carved into it instead.

If we don't finish what God has called us to do, He will raise someone else up to do it. If God has ordained it to be done, it WILL get done. In Revelation 3:11, we read, "Behold, I am coming quickly! Hold fast what you have, that no one may take your crown."

I have an assignment. If I don't complete it, that doesn't mean it won't get done. If God has purposed it, and I don't complete it, someone else will be raised up to finish it. And, they will get my rewards for that assignment.

Nope! Not going to happen. How about you? Let's carry on with what God has called us to do today.

# Intercessor

*"When a Christian shuns fellowship with other Christians,
the devil smiles. When he stops studying the Bible, the devil
laughs. When he stops praying, the devil shouts for joy."*
– Corrie Ten Boom

*And pray in the Spirit on all occasions with all kinds of prayers
and requests. With this in mind, be alert and always keep
on praying for all the Lord's people. (Ephesians 6:18)*

It is so powerful and humbling when I get a text message or an email from someone who has been praying for me. "Christy, the Lord put you on my heart and mind in the middle of the night. I don't know what you're struggling with, but I have been interceding for you." WHAT??!! I am always stunned to get those messages. I shouldn't be, but I am. Inevitably, it happens when I am being attacked in my mind or in my body. The person praying for me rarely knows what I am going through. They aren't aware of the invisible things invading my mind. They don't hear the whispers of the enemy in my ear. Yet, because they've made themselves available to the Holy Spirit, He uses them to fight for me.

Interceding, praying for the Lord's people, is something that all of us can do. I can testify to the power of it. I believe that on more than one occasion, the intercessory prayers of someone have saved my life.

Ask the Holy Spirit to bring to your mind, someone who is struggling. When He does, begin praying for that person.

# Beauty

*"The beauty of a woman must be seen in her eyes, because that is the doorway to her heart, the place where love resides." – Audrey Hepburn*

*Every part of you is so beautiful, my darling. Perfect is your beauty, without flaw within. (Song of Solomon 4:7)*

*H*ave you ever "played hard-to-get"? The biggest reason we play hard-to-get, is fear of rejection. We're afraid if we don't play hard-to-get, the pursuit will end, and all of us want to be pursued. Love stories always include pursuit. I believe that one reason so many marriages struggle is there's no more pursuit of each other.

There is a relationship that you can have where the pursuit never ends. God is pursuing you right now. He never stops pursuing. He longs to have "Come away, My darling" moments with you. He wants to "court" you. He longs to show you who you are. You don't have to play hard-to-get with Him. He's seen you naked and He still delights in you! He made you.

Every part of you is so beautiful. Every part. Perfect is your beauty. Believe that. Will you be still and listen to Him speak tenderly to you?

# The One Whom Jesus Loves

*"My deepest awareness of myself is that I am deeply loved by Jesus Christ and I have done nothing to earn it or deserve it." – Brennan Manning*

*One of them, the disciple whom Jesus loved, was reclining next to Him. (John 13:23)*

"The disciple whom Jesus loved…" John never actually named himself. Was he that arrogant? Did he actually believe that he was the only one who Jesus loved? Did he believe that Jesus loved him more than the others? I don't think so. I think John just really got what many never get. I believe he understood with a deep down, marrow-of-the-bone kind of understanding that, "This is who I really am." If John were to be asked by us today, "What is your primary identity in life?" He wouldn't reply, "I'm a disciple, an apostle, an evangelist, and an author of one of the four Gospels." I doubt he would even say, "Hello, my name is John." He would answer us, "I am the one whom Jesus loves." Sociologists have a theory called the looking glass self. You become what the most important person in your life (spouse, mother, father, child, boss, etc.) thinks you are. How would lives change if we truly believed the Bible's astounding words about God's love for us - if we looked in the mirror and saw what God sees?

My friend, you *are* the one whom Jesus loves. Choose to believe that today.

# Heaven On Earth

*"Let eloquence be flung to the dogs rather than souls*
*be lost. What we want is to win souls. They are not*
*won by flowery speeches." – Charles Spurgeon*

*…Christ in you, the hope of glory. (Colossians 1:27)*

There are people in your world who have no idea how to access heaven. There are also people in your life who may know Jesus and believe in Heaven. But they don't think Heaven is available while we are on Earth. Your life reveals to them what Heaven is like. In you, they can encounter Jesus. The world longs for a revelation of the sons and daughters of God. Everyone wants to belong somewhere. Many believe they have to behave in order to belong. But, those who understand their inheritance know they belong. Therefore, they behave like sons and daughters of God. They demonstrate to the world what it's like to belong in the Father's house. Like them, you can become the revelation the world is looking for!

Will you be the revelation? Will you let someone encounter Jesus through you today? I pray that the Holy Spirit would intersect your path, today, with someone who needs to encounter Jesus, even if it's the most unlikely person in the most unlikely of places.

# Provision

*"A firm faith in the universal providence of God is the solution of all earthly troubles." – B.B. Warfield*

*"…Peace be with you." After He said this, He showed them His hands and side. (John 20:19-20)*

From His peace, there came a new provision. Jesus showed Himself to be the "I am." All problems would pale in comparison to Him. Are you afraid? He has perfect love that casts out fear. Are you sick? He heals. Are there dead things in your life? He's alive. All issues have to go through the "I am." We experience His presence; and in His presence, we experience peace; and in His peace, we experience provision. Later, in that same verse it says, "Then the disciples were glad…" To put it another way, they got a new passion. They were suddenly operating from a place of abundance. Their environment had changed, and so had their outlook. No matter how sinful this world is, no matter how dark this world is; everything changes with His presence, peace, and provision.

What do you need today my friend? All of your issues have to go through the "I am." Like the disciples, aren't you glad? Let's live this day with a new outlook.

# APRIL 13

# Abundance

*"We make a living by what we get. We make a life
by what we give." – Winston Churchhill*

*"I have shown you in every way, by laboring like this, that you must
support the weak. And remember the words of the Lord Jesus, that
He said, 'It is more blessed to give than to receive.'" (Acts 20:35)*

*W*hen we get excited about a gift, it usually isn't because we're excited for the giver who will be blessed for it. It's for the receiver who got an unexpected blessing. Why is that? It's because many believers tend to live from lack, while longing for abundance. But, when we understand who we really are, we live from abundance. I wonder if many of us live from lack because we don't let God use us right where we are. Instead, we're waiting. You, child of God, have an inheritance. All of us long to access our inheritance, but we often live with the worldview of an orphan. We are focused on lack. We are trying to work *toward* abundance rather than working *from* abundance.

We have is a perception problem - a worldview issue. If you can make the switch from trying to work *toward* abundance to working *from* abundance, you'll not only get more joy from giving than receiving, you'll also be able to tap into what you need to accomplish what you are called to do. Fear keeps us from aligning with our assignment. But, our identity as sons and daughters, tells us the Spirit of the Lord is upon us and has anointed us.

# King Of My Heart

*"God loves each of us as if there were only one of us."*
*– Saint Augustine*

*"See, your King comes to you, gentle and riding on a donkey...*
*The crowds that went of Him and those that followed shouted,*
*"Hosanna to the Son of David! Blessed is He Who comes in the name*
*of the Lord! Hosanna in the highest heaven!" (Matthew 21:5, 9)*

*A*ll three of my children are in college right now. All in three different cities and states. When they come home, I can hardly stand the joy that overwhelms me! The extent of my joy is directly proportionate to how long they've been away. Typically, the longer I wait for someone to arrive, the more excited I am to see them and the greater my joy in their return. There was a jubilant atmosphere among the people of Israel on the day on which Jesus rode into Jerusalem on a donkey. The people had waited a long time for the promised Messiah. Israel had awaited the coming of their King, but this King didn't look as they had expected.

A donkey? Peasant clothes? The people expected a King of the land. It was what they wanted, but it wasn't what they needed. Jesus came to be the King of their hearts.

Is He the King of your heart today? Let Him reign...you'll never be the same.

# APRIL 15

# The Valley

*"You just can't beat the person who never gives up." – Babe Ruth*

*The hand of the Lord came upon me and brought me out in the Spirit of the Lord, and set me down in the midst of the valley... (Ezekiel 37:1)*

When the hand of the Lord came upon Paul, it raised him up to Heavenly places. When it came upon John, it carried him up to the New Jerusalem. But what happens when the hand of the Lord is upon you and rather than taking you up on a mountain, He sets you down in a valley? When I get in the Spirit and His hand allows me to go through a valley, and even causes me to go through low places, it's to make me feel, understand and turn my attention to people who are living in the low places. We can become so self-centered that we forget about people who are living in low places while we are high on the mountaintop. But, all along the journey, God will humble you. God says to all of us, "Look in this valley. Look into these low places. Look around you. Do you see the homeless? Do you see the addicts? Do you see the lonely men and women in the nursing homes? What about your neighbor?" The Spirit doesn't just take you to the high places. Sometimes the Spirit of God makes you sensitive about the valleys and low places in which people around us find themselves.

I challenge you mighty woman or mighty man of God! Look into the low places today.

# The Advocate

*"The reader is, as it were, blinded by the brilliance of His*
*image and comes away like a man who has looked long*
*at the sun – unable to see anything but its light."*
*– Edgar Bruns (The Art and Thought of John)*

*"I tell you the sober truth: it is much better for you that I go." (John 16:7)*

How could Jesus' departure benefit the community of believers? First, "because unless I go, the Advocate will not come to you, but if I do go, I will send Him to you." Second, while Jesus was still visible on earth, there was the danger that the apostles would be so attached to the sight of His human body they would trade the certainty of faith for the tangible evidence of the senses. To see Jesus in the flesh was an extraordinary privilege but "more blessed are they who have not seen and yet believed." (John 20:29) What a gift for us today! We have the Holy Spirit in us, and with us wherever we go. We have the Advocate interceding on our behalf.

Aren't you thankful for the Holy Spirit today? Aren't you thankful that Jesus loved us so much to send the Advocate in His place? What is the Holy Spirit speaking to you today?

## APRIL 17

# Here I Am To Worship

*"Isn't it a comfort to worship a God we cannot
exaggerate?" – Francis Chan*

*Now when they began to sing and to praise, the Lord set
ambushes against (the enemy), …and they were defeated.
(2 Chronicles 20:22)*

Jehoshaphat was surrounded on all sides. He fasted and prayed, and the Lord gave him instructions. Jehoshaphat bowed, with his face to the ground, and worshiped the Lord. When we open our mouths, despite what our situations look like, and start praising and worshiping, demons fall on their faces!

Have you ever felt the enemy breathing down your neck or nipping at your ankles? I sure have. It can make it very difficult to focus on anything other than your circumstances. You will always have a problem when you make a determination based on what you see. You need to get your eyes off that thing that's in front of you and fix your eyes and focus on the God Who, with just one word, can wipe out the enemy. No matter what the doctor says. No matter what you pulled out of the mailbox. No matter what your bank account says.

All you have to do is worship. All you have to do is give Him praise. God is still on the throne. God is still God. You will not have to fight this battle. This battle is His.

Father we begin this day in a posture of worship and with our eyes fixed on You. We choose to praise You despite our circumstances.

# Judging Yourself Unworthy

*"Life with God is not immunity from difficulties,
but peace within difficulties." – C.S. Lewis*

*Then Paul and Barnabas grew bold and said, "It was
necessary that the Word of God should be spoken to you
first; but since you reject it, and judge yourselves unworthy
of everlasting life, behold, we turn to the Gentiles.
(Acts 13:46)*

In Acts 13 Paul, the greatest evangelist the world has ever known is preaching Jesus Christ crucified for the sins of all mankind. He's preaching, "You can be forgiven! You can have His grace! His mercy is for you! You can have His acceptance! You can have His goodness! All of this is available to you!" And yet, the Bible says, "The Jews DID NOT receive Him." They opposed the things spoken to them *because they judged themselves unworthy.* They couldn't receive from God because they judged themselves unworthy. The challenge for them was not sin. The challenge for them wasn't even the devil. They didn't need the whisper of the enemy in their ear. The scripture says, "They judged *themselves* unworthy. They did it all by themselves.

Are you, like me, sometimes guilty of the same thing? Do you judge yourself unworthy because you think it's about *your* worthiness? Do you think it's about whether *you* perform well enough?

Father forgive us today for judging ourselves unworthy. Help us to remember that we were worth dying for.

# Expect

*"The only way to achieve the impossible is to believe it is possible." – Alice in Wonderland*

*Now if we are children, then we are heirs – heirs of God and co-heirs with Christ, if indeed we share in His sufferings in order that we may also share in His glory. (Romans 8:17)*

If we are co-heirs with Christ, that means we have a double-claim to every promise that is in His Word. We're not just heirs. We are joint-heirs. This knowledge should give you great expectation! We see the power of this expectation in Acts 3. The Bible says there was a lame man who brought to the temple and he was praying there daily. When we hear this story taught, usually the emphasis is on verse 6, "Then Peter said, 'Silver or gold I do not have, but what I do have I give you. In the name of Jesus Christ of Nazareth, walk." But notice that's not what activated the miracle. Notice that the miracle of the lame man was dependent on verse 5, "So the man gave them his attention, *expecting* to receive something from them." In other words, the man said, "I don't hope, I don't think…I *expect* to receive something from the Man of God."

Are you expecting today? Expect His glory! Expect His love! Expect His blessings! Expect His healing! Expect!

Father, we are so thankful for our inheritance! May we never forget we are co-heirs with Jesus! Thank you that we have claim to every promise in Your Word!

APRIL 20

# Poured Out

*"Consider what you owe to His immutability. Though you have changed a thousand times, He has not changed once." – Charles Spurgeon*

*...God's love has been poured out into our hearts through the Holy Spirit, Who has been given to us. (Romans 5:5)*

*H*is love is poured into every nook and cranny of our hearts. That means when you're in trouble, when persecution comes, when your heart is aching because you don't know which way to turn – that's when you must allow Him to do what He's been sent to do. That's what it means to walk in the Spirit. You just have to stop and say, "Holy Spirit, what are You going to do about this? Holy Spirit, this is above me; I need Your comfort." Do you think He's just going to sit by and do nothing? He was there when your parts were formed. He will rescue you! He will answer you. He'll give you a big drink of Jesus! He'll remind you that your bags are all already packed. You're not here for very long. So why get worked up about all this? Five seconds into eternity, you won't remember any of it. He tells you, "You are loved, and you are leaving! You have an eternal purpose and I'm here to see it through.

Do you need comfort today? Are you in trouble? Ask the Holy Spirit, "What are YOU going to do about this? And while You're working it out, I need the comfort that only You can provide."

APRIL 21

# On Tiptoe

*"We should be astonished at the goodness of God, stunned that He should bother to call us by name, our mouths wide open at His love, bewildered that at this very moment we are standing on Holy ground." – Brennan Manning*

*God brought you alive – right along with Christ! Think of it! All sins forgiven, the slate wiped clean, that old arrest warrant cancelled and nailed to Christ's cross.*
*(Colossians 2:14)*

There is nothing that stands between you and what you need from God. Anything that could stand between you and God was removed and nailed to the cross. And with that knowledge, the position that you should be in is on your tiptoes...in expectation of what God will do for you, in you and through you. There should be an expectation for God to pour out His Spirit on you and your family. There should be an expectation for healing. There should be an expectation for miracles and deliverance. You should be on your tiptoes expecting God to take care of your every need. There is more to what God did for you than your salvation. He wants you to live! He wants you to be alive and on your tiptoes with expectation of all that He has for you.

Do you have that expectation today? Or has life become a bit dull? Remember what He did for you! He brought you out of the grave right along with Jesus. Every sin from the past, the present, and the future have been wiped clean!

Jesus, we stand on tiptoes in expectation today!

# Follow The Leader

*"You might as well try to see without eyes, hear without ears, or breathe without lungs, as to try to live the Christian life without the Holy Spirit." – D.L. Moody*

*Paul and his companions traveled throughout the region of Phrygia and Galatia, having been kept by the Holy Spirit from preaching the word in the province of Asia. (Acts 16:6)*

They were *kept* by the Holy Spirit from preaching the gospel. They were *kept* by the Holy Spirit from doing a good thing! Not all good things are God things. And not all good things are meant for you. How do you tell what are the "God things?" In other words, how will you know where God wants you to go and what God wants you to do? Just like Paul, you have to be led by the Holy Spirit. When you ask Him to lead you and to teach you, He'll start putting "checks" in your life. There will be a prompting, a reminder, or a nudge giving you direction. You may say, "I have the Bible. Isn't that all I need?" We must have His Word, but we must also have the leading of the Holy Spirit. The Bible will you the characteristics you should look for in a spouse, but the Holy Spirit will lead you to the exact person that God has chosen for you.

Are you at a fork in the road? Do you need to make some decisions? Are you going to rush ahead of God or will you say, "Holy Spirit, I will wait to hear from You. I will 'follow the Leader.'"

APRIL 23

# Are You Pregnant?

*"Life is always a rich and steady time when you are*
*waiting for something to happen or hatch."*
*– E.B. White (Charlotte's Web)*

*"…what is conceived in her is from the Holy Spirit."*
*(Matthew 1:20)*

*I* have had several people come to me over the years and say, "I had a dream about you! You were pregnant!" My usual response has been, "I DO NOT receive that." But I now see that they were dreaming about a spiritual pregnancy, not a natural pregnancy. In Matthew 1 Joseph is ready end his relationship with Mary after he finds out that she's pregnant. Then, an angel of the Lord appeared to him in a dream and said, "Joseph, son of David, do not be afraid to take Mary home as your wife, because what is conceived in her is from the Holy Spirit." When the Holy Spirit births something new inside of you, don't be surprised if the people around you have a hard time getting on board with you. God-sized dreams are always bigger than we are, and are usually uncomfortable and unpredictable. It's not your job to convince the world of what God has called you to do or be. The purpose of what God is birthing in you is always about what God wants to do through you. What God is birthing in you is for the glory of HIS name and for the advancement of His kingdom – not yours. It helps to keep that in perspective as we pursue those things that we feel God is calling us to. If it's truly a God-birthed passion, it will be accompanied by God-sized results that will impact His kingdom far beyond your wildest dreams.

# Because I Said So

*"Faith is taking the first step even when you don't see
the whole staircase." – Martin Luther King, Jr*

*When He had finished speaking, He said to Simon, "Put out
into the deep water and let down the nets for a catch." "Master,
we've worked hard all night but because you say so, I will let
down the nets." When they had done so, they caught such a large
number of fish that their nets began to break. (Luke 5:4-6)*

Peter didn't feel like fishing anymore. His feelings told him that his situation wasn't going to change. But he said, "Jesus, because You said so, even though I don't feel like it, I'm going to obey." And guess what? Peter and his friends caught so many fish, their nets began to break. That's how it is with God. You may feel discouraged when you look at your situation, but when you trust Him and believe what He says, your feelings will change! You'll have so much joy and peace that your nets will break. Living by what you feel will always take you to a dead-end. Many people live dead-end lives because they live by feelings. Feelings fluctuate. "No one loves me." That may be how you feel, but what does God say about it? Doesn't He say that He loves you with an everlasting love? "There's no way I can do that." Yet, didn't your Father say that you "can do all things through Christ Who strengthens you?" You have a choice today. You can either live by your feelings or you can choose to live by what God says. I'm going to give you a head start for today. God says that, "surely goodness and mercy will follow you" all day today.

# What A Day That Will Be!

*"To go to heaven, fully to enjoy God, is infinitely better
than the most pleasant accommodations here."*
*– Jonathan Edwards*

*"For I say to you, I will no longer eat of it until it is fulfilled
in the kingdom of God." And then He took the cup, and gave
thanks, and said, "Take this and divide it among yourselves;
for I say to you, I will not drink of the fruit of the vine
until the kingdom of God comes." (Luke 22:16-17)*

*I* was born in the hills and NOT raised with good table manners! But, I raised my kids to have good table manners. They've been taught to wait to begin eating until everyone is served. Jesus tells us that He will wait, as well. He looked at His disciples that night and said, "I'm going to Heaven and I will wait for you there. I will wait until all of us are sitting down together, and then I'll eat again with you." What a promise! That promise must have helped the disciples through some of their darkest moments. "No matter what we are going through right now, we WILL sit down with Jesus again."

There will be a day when we will see Jesus face-to-face. In the meantime, He is waiting for us to join Him for the best meal we will ever eat. He won't begin until we are all seated at the table. What a day that will be!

# Father's Child

*"His heart is the most sensitive and tender of all. No act goes unnoticed,
no matter how insignificant or small. A cup of cold water is enough
to put tears in the eyes of God. Like the proud mother who is thrilled
to receive a bouquet of wilted dandelions from her child, so God
celebrates our feeble expressions of gratitude." – Richard Foster*

*For those who are led by the Spirit of God are the children of God.
The Spirit you received does not make you slaves, so that you live in
fear again; rather, the Spirit you received brought about your adoption
to son-ship. And by Him we cry, "Abba, Father." The Spirit Himself
testifies with our spirit that we are God's children. (Romans 8:14-16)*

*I* am so thankful that Jesus loves sinners, outcasts and misfits. I'm
thankful because I am a sinner, and outcast and a misfit. He loves
me because His Father loves me. He loves you because His Father loves
you. He does nothing on His own…only what His Father tells Him. In
scripture it was through meal-sharing, preaching, teaching, and healing,
that Jesus acted out His understanding of the Father's indiscriminate
love – a love that causes His sun to rise on bad men as well as good and
His rain to fall on honest and dishonest men alike (Matthew 5:45)

Aren't you thankful? Be at peace today knowing you are Abba's child
and He is well pleased with you.

# Causing To Stumble

*"The Christian ideal has not been tried and found wanting. It has been found difficult; and left untried." – G.K. Chesterton*

*"If anyone causes one of these little ones – those who believe in me – to stumble, it would be better for them to have a large millstone hung around their neck and to be drowned in the depths of the sea." (Matthew 18:6)*

*I* will assume that I am writing to mature believers today. The world is watching you. Other believers are watching you. I don't mean that to sound creepy, but we are observers by nature. Too often I will see someone behaving one way in church and barely recognize that same person in a public place. As believers, you and I are held to the highest of standards. The world is watching us. They want to know how we will handle ourselves in a tragedy. How will we handle ourselves on the job? How will we treat the server in a restaurant who is having a bad day?

More than a bible verse or a sermon, how we treat people and what they see in us, can have more impact on winning a lost soul or demonstrating to less mature believers how the Christian life is supposed to look.

I know we are all humans and don't have supernatural power. Wait! Yes, we do. We have the power of the Holy Spirit!

# I Speak Jesus

*"If you had a thousand crowns you should put them all on the head of Christ! And if you had a thousand tongues they should all sing His praise, for He is worthy!" – William Tiptaft*

*"What I tell you in the dark, speak in the daylight; what is whispered in your ear, proclaim from the roofs."*

*(Matthew 10:27)*

It is not enough to live by the word spoken from the preacher on Sunday. We need to talk to Jesus ourselves. It will be the secrets He speaks to you in private that will not only sustain you, but will change your life. A personal relationship with Jesus is supposed to be just that... personal. For a personal relationship to be successful, there must be one-on-one communication. Talking and listening to the Holy Spirit in your secret place will bring peace because He *is* peace, and there is peace within His presence.

He will whisper things to you in the secret place that He wants you to shout in public. It's in the secret place that He speaks hope and freedom. And when you speak that same hope and freedom in the public places, addictions begin to break.

He longs to meet you in private so He can strengthen you in public. The Holy Spirit will always give you the words to say.

# Go!

*"Every Christian is either a missionary or an imposter."*
*– Charles Spurgeon*

*The woman left her water jar beside the well and ran back to*
*the village, telling everyone, "Come and see a Man Who told me*
*everything I ever did! Could He possibly be the Messiah?" So the*
*people came streaming from the village to see Him." (John 4:28-30)*

This woman became the first evangelist in the gospel of John. She went and told her people about Jesus, and brought them to Him. A foreign, single woman who had had five husbands, now living with a man who was not her husband, was the one that Jesus chose to bring a town in Samaria to Him so that they could say, "We have heard for ourselves, and we know that this is truly the Savior of the world." This woman had a divine appointment that had been scheduled before the beginning of time.

What about you? Do you realize there is a divine appointment for you as well? Jesus knows all about every detail of your life – the good, the bad, and the ugly. He has chosen you because of all those things. He has living water for you today. He wants you to drop your water pots and go!

## APRIL 30

# He Had To Go There

*"When fear has risen within her, she will raise her hands*
*even higher, taking deep and careful breaths, as the*
*daylight reminds her: She is guided. She is seen. And by*
*grace she will make it through all of these things."*
*– Morgan Harper Nichols*

*"I am He." (John 4:26)*

Jesus reveals Himself to a woman that is considered an outcast. She's getting insight that most religious people didn't get. Jesus actually hid from religious people. I wonder if He does that today? Jesus chose to share His intimate secrets with a colossal sinner. He chose to hang out by a well with the very least of these…a misfit. Not only is *she* shocked. The disciples are shocked. My favorite part of this story is earlier in the chapter. "But Jesus *had to* go through Samaria." (John 4:4) The Greek word for "had to" is edei. The use of edei (had to) makes it clear that this is a divine appointment. Jesus *had to* go through Samaria because He had a divine appointment with a downcast woman. This woman wasn't looking for Jesus. But Jesus was looking for her. Jesus loves the people the world loves to hate.

No matter what you've ever done, Jesus wants to reveal Himself to you. He wants to use you to reveal Himself to the people that the world loves to hate.

## MAY 1

# There's Another Side To His Love

*"We often learn more of God under the rod that strikes us than under the staff that comforts us." – Stephen Charnock*

*For the Lord disciplines those He loves, and He chastens each one He accepts as His child. (Hebrews 12:6)*

In our current church culture, God's love has often been reduced to a bumper sticker, surface kind of love. The sunny side of the street has been presented with nothing of the other side ever mentioned. That "love" of God that's been presented sounds like sugar-sweet love that's only interest is to make us happy rather than that "love" that does what's best for us. It's a watered-down love rather than a tough love. You see, there's another side of God's love. It's a love that deals with us according to our needs. God will allow us to be cut in order to remove any sin or hindrances to our growth in Him. He will do whatever it takes to get us wherever He wants us to go. But He loves as much when he "cuts" us as when He blesses us. His love will always seek our best interest. His love will always place our eternal security above any temporary comfort or pleasure.

Do you feel chastened? Chastened means "child-trained." You are His child, and because He loves you, there are seasons of "training." Let's make sure we learn the lesson!

# Never Closer

*"He remembers our frame and knows that we are dust. He may sometimes chasten us, it is true, but even this He does with a smile, the proud, tender smile of a Father who is bursting with pleasure over an imperfect but promising son who is coming every day to look more and more like the One whose child he is." – A. W. Tozer*

*"I am the true grapevine, and my Father is the gardener. He cuts off every branch of mine that doesn't produce fruit, and He prunes the branches that do bear fruit so they will produce even more." (John 15:1-2)*

The Gardener always prunes or cuts out that which is not fruit bearing. And so does our Father in Heaven. And it is never comfortable. It can be very painful. But a gardener is never closer to the branch than when he is trimming it. Likewise, your Father is never as close to you as when He is reaching in and removing, from your heart and life, things that offend.

Are you in the pruning process right now? As difficult as it is, remember this - your Father "trims" your branches with tenderness and love. This is for your good, so that you will produce and look more like Him. Pruning is impossible without His hands on the "branch." Take comfort that He holds you even as He "cuts."

MAY 3

# They're Gone!

*"When we stray from His presence, He longs for you to*
*come back. He weeps that you are missing out on His love,*
*protection and provision. He throws His arms open, runs*
*toward you, gathers you up, and welcomes you home."*
*— Charles Stanley*

*"Sing, O daughter of Zion! … Be glad and rejoice with all*
*your heart… The Lord has taken away your judgments.*
*He has cast out your enemy. The Lord is in your midst: you*
*shall see disaster no more." (Zephaniah 3:14-15)*

The little book of Zephaniah opens with a message of judgment to the people because of their idolatry. Then, at the end of his indictment, comes an amazing shift. There's a shift because the Lord has issued a pardon. The judgments are turned aside and the people are set free. They are not only forgiven, but "The Lord is in their midst." The Lord is with them.

No matter how low you've fallen, yesterday or today, He loves you. And if you're His child, there is no judgment! And not only that, He is with you. Right now. Right where you are this moment. He is in your midst. He has cast out your enemy. So sing! Be glad and rejoice today, because your sin has been removed as far as the east is from the west.

MAY 4

# Positively

*"The devil knows how to quote Scripture to his purpose!"*
*— Shakespeare*

*For they don't understand God's way of making people right with Himself. Refusing to accept God's way, they cling to their own way of getting right with God by trying to keep the law. (Romans 10:3)*

The enemy loves to bring negative Scriptures to your mind. Satan will tell you that there is no grace for you because you don't meet all the qualifications. He will try to convince you that grace is dependent on your own righteousness. But the Word says that none of us will ever be made right with God except by our faith in Jesus Christ. The devil is a thief and he will come and try to take away the Word and the promises that God has just for you. But the Holy Spirit reminds us of the unchanging nature of God. He reminds you of His unwavering love towards you. He confirms that God remains faithful to His promises even when we prove faithless. The Spirit reassures us that there is no law that is effective against those who rely on Christ's work.

"He cancelled the record of the charges against us and took it away by nailing it to the cross" (Colossians 2:14).

Praise Him today for His unwavering love towards you!

# He Sings Over You

*"You would not have called to me unless I had been calling to you," said the Lion. – C.S Lewis (The Silver Chair)*

*The Lord God in your midst, the Mighty One, will save; He will rejoice over you with gladness, He will quiet you with His love, He will rejoice over you with singing. (Zephaniah 3:17)*

"*H*e rejoices over you with singing." In Hebrew, this literally means to spin around under the influence of great emotion. Have you ever been so happy that you spun around? God delights in you. He rejoices over you with gladness. He rejoices over you with singing. It doesn't matter if you're struggling. It doesn't matter if your attitude is terrible. It doesn't matter if you're depressed. It doesn't matter if you're disappointed. God delights in you. It doesn't matter if you're having a pity party today. It doesn't matter if your friends or family have abandoned you. It doesn't matter if your kids are a mess. It doesn't matter if it feels like your life is a disaster. God delights in you so much that He rejoices over you with singing. He spins around under the influence of great emotion.

Can you feel the wonder of that today? That God is rejoicing over you with loud singing?

# Lifeblood

*"Life is wasted if we do not grasp the glory of the cross, cherish it for the treasure that it is, and cleave to it as the highest price of every pleasure and the deepest comfort in every pain. What was once foolishness to us – a crucified God – must become our wisdom and our power and our only boast in this world." – John Piper*

*Jesus said, "I am the way and the truth and the life. No one comes to the Father except through Me." (John 14:6)*

There is a world that needs to hear, experience, and believe those words. To a soul that is void of real love and family, these aren't mere idle words – they are lifeblood. They are words that can introduce people to truth that will, in turn, nourish their lives and ultimately give them safe passage home, where they need to be. Home is where we flourish. And, home is where God does His finest work. The reality of life is that not every natural or spiritual household is fabulous, lovely or conducive to growth and fruitfulness. Not every home is the garden God would have it to be. Our churches need a spiritual welcome mat at every door that receives and embraces everyone. But if they don't, we all have a very sobering responsibility to create an environment of life around us. It should be like a garden where God can facilitate His heart toward men, women and families which will spread and nurture the heart of others in a manner that will cause men, women and children to flourish in everything they put their hands to.

Will you speak life today?

MAY 7

# Rock Bottom

*"If you're going through hell, keep going."*
*— Winston Churchill*

*Remember, dear brothers and sisters, that few of you were wise in the*
*world's eyes or powerful or wealthy when God called you. Instead,*
*God chose things the world considers foolish in order to shame those*
*who think they are wise. And he chose things that are powerless to*
*shame those who are powerful. God chose things despised by the*
*world, things counted as nothing at all, and used them to bring to*
*nothing what the world considers important. As a result, no one*
*can ever boast in the presence of God. (1 Corinthians 1:26-29)*

Have you ever felt like you've hit rock bottom? And, when you were there, thought you'd never be able to get up? And you don't need anyone else to beat you up because you do a great job of that all by yourself? Blame, shame, guilt, condemnation… "If only I would have…" "If I could just go back…" "If I could take it back…" "If I hadn't said…" "If I hadn't done that…" "If I hadn't went there…" "If I hadn't met him or her…" Have you ever hit rock bottom, thinking you were as low as you could possibly get, only to have *that* bottom fall out from under you as well? I sure have. But today I can say with all integrity, I wouldn't exchange any of it. I thank God for rock bottom, because when you truly hit it, He's the only way out of it. And, when He brings you up from it, He *will* bring you out of it, He makes all things new. He restores what was lost. And, He puts you to work.

# You Are Called

*"God will meet you where you are in order to take
you where He wants you to go." – Tony Evans*

*Remember, dear brothers and sisters, that few of you
were wise in the world's eyes or powerful or wealthy
when God called you. (1 Corinthians 1:26)*

"When God called you…" When you think of someone "called by God," whom do you think of? Do you think of someone who is squeaky clean with no past criminal record? Do you think of someone raised in a Christian home? Do you think of someone educated, or someone with a perfect spouse, perfect kids and money in the bank? I grew up in church. And, quite honestly, I could never relate to most of the pastors I heard preach. I believed the Word of God, but I was never able to apply it to my life. But one day, as an adult, I heard a female pastor. Intertwined in her sermon was her life story – her past mistakes, regrets and struggles. For the first time in my life, I felt something come alive and awake in my spirit. For the first time in my life, I heard a smiling small voice whisper to me, "You are also called, my daughter." Maybe it's hard for you to imagine that you are called by God for a purpose. But I'm here to tell you today that there is a plan. That which you've gone through and the place in which you find yourself now are absolutely a part of that calling. No matter how you may appear in the world's eyes, you, child of God, are called.

# Powerless

*"Relying on God has to start all over every day, as if nothing has yet been done." – C. S. Lewis*

*Instead, God chose things the world considers foolish in order to shame those who think they are wise. And he chose things that are powerless to shame those who are powerful. (1 Corinthians 1:27)*

*H*ave you ever felt powerless? The definition of powerless is "without ability, influence or power." Some synonyms of the word powerless are helpless, inadequate, ineffective, useless, defenseless, vulnerable, feeble and weak. Weak? Sounds very negative, right? But powerless is really the opposite. Powerless is the best place you can be. When you are powerless, there is no way out except Him leading you out. "But the Lord said to me, 'My grace is sufficient for you, for my power is made perfect in weakness (in powerlessness). Therefore I will boast all the more gladly about my weaknesses, so that Christ's power may rest on me. That is why, for Christ's sake, I delight in weaknesses (powerlessness), in insults, in hardships, in persecution, in difficulties. For when I am weak, then I am strong.'"

Thank God that you are powerless today. That's exactly where He wants you. He always shows up mightily when we are powerless.

# Despised

*"Hatred paralyzes life; love releases it. Hatred confuses life; love harmonizes it. Hatred darkens life; love illuminates it."*
*– Martin Luther King Jr.*

*God chose things despised by the world, things counted as nothing at all, and used them to bring to nothing what the world considers important. As a result, no one can ever boast in the presence of God. (1 Corinthians 1:28)*

"God chose things despised…" This was the phrase that did me in. This is the phrase that has become one of my life verses. God chose things despised - things counted as nothing at all - and used them to bring to nothing what the world considers important. I came into this world despised. I grew up feeling despised. But, when I read this, I realized that because "the world" despised me, God's chosen me for a very special assignment. And, although "the world" may despise me, God does not! God has called me. I am chosen. I am not despised by God. My friend, you are called. You are not despised by God. You may have felt despised or considered unimportant. But God has called you for a divine assignment. When you tell people what you've come through, where you've been, and where you're heading, they will know that it has nothing to do with you! "So that no one may boast…"

You are chosen, and you are called.

## MAY 11

# Boasting In Jesus

*"We are all faced with a series of great opportunities brilliantly
disguised as impossible situations." – Chuck Swindoll*

*It is because of Him that you are in Christ Jesus, Who has become for us
wisdom from God – that is, our righteousness, holiness and redemption.
Therefore, as it is written: "Let the one who boasts boast in the Lord."
(1 Corinthians 1:30-31)*

*I*t is because of Jesus that you are wise. It is because of Jesus you have
power. It is because of Jesus that you are righteous. It is because of
Jesus that you are holy. It is because of Jesus that you are redeemed...
so that no one can boast. "Let the one who boasts boast in the Lord."
God can't work with people who think they have it all together on their
own. God can't work with people to whom other people can't relate.
God CAN work with broken people. And God loves to use people who
are weak. Do you not understand all the glory that He plans to get
because of you, my friend? You may say, "How could He allow me to
go through what I'm going through?" How could He not? He has an
assignment for your life that has a connection to your situation. I am a
messenger sent to you today, from the Lord to tell you, "He has a plan
for you, plans to prosper you and not to harm you, plans to give you a
hope and a future." (Jeremiah 29:11)

# He's Wild For You

*"He is the playfulness of creation, scandal and utter goodness, the generosity of the ocean and the ferocity of a thunderstorm; he is cunning as a snake and gentle as a whisper; the gladness of sunshine and humility of a thirty-mile walk by foot on a dirt road." – John Eldredge*

*Be here – the King is wild for you. (Psalm 45:11)*

The King is wild for you. The Jesus we speak of is the lover of every human soul who has ever walked this earth. He is the pure and majestic Prince of Heaven, the bright Morning Star spoken of in Revelation, and the One who bottles our every shed tear. He is the Bridegroom for whom all heaven and Earth await, and the One who will one day return for those who love and long for Him. He's the King who laid aside His throne and came riding to our rescue. He's the One who gave all because Father, Son, and Spirit would not forget nor abandon their love for us.

Before the busyness of your day begins, "be here." Be with Him. He *is* wild for you. He wants to talk with you and spend time with you. He wants to show you His wild love for you.

# The Comforter

*"Remember that grace and truth cannot finally be crucified. Remember
that all the high things that make humanity beautiful cannot be
forever laid in the dust, spattered with blood. And most of all,
remember that He who rose from the dead, rose to pour out His Holy
Spirit into human lives, and, by that Spirit, to make available to any
individual all the fullness of Himself, twenty-four hours a day."*
– Ray C. Stedman

*But the Comforter, which is the Holy Ghost, whom the Father will
send in My name, He shall teach you all things, and bring all things
to your remembrance, all that I have said to you. (John 14:26)*

By calling the Holy Spirit the Comforter, Jesus was giving them,
and us, an infallible prediction. If He is sending us a Comforter,
then there's going to be discomfort. He knew there would be a lot of
hurt and pain in the body of Christ. Some trials are so painful, so big,
that there is no way to get relief. Not from your family. Not from your
friends. Not from the doctor. Not from the counselor. Not from the
medication. Not from the seminar. Not from the self-help books. There
are just some trials that there is only one way to get comfort. That way
is from The Comforter.

Have you ever been through a trial that was so painful that you
couldn't get relief, no matter where you turned? Maybe that's where you
find yourself today. Jesus sent The Comforter so that we would never
be alone, to comfort and to teach us all things.

## MAY 14

# Focus

*"Focus on giants – you stumble. Focus on God
– giants tumble." – Max Lucado*

*"For the eyes of the Lord run to and fro throughout the
whole earth... To show Himself strong on behalf of those
whose heart is loyal to Him..." (2 Chronicles 16:9)*

*W*hen it says His eyes "run" it means they are on an aggressive, high-speed search. Scripture says that God has seven eyes, and all seven scour the earth looking for those whose gaze is lifted to Him for help. When God finds this kind of loyalty of heart, He shows Himself strong on their behalf. He fights for them. The context of the verse is all about deliverance from enemy invasion. When the thief comes to steal, kill and destroy, God wants to answer by demonstrating His military strength and awesome delivering power. But, He's looking for singular focus.

How is your focus? Where or to whom are you looking to for help? May I implore you, based on personal experience, to fix your focus on Jesus? I can testify that God loves to show Himself strong when we focus completely on Him. He *will* fight for you. He *will* deliver you.

Let that sink in today. The eyes of God run to and fro throughout the whole earth, to show Himself strong on *your* behalf!

# Not By Sword

*"God gives where He finds empty hands." – Saint Augustine*

*"All those gathered here will know that it is not by sword or spear that the Lord saves; for the battle is the Lord's, and He will give all of you into our hands." (1 Samuel 17:47)*

I was never a Girl Scout. I failed Brownies so I knew I would never cut it as a Girl Scout. But I love the motto, "Be prepared." I love to be prepared. If I'm speaking somewhere, I like to know my audience, how long I am to speak, where I am in the order of service, the theme of the event, etc… There's comfort in being prepared. Being prepared for me is having the necessary tools that I may need for what I'm expected to do. Sometimes that can be information, a certification, a title, research, money, and more. In 1 Samuel 17, we have the story of David and Goliath. The Philistines and the Israelites were ready to go to battle with each other. We see David fighting for the Israelites. David is young and small and has nothing but five smooth stones. Goliath is almost ten feet tall. He was wearing armor weighing almost one hundred twenty six pounds, and the Bible says that just the tip of his spear weighed fifteen pounds. In my opinion, David was not at all prepared. Sometimes, though, it may seem that we do not have the tools we need to do what God has called us to do. But there's a reason - that "all those gathered here will know that it is not by sword or spear that the Lord saves; for the battle is the Lord's, and He will give all of you into our hands." Will you trust Him today, even if it would seem as if you have no tools to do what He's called you to do?

# Giants Will Fall

*"Don't lose hope. When it gets darkest the stars come out."*
*– Unknown*

*When Saul and his troops heard the Philistine's challenge,*
*they were terrified and lost all hope. (1 Samuel 17:11)*

*H*ave you ever been there? Have you ever lost all hope? Have you known that you were called to do something? Have you known that you were supposed to step out, step up and do something? But you looked at *that something*. And then you looked at yourself. *That something* looks like a giant. And sadly your muscle mass doesn't come close to Goliath's! You're not big enough. You don't have enough. You're not smart enough. You're not attractive enough. You're not spiritual enough. I love the next verse. After 1 Samuel tells us that "they were terrified and lost all hope." verse 12 says, "Enter David." That's it. Just "enter David". You know he's going to do something great. You just know it. David is little. David doesn't really have any tools except a sling and five smooth stones. David is not prepared to face a giant, but God is. And David remembers how God has shown up and saved him before. David remembers how God has provided exactly what he needs exactly when he needed it.

How about you today? Have you lost hope? Are you afraid? I encourage you to look beyond what you can see. If God showed up for David and defeated a ten-foot-tall giant, He will show up and defeat your giant as well.

# The Meltdown

*"It's not the falling down, but the getting back
up that's important." – Christy Sawyer*

*When Saul and his troops heard the Philistine's challenge,
they were terrified and lost all hope. Enter David.
(1 Samuel 17:11-12)*

*H*ave you ever had a meltdown? I've had plenty. I recently had a slight inner meltdown. No one saw it, and it didn't last much longer than an hour. If anyone ever tries to make you feel unspiritual because you have a human moment, I would question whether they are human at all. I define a meltdown as falling down, tripping, or stumbling. The reason I told you that it was a slight meltdown is this: First of all, you need to know it's normal to fall down. And you need to know it's okay to fall down. Falling down is not what's important. Getting back up is what's important. My "getting back up," gets quicker and quicker as my faith gets stronger and stronger. I'm learning to quickly call out for help when I fall. And, God *always* shows up. He *always* reaches as far down as He has to in order to pull me back up. He always has. The difference is that my hand goes up for help much faster than it used to. I wonder what David's thoughts were when the reality set in that he was actually going to face ten-foot-tall Goliath. Did he have a meltdown? I wonder, even if he had just a slight meltdown, if he quickly recalled all the other times that God had shown up to rescue him. I see him rising up and stepping out to face his giant. "*They* were terrified and lost all hope. *But enter (insert your name)."*

# Who Will Go?

*"If God is your partner, make your plans BIG!" – D. L. Moody*

*"The Lord looks down from heaven on the children of man, to see if there are any who understand, who seek after God." (Psalm 14:2)*

I believe that God was and is in highest heaven, far above all the nations, looking for a company of believers. He's looking to see if there are any who understand and take the value, rescue, and redemption of His sons and daughters all over the world seriously. I imagine a dark night. I imagine His eyes roaming the earth. I imagine God looking down and pondering these questions from highest heaven: "Who is going to understand? Who is going to roll up their sleeves? Who is going to count the cost and pay the price? Who is going to influence and rescue the sons and daughters that I know are struggling right now? Who is going to pay attention to those weeping behind closed doors? Who is going to pay attention to those trapped in closed nations? Who is going to step into the aftermath of past and present tragedy? Who is going to change the generational curses that oppress and bind My sons and daughters? Who is going to rescue the precious ones who, right now, are looking into this night sky and are wondering if I exist and if I care? Who is going to intervene for the one who is being abused? Who is going to intervene for the ones who are held captive? Who is going to intercede for the ones being stalked for purposes they were never created to endure? Who is going to pray? Who is going to care? Who is going to go?" I will. Will you?

## MAY 19

# No More Tears

*"Heaven knows we need never be ashamed of
our tears..." – Charles Dickens*

*Then David and his men lifted up their voices and
wept, until they had no more power to weep.
(1 Samuel 30:4)*

David is on the run from Saul who wants to kill him. David has to run away from home and leave his family to escape the brutality of the king. David runs and hides in a cave with a bunch of rejects. Misfits. Outcasts. The Bible says they are discontent, in distress, and in debt. They are troubled men who ask David to become their leader. So, David and his troubled men become soldiers in the Philistine army. (The very same army in which Goliath had been.) The Philistine army is about to do battle with the Israelites but the general inspects his soldiers and finds these Jewish men in his army. He immediately dismisses them. So, David and his discontent Israelite men leave and find their way back to their own city. When they get there they are shocked to discover that the enemy has invaded their city, burned it down, and kidnapped their wives and children. They are devastated. They cried. They cried so much that they had no more tears to cry.

Have you ever been there? Have you wept until you had no more power to weep? Sometimes we live through things in this life that are hard to handle, frustrating, devastating and unexpected. If that is you, I encourage you to get in the Word of God and strengthen yourself with His Word.

# Flourish, Baby, Flourish!

*"Our old history ends with the cross; our new history
begins with the resurrection." – Watchman Nee*

*"Listen carefully; unless a grain of wheat is buried in the ground, dead
to the world, it is never any more than a grain of wheat. But if it is
buried, it sprouts and reproduces itself many times over. In the same
way, anyone who holds on to life just as it is destroys that life. But if you
let it go, reckless in your love, you'll have it forever, real and eternal."*
(John 12:24-25)

If I hold seeds in my hand, they'll always be seeds. But if I bury them in the ground, they become tomatoes, cucumbers, squash, onions and carrots. Once I bury them, I have to trust what I *can't* see happening. If I insist on holding it to watch, the seed will stay a seed. But when I let it go, the seed is transformed. It ceases to be a seed in order that a plant may live. It can no longer find its identity in that of its old self…a seed. It becomes something far different and lives a new kind of life. From the "potential" of life that is contained within a seed, comes a new life that is now capable of producing fruit.

Are there things that you need to let go of today? Things that you need to "bury"? If we hold on to things, we destroy them. But "if you let it go, reckless in your love, you'll have it forever." It will become so much more than the thing that you buried! It will flourish!

## MAY 21

# Talk To Yourself

*"A true friend never gets in your way unless you
happen to be going down." – Arnold Glasow*

*But David strengthened himself in the Lord his God.
(1 Samuel 30:6)*

"Strengthened himself" is a Hebrew phrase that means "he talked to himself." There comes a time in life when you have to talk to yourself. When your money seems to be gone, when your family is all to pieces, when your children are acting crazy, and when your friends have turned their backs on you, it's time to talk to yourself. When you feel discouraged, defeated and depressed, what do you do? You have to learn to speak to yourself! You have to learn to strengthen yourself! You have to learn to encourage yourself! The problem may be that you're talking to everybody else. And sometimes the people you're talking to are not the people you need to be talking to! Maybe you have friends like Job's friends – friends that are telling you the wrong thing, telling you that it's your fault, telling you that you're the reason all hell has come against you. David finds himself with friends that want to kill him. They're talking about him behind his back. David was discouraged. That's when Scripture says: "BUT…" (1 Samuel 30:6). Anytime you see the word "but" in Scripture, there's a shifting about to take place. "But David strengthened himself." What do you need to say to yourself today? What part of God's Word do you need to speak over yourself today?

MAY 22

# The Dead Sea

*"Some of us are like the Dead Sea, always taking in but never giving out, because we are not rightly related to the Lord Jesus." – Oswald Chambers*

*"The words that I speak unto you are spirit, and they are life." (John 6:63)*

I love Israel. I've had the privilege of visiting several times. I'm fascinated by the Sea of Galilee, the Dead Sea and the Jordan River that connects the two. The Dead Sea is so high in salt content that the human body can float easily. All that saltiness means that there is no life at all in the Dead Sea. Both the Sea of Galilee and the Dead Sea receive their water from the Jordan River. Yet, they are very, very different. Unlike the Dead Sea, the Sea of Galilee is pretty, resplendent with rich, colorful marine life. There are lots of plants as well. So, you have the same region, the same source of water, and yet while one sea is full of life, the other is dead. How come? The Jordan River flows into the Sea of Galilee and then flows out. The Sea of Galilee has an inlet AND an outlet. The Dead Sea only has an inlet. The Dead Sea takes, but it never gives. As a result, it has no life at all. Likewise, if we are only taking in but never pouring out, we are not life-givers. We become the Dead Sea. The one who refreshes and blesses others is the one who not only "takes in" all he or she can, but also generously "gives out" to others.

I don't want to be a "dead sea." How about you? Make sure you're taking in, but make sure you are pouring out.

## MAY 23

# Pray For Yourself!

*"Let God's promises shine on your problems." – Corrie ten Boom*

*Then David said to the priest, "Please bring the ephod here
to me." And the priest brought the ephod to David.*
*(1 Samuel 30:7)*

What is an ephod? When the priest went in to do his duties, he would put something over his clothes called an ephod. The ephod would hang over his shoulders and hang down just below his waist. Before David went about the business of the Lord, he put the priestly garment on. If you are a child of God, you carry a priestly anointing, and you need to put your ephod on! What does that mean? That means that you don't need to have someone else pray for you. You can pray for yourself. Sometimes you just can't get to your pastor. Sometimes no one will answer the phone. And sometimes, you just can't always share your challenges with everyone. Not everyone can handle them. But you have a priestly anointing. You can put your ephod on and you can lay hands on yourself. Pray for yourself. Strengthen yourself. Encourage yourself. Mighty child of God, you have the authority! You have the access! You have the power of the Holy Spirit! Sometimes you just have to pray for yourself. You need to understand that you can get your own prayers through to heaven. You don't have to have anyone else to do that for you!

Maybe today you need to lay hands on yourself! God will incline His ear to your cry!

MAY 24

# Who Said That?

*"The indwelling Spirit shall teach him what is of God and what is not. This is why sometimes we can conjure up no logical reason for opposing a certain teaching, yet in the very depth of our being arises a resistance." – Watchman Nee*

*Therefore, there is now no condemnation for those who are in Christ Jesus. (Romans 8:1)*

Who are you listening to? There's a huge difference between the voice of the enemy and the voice of the Holy Spirit. Condemnation from your enemy sounds nothing like conviction of the Holy Spirit. Beloved, let there be no confusion. The Holy Spirit works to convict us (to advise and urge us, to warn us of something to be avoided) to push away from doing wrong and towards God. The condemning spirit of the enemy of our faith works to push us away from God. He does this with shame and condemnation. He knows this will lead us to more hopelessness; which will make us more prone to continue to do what we shouldn't. We are all human. I hate to break it to you my friend, but we're all going to sin. There are two feelings we can experience after we've sinned. One is conviction and the other is condemnation. Conviction is from the Holy Spirit, urging us to come get it off our chest, to come clean with whatever it is, so we can get back to intimacy with God. Condemnation is from Satan, trying to convince us that we're no good and that God will never forgive us. His purpose is to keep us away from God by making us feel guilty.

Who are you listening to today?

❧

## MAY 25

# Loyal

*"Most Christians long to see miracles, but they don't want to be put in a position where they will need one." – Rick Joyner*

*"For the eyes of the Lord run to and fro throughout the whole earth… To show Himself strong on behalf of those whose heart is loyal to Him…" (2 Chronicles 16:9)*

"The Lord is looking to show Himself strong on behalf of those whose heart is LOYAL to Him." The word "loyal" comes from a Hebrew word that has various English translations: perfect, true, whole, completely His, fully committed, blameless. The meaning is that those who look to God alone for deliverance in the hour of an enemy invasion are demonstrating a loyal, perfect, and true heart towards Him. God is actively looking for this kind of loyalty.

One of the best gifts I've received several times throughout my life is the gift of having absolutely no options but Jesus…having no one to turn to but Almighty God and absolutely no power of my own but through the power of the Holy Spirit.

Have you ever been there? If so, that's great news! Those who look to God alone for deliverance in the hour of trouble are exactly to whom God wants to show Himself strong.

# Conviction Versus Condemnation

*"A true physician makes incisions only in order to effect cures,
and a wise minister excites painful emotions in men's minds
only with the distinct object of blessing their souls."*
– *C. H. Spurgeon*

*If we say that we have no sin, we deceive ourselves, and the truth is
not in us. If we confess our sins, He is faithful and just to forgive us
our sins and to cleanse us from all unrighteousness. (1 John 1:8-9)*

"*H*e is faithful and just to forgive." Just like that. Immediately. No games. Any bad feelings we have after that are feeling of guilt from Satan. So if you're being drawn closer to God, you're feeling the conviction of the Holy Spirit. But if you feel like hiding from God and begin to doubt His love for you, you're feeling condemnation from the devil. In James 4:7 we read, "Resist the devil, and he will flee from you." I love the Message translation: "Yell a loud no to the devil and watch him scamper. Say a quiet yes to God and He'll be there in no time. Quit dabbling in sin. Purify your inner life. Quit playing the field. Hit bottom, and cry your eyes out. The fun and games are over. Get serious, really serious. Get down on your knees before the Master; it's the only way you'll get on your feet."

Maybe today you need to get with the Master. "He is faithful and just to forgive." Instantly. Draw close to Him and He will draw close to you. Resist the devil!

# Tone Of Voice

*"If it excites you, if it makes you feel good, it's
God speaking to you." – Wayne Dyer*

*With the arrival of Jesus, the Messiah, that fateful dilemma is
resolved. Those who enter into Christ's being-here-for-us no longer
have to live under a continuous, low-lying black cloud. A new power
is in operation. The Spirit of life in Christ, like a strong wind, has
magnificently cleared the air, freeing you from a fated lifetime of
brutal tyranny at the hands of sin and death. (Romans 8:1)*

How do you tell the difference between the voice of the enemy of our faith and the voice of the Holy Spirit? The tone of our enemy is always accusing and nagging – it's a voice that produces fear and shame. It gives a sense of rejection and asks questions like: "Has God indeed said?" Our enemy is the father of lies. He's deceitful. In contrast, the tone of voice of the Holy Spirit is the loving voice of our Father. He's urging our return to Him. He says, "Come to me all who are weary and heavy burdened. I will draw all men to Me."

What tone of voice do you hear today? Is it accusing you and mocking you? That is not your Father. Your Father's tone of voice is a loving voice and it's urging you to draw near Him.

MAY 28

# Mixed Messages

*"The Spirit of God first imparts love; He next inspires hope,
and then gives liberty; and that is about the last thing we
have in many of our churches." – Dwight L. Moody*

*And do not turn aside; for then you would go after empty things,
which cannot profit or deliver, for they are nothing. For the Lord
will not forsake His people for His great name's sake, because it has
pleased the Lord to make you His people. (1 Samuel 12:21-22)*

Satan's messages are vague and general. He causes a choking sense of general guilt. He makes it seem as though everything is wrong and there's nothing you can do to overcome. A sense of complete hopelessness and weakness often wins. The enemy attacks every part of you that he can. You can't see a light at the end of the tunnel. You feel helpless and hopeless focusing on half-truths. But, the Holy Spirit is specific. The Spirit says, "Fix this one thing and you'll be free." He urges you to take one specific action - to make a choice of your will. The conviction/urging of the Spirit is specific to the sin. The Spirit defends you against your mind. The Holy Spirit draws you to God.

What message are you receiving today? If you are feeling a sense of hopelessness, then you are hearing a lie from the enemy of your soul. You have a Defender that is urging you to draw near to your Father. He is specific and wants to set you free.

# Be Encouraged

*"You serve a God Who is greater than any enemy
you will ever face." – John Hagee*

*The accuser of our brethren, who accused them before our God
day and night, has been cast down. (Revelation 12:10)*

Discouragement is the message of the enemy of our soul. He feeds anxious feelings. He schemes against you sending discouragement like fiery darts. He is the author of confusion and chaos. In contrast, the Holy Spirit's message is encouragement. He encourages you to rely on God's power, not on your own strength. The Holy Spirit encourages you to be anxious for nothing. He comforts and encourages the broken-hearted and proclaims liberty for the captives. He intercedes for you. He prays for you even when you don't have the strength to pray for yourself.

Are you anxious today? Cast your cares upon Him today. He comes to give you comfort and encouragement. He wants to heal broken hearts and set the captive free. Are you so discouraged that you don't even have the words to pray? That's okay. The Holy Spirit has the words. He makes intercession for you. I pray that this word helps you to discern the difference between the voice of the enemy and the voice of your loving Father.

MAY 30

# "What Sin?"

*"The waters are rising, but so am I. I am not going under, but over." – Catherine Booth, co-founder of the Salvation Army*

*He has removed our sins as far from us as the east is from the west. (Psalm 103:12)*

If you could erase one thing from your past, what would it be? The enemy says, "Remember the past." He will replay the videos of your past memories of sin, guilt, and shame. He brings up accounts of your past failures that are *all* under the blood. But the Holy Spirit says, "Forget the past." The Spirit tells you that your sin is forgotten. Your sin is cleansed. Your sin is removed. Your sin is covered and *never* to be held against you.

He will trample our sins under His feet and throw them into the depths of the ocean (Micah 7:19).

He'll never again remember…(Hebrews 10:17).

This is great news! Do you keep bringing up your sins? Your Father in heaven says, "What sin, My child? I don't even know what you're talking about!" Your past has been erased! You have been washed white as snow!

## MAY 31

# Forever Father

*"The Bible is alive, it speaks to me; it has feet, it runs after me; it has hands, it lays hold of me." – Martin Luther*

*Do not be afraid or discouraged. For the Lord your God is with you wherever you go. (Joshua 1:9)*

Have you ever felt rejected? Have you ever been tempted to "do" things to be accepted? The message of your enemy is rejection. The devil disguises himself as an angel of light. He gives you the feeling that God has rejected you as unworthy. Satan speaks of God as your condemning judge and you as a miserable sinner. He emphasizes "good works" instead of God's grace. The message is to "do, do, do". And yet you can never "do" enough to "measure up." But the Holy Spirit draws you to God. He produces in you an unexpected kindness, love, long-suffering, forgiveness with God's help. The Holy Spirit speaks of your permanent relationship with God, drawing you to the Son of your Father. The Holy Spirit's emphasis is to experience and live under the covering of God's grace and forgiveness.

There is nothing that you've ever done or will ever do that will be a deal-breaker for God. You are His. You will always be His. If you have repented, you are forgiven. You have grace, grace and more grace!

# I Will Undo

*"Jesus comes not for the super-spiritual but for the wobbly and the weak-kneed who know they don't have it all together, and who are not too proud to accept the handout of amazing grace." – Brennan Manning*

*"Behold, at that time I will undo all that has afflicted you: And I will heal all your hurts, and gather the outcasts; and I will get them praise and fame in every place where they were put to shame. (Zephaniah 3:19)*

"I will UNDO all that has afflicted you..." What a promise! I love the word "undo". How can all that I've done and all that's been done to me be undone? That's why Jesus came! He came to undo all of my sins, my shame and all that's ever been done to me. He died so that my past could be undone! Are there parts of your past that you'd like to be erased? Jesus paid the price so that every single sin can be removed as far as the east is to the west. And He came that we might be healed. Every hurt and every affliction...healed. He is the Healer. And He gathers the outcasts. Have you ever felt that you didn't belong? Have you ever felt rejected or abandoned? He comes to gather all that have been driven out and brings them to Him. And He says that in every place that you were put to shame, He will undo that as well. He will replace your shame with praise.

May you be blessed with the peace and the promise of the One that will undo all that has afflicted you. May you totally trust that the promises of Zephaniah 3:19 are for you today.

## JUNE 2

# He's Here Now

*"You are never left alone when you are alone with God."*
*– Woodrow Kroll*

*But the Comforter, which is the Holy Ghost, whom the Father will*
*send in My name, He shall teach you all things, and bring all things*
*to your remembrance, all that I have said to you. (John 14:26)*

In this passage, Jesus is talking to His disciples. Up to this point, the
only comfort they'd received had come from Him. But Jesus could
only comfort them while He was with them. He wants to comfort all
of us, everywhere, all the time. So that's why He sent us a Helper, the
Holy Spirit, to be our Comforter. Of the Godhead, the Holy Spirit is
the most ignored. But, realize this: God is in heaven with Jesus at His
right hand. The Holy Spirit is the one that's here. Jesus knew what we
were going to face. He said, "I'm not going to leave you powerless. I'm
not going to leave you comfortless. I will come to you." It's easy to read
and to believe that the Holy Spirit was sent to the world. It's harder to
believe that the Holy Spirit has been sent just for you. And that's the
Word God has for you today. You've been adopted. You are no longer
an orphan. You are His, and you have an inheritance. And part of that
inheritance is the Comforter.

Do you believe that the Holy Spirit was sent to you? I pray that you
will let Him comfort you and teach you all things this day.

JUNE 3

# Empty-handed

*"Sometimes God speaks a thing before it is a thing. Faith is believing the thing before you see the thing. Faith is being willing to go empty-handed, trusting that at just the right time, just the right thing will be put into your hands."*
*– Christy Sawyer*

*Enter David. (1 Samuel 17:12)*

Sometimes, God *speaks* a thing before it *is* a thing. You want Him to give you some evidence, some insurance, or even some full-proof-tools. When you look down, all you see are empty hands. I was recently privileged and honored to speak at an international pastor's conference. I did everything that I could do to prepare to speak twice at this event. But the day before the event, I still did not know what time the event was, what time I would speak, or even how I was to get to where I was to speak. I had yet to meet my translator or spend any time with this person who would be my voice. I had a small meltdown in my hotel room, and asked God a few questions: "Why would you bring me here and give me no tools to work with? Do you want me to make a fool of myself? Why do the other pastors have the tools that they need? Am I not good enough to have tools?" (I'm a brat. I know this.) God reminded me of the story of David and Goliath. And how he called David a giant-slayer before David ever picked up a slingshot. He reminded me of all the times that He's shown up with what I need at just the right time. Faith is believing a thing before you see a thing. Faith is being willing to go empty-handed; trusting that, at just the right time, just the right thing will be put into your hands.

# Connect

*"You were made for mutually self-giving, other directed love. Self-centeredness destroys the fabric of what God has made." – Tim Keller*

*There's one just over there, and there's one over there to the right, and no one, not one of these, gives me a passing thought. No one will help me. No one cares one bit, what is happening to me. (Psalm 142:4)*

*I*n this passage we find David sitting in the midst of four hundred-plus men in a cave. As he looked at these men, he had this thought: "I'm sitting in a crowded place and no one is giving me a passing thought. No one knows what's going on in my life. No one has any idea of what's going on inside of me. Though they may see me on the outside, they have no idea what's happening on the inside. I'm surrounded by a bunch of people, yet I feel no connection to them at all." Not only could this happen thousands of years ago in a cave to a man after God's own heart, this can happen in our own churches today. You can look to the right and to the left and say, "They don't really know me. They have no idea what's going on in my mind and in my life." Similar to David and his four hundred-plus men pursuing the same objective, we can still be singing the same worship songs and still feel disconnected. Can I just tell you something? The body of Christ is *so* valuable to our lives. For us to be in the midst of our brothers and sisters in Christ and not be connected to them or to feel that people don't care for us would be a tragedy. Will you make the first move? It will be medicine for your own afflictions!

# You Are Crucial

*"Your greatest fulfillment in life will come when you
discover your unique gifts and abilities and use them to
edify others and glorify the Lord." – Neil T. Anderson*

*Just as there are many parts to our bodies, so it is with
Christ's body. We are all parts of it, and it takes every
one of us to make it complete. (Romans 12:4-5)*

*Y*ou are a vital part of Christ's body. Every gift that God has given
to you is important. Your gifts are needed and crucial. From being
kind, to smiling at the person next to you, to volunteering to help with
an event, to visiting someone in the hospital – everyone is important
to Jesus. Everyone is important to the body of Christ. Don't ever sell
yourself short. Everyone has a place. If you are breathing, God has
something for you to do.

What do you love to do? What do you feel passionate about? Whatever *that* is, God gave you that gift and that desire. Are you using it to
serve the body of Christ? Will you pray about that today? Ask the Holy
Spirit where and how He would like to use you. You are needed. You
have a significant role to play. There is no small part. If you want to
experience the greatest fulfillment in life, use your gifts and abilities to
serve others and give God glory.

# We Are Better Together

*"Anyone can love the ideal church. The challenge is to love the real church." – Bishop Joseph McKinney*

*He who separates himself seeks his own desires and he quarrels against all sound wisdom. (Proverbs 18:1)*

"He who separates himself seeks his own desire." One of Satan's greatest goals is to isolate us. He does everything possible to get you away from everyone and make you think you are the only one who struggles and hurts. It's a tactic that is as old as time. He did this with Eve. He isolated her from her own husband. He got her alone and started whispering lies. This verse is a telling verse. The writer is telling us that isolation is a form of selfishness. Ouch. I struggle with this myself. Isolation is a very real issue for me. When you're not willing to be with people or to be a part of people's lives, the text says that we are seeking our own desires and not what Christ wants. Christ wants us to be connected to each other. None of us are perfect. No church is perfect. No church is ideal. The *real* church has issues. The *real* church can be messy. The *real* church can be like Noah's Ark - the stench on the inside would've been unbearable, were it not for the storm on the outside.

He brought us together to do His work and grow His Kingdom. We are better together.

# Stay Hydrated

*"Dearest Daughter. I knew you would not be long*
*in coming to Me. Joy shall be yours."*
*– C. S. Lewis, The Horse and His Boy*

*"Whoever drinks of this water will thirst again, but whoever*
*drinks of the water that I shall give him will never thirst. But*
*the water that I shall give him will become in him a fountain*
*of water springing up into everlasting life." (John 4:13)*

Have you ever been without water? I have. I've been without water as a result of storms and home remodeling. But in all honesty, I've also been without water because I couldn't afford to pay my water bill.

In this text, Jesus is speaking to a woman who comes to a well in the heat of the day to collect water. (She comes in the heat of the day to avoid the other women. Let's just say she doesn't have the best reputation in town.)

Jesus offers her *living water* that will NEVER run dry. This *living water* is forgiveness for every mistake we've ever made. It's rest from all of our needless striving. It's life, but not just life…abundant life! Eternal life! Joy unspeakable and mercies new every morning!

How about you, my friend? Do you have a need in your life? Does your "well" seem to have run dry? When we surrender to Jesus, there's not a need that He will not meet and He will give you a fountain of living water that will spring up into everlasting life.

## JUNE 8

# Get Wisdom

*"It is a great misfortune to be alone, my friends; and it must be believed that solitude can quickly destroy reason."*
*— Jules Verne (The Mysterious Island)*

*Where there is no guidance the people fall, but in the abundance of counselors there is victory. (Proverbs 11:14)*

When you live isolated, *you* counsel you. *You* talk to you. So if there's wisdom in a "multitude of counselors", how do you get wise in isolation? Solomon was the one who wrote this in the book of Proverbs. Next to Jesus, Solomon was the wisest man who ever lived. He is telling us that we get smarter when we surround ourselves with wise people. It's very dangerous to make decisions without wise counsel. Isolation from the body of Christ removes you from a wisdom stream.

I can't be a wise person without the counsel of Godly people in my life. I can't be a growing Christian without people of God around me. We need each other. God has put us together. We are in this together. And, we have to look out for one other. There is nothing more dangerous as when have isolated myself and started talking to myself or counseling myself. "Where there is no guidance the people fall…" If you need victory today, reach out to a Godly man or woman for wise counsel. God speaks through His Word, but He also speaks through His sons and daughters.

Come out of the cave today!

# Let's Walk Together

*"Friendship needs no words – it is solitude
delivered from the anguish of loneliness."
– Dag Hammarskjold*

*A man who isolates himself seeks his own desire; he
rages against all sound wisdom. (Proverbs 18:1)*

When we alienate or isolate ourselves, we are elevating ourselves. When we elevate ourselves, we begin to think we have all the answers and begin to lose the voice of sound wisdom. We all need people in our lives who will walk with us and share with us. And it's really important to find people who don't necessarily agree with you all the time. And it's important to have people in your life who hear from the Lord. Who do you have in your life that will speak truth to you? Sometimes we head into the cave of isolation because we don't want to hear the truth, or we can't hear the truth without getting offended.

How about you? Do you have people in your life that will walk with you through the tough situations? Do you have someone who you can share your burden? Do you have someone who will speak truth to you? I pray that you do! We all need a wise and Godly person in our lives! If you don't, ask God to send you someone. Iron sharpens iron!

# Two Are Better Than One

*"Our love to God is measured by our everyday fellowship
with others and the love it displays." – Andrew Murray*

*Two are better than one because they have a good return for their labor;
if either of them falls down, one can help the other up. But pity anyone
who falls and has no one to help them up. (Ecclesiastes 4:9-10)*

This Christian life is a battle. There's a fight all the time. We all have to fight them. The Bible says that one can put one thousand to flight, but two can put ten thousand to flight. So guess what? You make me ten times better! When you're connected, strength comes. But when you're in isolation, there's no one there to help. When you're not connected who will pray for you? In whom can you confide? Who will give you strength? Who will lift you up? Who can you call in a tragedy? That is why we need to be connected to the body of Christ. The body of Christ is to be made up of you and me. You have an assignment, and it's the same as mine - serve the body of Christ. One of the best ways to combat loneliness and depression is to serve someone else. Jesus uses us to help each other. We are not only to help each other but we are to share our struggles. When you're by yourself, you can feel like a failure. But when we share our struggles, then we know that we are not alone. We all need someone in our lives to say, "I've been there. I've been where you are. You *can* and you *will* make it." Maybe you need to be that person for someone today. You truly have the ability to change and to save someone's life with your words of encouragement.

# Guard Your Heart

*"A kind heart is a fountain of gladness, making everything in its vicinity freshen into smiles." – Washington Irving*

*Above all else, guard your heart, for everything you do flows from it. (Proverbs 4:23)*

If I watch TV that is vile, then that is what will flow out of me. If I listen to music with lyrics that are dark and promote infidelity and abuse, then that is what will flow out of me. If I read fantasy novels about adultery and unrealistic expectations of men and relationships, then those unrealistic expectations will flow out of me. If I listen to my co-workers' for advice, and she's not even sure if she could find a Bible in her house if her life depended on it, then it will be her ungodly and ignorant words that will flow out of me. However, if I am drinking deep from the deepest part of the living waters that God has given to me, then it will be life that flows from me. If I watch things that promote Godly values and relationships, then it will be those principles that flow from me. If I read things that are beautiful, peaceful, and lift up the name of Jesus; then it will be beauty, peace, and Jesus that flow from me. If I get counsel from wise, Godly women who are Spirit-filled and have the scars to prove the battles they've overcome, then it will be wisdom and encouragement and hope that will flow from me.

What are you watching? To whom are you listening? What are you drinking and from where are you drinking? What are you thinking about? What are you allowing to flow into your mind? *That* is what will flow from your heart.

## JUNE 12

# A Beautiful Mind

*"Live in the sunshine, swim the sea, drink the wild air."*
*– Ralph Waldo Emerson*

*Summing it all up, friends, I'd say you'll do best by filling your minds and meditation on things that are true, things that are noble, things that are reputable, things that are authentic, things that are compelling, things that are gracious – the best, not the worst; the beautiful, not the ugly; things to praise, not things to curse. Put into practice what you learned from me, what you heard and saw and realized. Do that, and God, Who makes everything work together, will work you into His most excellent harmonies.*
*(Philippians 4:8-9)*

Whatever you allow to flow into your mind will be what flows out of your heart (and your mouth). If lies flow in, lies will flow out. If truth flows in, truth will flow out. If vile flows in, vile will flow out. If reputable flows in, reputable will flow out. If the best flows in, the best will flow out. If ugly flows in, ugly will flow out.

What are you meditating on today? Whatever that is will be what flows from your heart. It's never too late to change what you allow in your mind. Let's fill out minds with things that are true and beautiful and reputable and authentic and watch what flows from our hearts and mouths as a result.

# Rivers And Swamps

*"Always drink upstream from the herd." – Will Rogers*

*My dear friend, with our tongues we speak both praises and curses.
We praise our Lord and Father, and we curse people who were
created to be like God, and this isn't right. Can clean water and
dirty water both flow from the same spring? (James 3:9-10)*

You can't have fresh and contaminated coming from the same source.
If fresh water flows in, then fresh water flows out. If contaminated
water flows in, then contaminated water flows out. It's like the difference
between a river and a swamp. Water in a swamp moves very slowly. The
water can be brackish and the oxygen levels are very low. A swamp is like
a "container". A river is like a "hose", and the water flows freely. Because
swamps have very little oxygen, there's very little life. There's disease,
death, and decay because the water is stagnate. Rivers have fresh water
and living things. Low-oxygen conditions prevent growth and change
and cause illness and death. Fresh water and oxygen promote life.

Today, do you find your present situation to be more like a river or a
swamp? Praise God if it's a river! The Bible says, "Where the river flows,
everything will live." But if it's more like a swamp, you can change that
by what you allow to flow "in". Choose life-speaking and life-giving
things to flow into your mind, your home, and your life today.

# Everything Will Live

*"Our Lord has written the promise of the resurrection, not in books alone but in every leaf in springtime." – Martin Luther*

*Swarms of living creatures will live wherever the river flows. There will be large numbers of fish, because this water flows there and makes the saltwater fresh; so where the river flows everything will live. (Ezekiel 47:9)*

Ezekiel was given an incredible vision. But earlier, in the vision, he is led through waters. He starts ankle deep. Then, he gets knee deep. Then, he gets waist deep. Then, he describes the water as, "a river that I could not pass over." In other words, it's over his head. Images of water in the Bible almost always represent the Spirit of God, and this vision clearly reveals a mighty outpouring of the Holy Spirit in the last days. The vision was so powerful and overwhelming in scope that Ezekiel couldn't even comprehend it. In fact, before the vision was finished, the Lord stopped and asked Ezekiel in verse 6, "Son of man, do you see this?" In other words, God was asking Ezekiel, "Do you grasp the magnitude of what you're seeing? Are you able to comprehend the prophetic power of this vision? Do you see what these rising waters speak of? Don't miss this."

We have been given an incredible gift – the gift of the Holy Spirit. Wherever you have "dead things" or "barren things" in your life, invite the Holy Spirit. Because "where the 'river' flows, EVERYTHING will live."

## JUNE 15

# Rivers

*Like a tide, it is rising up deep inside
A current that moves and makes you come alive.
Living water that brings the dead to life
– Lyrics "The River" by Jordan Feliz*

*"Where the river flows everything will live." (Ezekiel 47:9)*

*I* don't think the true body of Christ is going to weaken and sputter as we approach the return of Christ. I don't think it's going to dwindle in numbers. I don't think it's going to decrease in power or spiritual authority. I think His church is going to go out in a blaze of power and glory in the last days. There's coming forth a body of believers who will swim in the rising waters of the Lord's presence. His presence among His people is going to keep increasing! Don't miss it! God never intended you to get refreshed by just a trickle of water. He's given you deep rivers in which to swim. The very spring and foundation of this river is the cross. He gave us the gift of the Spirit. And we were given a promise that He would be a river of life springing up in us, and that river would flow out into all of the world. Today, you may be distracted. You may be facing challenges. But, I want to remind you that there is a river from which you can drink deeply. You may be content with your present revelation of Jesus and the Holy Spirit. But my friend, you haven't seen anything yet! He's going to pour out on us as much as we can possibly stand without already being in our glorified bodies.

Dive in!

# Don't Be Left For Salt!

*"Oh, Eeyore, you are wet!" said Piglet, feeling him. Eeyore shook*
*himself, and asked somebody to explain to Piglet what happened when*
*you had been inside a river for quite a long time." – A. A. Milne*

*...So where the river flows everything will live. But the swamps and*
*marshes will not become fresh; they will be left for salt. (Ezekiel 47:9, 11)*

*E*zekiel is describing mud puddles, full of dirt and mire. As the river flows over these marshes, they're not healed. Eventually, the river will completely pass them by, leaving them so dry they'll turn to salt. In the Old Testament, salt is a symbol of rebellion and barrenness. The salt marshes Ezekiel describes here represent those of God's people who feel deeply but don't change. These people may weep over sin and death, but they don't obey God's Word to seek His life. They may make promises and resolutions to change, but they don't follow through on them. They've stood in His river of life, but they haven't allowed it to touch their innermost being. As a result, the life of Jesus doesn't spring forth from them. Instead, out of their bellies flows a steady stream of filthy gossip, insincere flatteries, lies and distortions. Such people aren't life-givers. On the contrary, everything around them is touched with strife and bitterness. They wallow in self-pity. They profess life, but they're stuck in a swamp. Instead of rivers of life, they are "left for salt." Are you in a place of barrenness today? Find a fresh water source! Dig into God's Word, and surround yourself with others who are "river dwellers".

# Blessed Is She Who Believed

*"We are what we believe we are." – C. S. Lewis*

*"Blessed is she who believed, for there will be a fulfillment of those things which were told her from the Lord." (Luke 1:45)*

I was told that I was a mistake, a complication, and a grubby little girl. I was told that I could never serve in ministry because of the mistakes of my past. I believed those things and so those things became *my* truth. But *the* Truth tells me something completely differently. Not only does *the* Truth tell me who I am, it also tells me all the things that are promised to me. There is only one Truth. God is Truth.

What if we chose to believe God and no one else? What if we chose to believe that His promises are for us? Young Mary was blessed because she chose to believe. God's promises to us are so big that they could never be fulfilled through our own effort. The angel Gabriel makes Mary a promise that is outrageous. And Mary does something equally outrageous. She believes. She chooses to believe what God tells her.

Who does God say that you are? What promises has He spoken to you? Believing is the hardest part. But if you will dare to believe, you will be blessed and those promises from the Lord will be fulfilled.

# Hope

*"If you're going through hell, keep going."*
*– Winston Churchill*

*And you will feel secure, because there is hope; you will look around and take your rest in security. You will lie down, and none will make you afraid; many will court your favor.*
*(Job 11:18-19)*

*I* 've been called an influencer. Perhaps you have, as well. But, the person who has the most influence is the person who has the most hope. Hope leaves the door open for God to fight for us in our circumstances. Without hope, our faith diminishes. Hope brings boldness and confidence in God. As we use this weapon called hope, it allows us to pray with faith and receive God's grace - even after we make a mess. Hope empowers us to believe and pray into the deliverance from impossible situations. When we dare to believe Him, He is honored. When we dare to hope in Him, He is glorified. *Then,* His promises begin to unfold.

What promises are you holding on to? What miracle do you need today? What do you need that is so big that there's no way it can be accomplished apart from Him?

# Adopted

*"The Gospel is not a picture of adoption, adoption
is a picture of the Gospel." – John Piper*

*For you did not receive the spirit of bondage again to
fear, but you received the Spirit of adoption by whom
we cry out, "Abba, Father." (Romans 8:15)*

*I* was adopted as a newborn baby in West Virginia. In a drawer in
the home of my adopted parents, are papers that prove that I am
legally their child. But, you and I have *real* adoption papers…the Bible!
If you've received the Lord Jesus Christ as your Savior, then you are also
adopted! And with this adoption agreement, you are entitled to some
incredible things. One of those things is comfort. The Holy Spirit has
been sent on a love mission to comfort His children in the absence
of Christ. Abba Father is so concerned about getting His kids to the
marriage supper and bringing you to glory that He sent the Holy Spirit
to you to keep the devil's hands off you. It's as if He has sent your very
own bodyguard. He says, "You're mine and I'm sending My very Spirit
to keep you." The Holy Spirit gives you liberty when you pray. He takes
you straight to your Father. You may be struggling today. You may be
carrying the load of your life. But, God is saying, "Don't live below your
privileges, or below your inheritance." Your Father sent you the Holy
Spirit with all of His power. He *never* leaves you.

Child of God, be comforted today. You belong. And you have access
to everything that you need.

## JUNE 20

# Like A Mother

*"In the midst of the awesomeness, a touch comes, and you know
it is the right hand of Jesus Christ. You know it is not the hand of
restraint, correction, nor chastisement, but the right hand of the
Everlasting Father. Whenever His hand is laid upon you, it gives
inexpressible peace and comfort, and the sense that "underneath
are the everlasting arms," (Deuteronomy 33:27) full of support,
provision, comfort and strength. – Oswald Chambers*

*As a mother comforts her child, so will I comfort you…
(Isaiah 66:13)*

God is speaking to a very stubborn and rebellious people in this verse.
So, even to us, who are hardheaded (me), God says to us, "I come
to comfort you as a mother comforts her child." *Good* mothers don't
give up. That's the kind of love the Father has for you. No matter what
you do. No matter how low you go. No matter how far you run. No
matter how dirty or lost you feel. He says, "You can't shake Me off!"
Your Father has His eye on you. He has adopted you.

I don't know where you are today or what you may be going through.
You may have had a hard time even getting out of your bed because
of guilt and shame or because of the mistakes you made yesterday. I
can testify to you today that no matter what happened yesterday, no
matter what you did, and no matter how you *feel;* your Father comes
to comfort you, as a *good* mother comforts her child. Let Him do it for
you, my friend.

# The Hound Of Heaven

*"God never hurries. There are no deadlines against which he must work. Only to know this is to quiet our spirits and relax our nerves."*
*– A. W. Tozer*

*As a mother comforts her child, so I will comfort you… (Isaiah 66:13)*

Here's an excerpt from a poem written in the 1800's: "*I fled Him, down the nights and down the days; I fled Him, down the arches of the years; I fled Him down the ways of my own mind; and in the midst of tears I hid from Him…*" The poet that wrote this spent his whole life addicted to drugs. He was addicted to opium and in total bondage. Even in that condition, he said that God chased him and pursued him. He's the one that termed Him the "hound of Heaven". Even at his lowest, and even when he turned the farthest from God, God was on his tracks. God was pursuing him. God was a hound dog. God came after him. God wouldn't let him go.

So I say to you parents and grandparents, God's looking out for those children and grandchildren that you worry about. Even if they're going in the wrong direction, the Holy Spirit is still trailing them. He is on their tracks. The "hound of Heaven" is on their heels. So today, give that burden to God. Don't lose one more night's sleep. The Holy Spirit knows right where they are.

## JUNE 22

# It's Personal

*"Even if you're on the right track, you'll get run
over if you just sit there." – Will Rogers*

*May the God of hope fill you with all joy and peace as
you trust in Him, so that you may overflow with hope
by the power of the Holy Spirit. (Romans 15:13)*

It's personal. If only we really believed that, and not just when we are in church together. Rather, if we could take it back into our homes and into our workplaces. If we could really say and really believe: "Holy Spirit, I know that you came for the whole world, but if I was the only one, you would have still come just for me. God, I know you are Father to the whole world, but I was the only one, you would still be my Father. Jesus, I know you died for the whole world, but if I was the only one, you would still have died just for me." It's personal! Make it personal! Let the Holy Spirit be personal to you.

Do you need comfort today? If you will make it personal and let the Holy Spirit make it personal, He will send you the comfort that you need, every time you need it, just in the nick of time. If you are not reaching out for Him, you are living below your inheritance. You don't have to go anywhere special for this to happen. It can happen right now, right where you are. He's inside of you! There are rivers of living water inside of you.

# The Refreshing

*"Pain insists upon being attended to. God whispers to us in our pleasures, speaks in our consciences, but shouts in our pains. It is his megaphone to rouse a deaf world."*
– C. S. Lewis

*For with stammering lips and another tongue He will speak to this people, to whom He said, "This is the rest with which you may cause the weary to rest," and, "This is the refreshing…" (Isaiah 28:11-12)*

When I pray in the spirit, I feel refreshed, rested and light. It's like a hundred pound weight has been lifted off of me. Have my circumstances changed? Not necessarily. But, I'm different…I'm safe. That is a witness of the Holy Spirit. Jesus is in charge of everything and everything is going to be all right. There are just some obstacles in my life that are bigger than I am. When I let the Holy Spirit do the praying for me, there's a rest and refreshing that comes to my soul. I can stop fighting. I can rest on what Christ has done for you. I can rest in the Spirit. I can rest my frustration, anxiety and weariness by praying and praising in the Spirit. Where do you get your comfort? You don't have to find comfort in escapes like television, food, drugs, alcohol, books or anything else. Jesus sent the Comforter to come alongside of you to be with you forever, teach you all things, and to give you refreshment. He came to give you rest.

## JUNE 24

# Open-Handed

*"God spared my life not so that I could live for me but so that I could just give everything to Him. You know, God's not asking for much. He's asking you to give up something you were never created to be so that you can become who he says you are. It's really not that much. I mean, Mercy woke us up today so that Love gave us one more day to manifest Him and not us." – Todd White*

*When Jesus had called the twelve together, He gave them power and authority to drive out all demons and to cure diseases and He sent them out to proclaim the kingdom of God and to heal the sick... So they set out and went from village to village, proclaiming the good news and healing people everywhere. (Luke 9:1-2, 6)*

Jesus has absolutely no need to be the center of the action. He was not threatened to send His friends out to do the very things He does. He launched them. He gives them a major role in His ministry. He said, "You go do it. Do everything you see Me doing." This is both humble and extraordinarily generous. However, this is how all ministry MUST be done - not tight-fisted. Where is there room to receive anything else, when you're tight-fisted? Jesus is absolutely open-handed with His kingdom. There is no need for it all to be about Him. Most men and women who get power crave more power. As their stars rise they can't bear to have others in the spotlight. One of the most revealing sides of anyone's character is how they handle people. I believe the way a person handles others is an indicator of their true nature. We must model our character after Jesus and of His goodness.

# Like A Child

*"It is a masterpiece of the devil to make us believe that
children cannot understand religion. Would Christ have mad
e child the standard of faith if He had know that it was not
capable of understanding His words?" – D. L. Moody*

*One day, children were brought to Jesus in the hope that He would
lay hands on them and pray over them. The disciples shooed them
off. But Jesus intervened: "Let the children alone, don't prevent
them from coming to me. God's kingdom is made up of people like
these." After laying hands on them, He left. (Matthew 19:13-14)*

This is a very "Sunday School" story. We've made it a precious moment
and missed both the true message and the beauty. Think about
instances in church when a child is crying and how uncomfortable it
makes everyone. First, we're thinking about the pastor. And honestly,
it's probably irritating and distracting to anyone speaking. How do you
feel when people are rude in the checkout line? Or when someone rides
the back end of your car to persuade you to go faster? Or the co-worker
that is so negative you call her Eeyore behind her back? Or the spouse
with habits that get on your last nerve? These things anger us because
they feel like an intrusion. But not Jesus…He welcomes intrusion. In
Luke's version of the story, the disciples think they are protecting Jesus
by shooing off both parents and kids, but Jesus "called them back."

His goodness is almost heartbreaking. I want to be like that. I want
to be the child that doesn't hesitate to go straight to Jesus. And I want
to be like Jesus, always in the moment. Always understanding that there
really are no "interruptions."

☽

# The Holiness Of Jesus

*"The greatest test of whether the holiness we profess to seek or to attain*
*is truth and life will be whether it produces an increasing humility in*
*us. In man, humility is the one thing needed to allow God's holiness*
*to dwell in him and shine through him. The chief mark of counterfeit*
*holiness is lack of humility. The holiest will be the humblest."*
*– Andrew Murray*

*One of the Pharisees asked Him over for a meal. He went to the*
*Pharisee's house and sat down at the dinner table. Just then a*
*woman of the village, the town harlot, having learned that Jesus*
*was a guest in the home of the Pharisee, came with a bottle of*
*very expensive perfume and stood at His feet, weeping, raining*
*tears on His feet. Letting down her hair, she dried His feet, kissed*
*them, and anointed them with the perfume. (Luke 7:36-38)*

What is incredible to see in this account is this woman knew herself to be anything but holy. But she found the holiness of Jesus approachable, loving, accepting and completely appealing. Jesus' holiness was magnetic not repellent. What if we all understood holiness this way? Think of this Jesus when you're praying for your loved ones. Think of this Jesus when you think of yourself. I want to be more like Him. His immense goodness captures us. Genuine goodness is captivating. You can tell a lot about a person by their effect on others.

# Beautiful In Its Time

*"We never noticed the beauty because we were too busy trying to create it."*
*– Anonymous*

*He will make everything beautiful in its time.*
*(Ecclesiastes 3:11)*

*H*e will make everything beautiful in its time – even the tragedies, even the losses, even the heartaches. If you've ever walked with someone who is ill and you pray and you pray and they don't get better. But you pray and what it does is it sweetens the atmosphere so that everyone can bear it, so that you can stand it. And then you begin to trust, "He'll make all things beautiful." You begin to believe that all things are working together for your good. "I don't understand this right now, but I'm going to pray and send up the sweet aroma of praise and let God turn it into something beautiful. I trust you God, even when You don't answer my prayers the way I thought You would." There is power in prayer. There is sweetness in prayer. It doesn't always change the situation, but it always changes the atmosphere. And, prayer always changes you! If you will pray, then "He will make everything beautiful in its time."

Talk to Him today. Just tell Him about it. The situation may not change right away, but you will change. And, the atmosphere around you will change.

## JUNE 28

# Bearing The Unbearable

*"Our prayers may be awkward. Our attempts may be feeble. But since the power of prayer is in the one who hears it and not in the one who says it, our prayers do make a difference." – Max Lucado*

*"Father, if it is Your will, take this cup away from Me; nevertheless, not My will, but Yours, be done." (Luke 22:42)*

The cup wasn't removed. The cup wasn't taken away. But, something happened when Jesus prayed that sweetened the atmosphere and caused Jesus to be able to get through the ordeal through which He had to go. He was able to bear the unbearable. And, I'm so glad He did. Aren't you? When He prayed, the angels came and ministered to Him. That's what prayer does. Prayer may not solve every problem in your life instantly. Prayer will bring joy to you soul strength to your life. Today, you may have trouble on every side. But, if you will pray about it, you will be able to bear the unbearable.

Sometimes, things can be so unbearable, that you can't even figure out what to pray. May I challenge you? For one week, pray the Lord's Prayer (Matthew 6:9-13), out loud, three times per day. Be prepared that, after a while of doing this, the first thing on your mind in the mornings will be: "My Father, Who art in Heaven...I don't know what this day is going to bring, but I'm going to be prepared for it because I've created a sweet aroma and incense of prayer and praise, and whatever comes my way today, so be it."

JUNE 29

# Encourage Yourself

*"A teardrop on earth summons the King of heaven."*
*– Chuck Swindoll*

*But David strengthened himself in the Lord his God.*
*(1 Samuel 30:6)*

Sometimes we go through seasons where we thought life would have been so much better, so much easier, and so much different. Perhaps you are discouraged or downcast today; downcast because life has turned out to be worse than you thought it was going to be. In this passage, David and his men had just found their city burned to the ground and their families had been taken from them. The Bible says they wept until they could weep no more. It had to be devastating. Life has a way of doing that sometimes. The Bible says, "Now David was greatly distressed." (1 Samuel 30:6) He was in a place of disappointment not only because of what he had just discovered, but also because his own men were speaking of stoning him. They wanted to kill him because they were grieved for their own sons and daughters. What do you do when you find yourself in a situation like David's? There will be times when you will be rejected. There will be times when you feel like people are throwing stones at you. There will be times when it feels like nothing is going right and everything is going wrong. There will be times when the people who should be supporting you turn on you and talk about you badly. What do you do when life is just not going in the right direction? The Bible says, "David strengthened himself in the Lord his God." If you are discouraged today, you may need to encourage yourself in the Lord your God.

# Seeking Refuge

*"I have a word for you. I know your whole life story. I know
every skeleton in your closet. I know every moment of sin, shame,
dishonesty and degraded love that has darkened your past. Right
now I know your shallow faith, your feeble prayer life, your
inconsistent discipleship. And My word is this: I dare you to trust
that I love you just as you are, and not as you should be. Because
you're never going to be as you should be. – Brennan Manning*

*For I will leave in the midst of you a people humble and lowly. They
shall seek refuge in the name of the Lord. (Zephaniah 3:12)*

There is a connection between God's delight in His name and His
delight in you. When you take refuge in His name, Zephaniah 3:17
says, "He rejoices over you with singing." When you seek your own
glory, you have your reward. If you bank on your own goodness, you
have your reward. But, if you humble yourself and seek the glory of God
above all things, and if you hid your name in the name of God clothe
yourself with the righteousness of Jesus, then your Father will reward
you beyond all imaginings and rejoice over you with gladness. He will
rejoice over you with loud singing.

Today, I pray you come to the awareness of how deeply you are loved
by God. May you allow God to love what you have deemed un-loveable
in your life.

# World-Changers

*"You have within you the strength, the patience, and the
passion to reach for the stars to change the world."*
*– Harriet Tubman*

*For as the earth bursts with spring wildflowers, and as a garden
cascades with blossoms, so the Master, God, brings righteousness into full
bloom and puts praise on display before the nations. (Isaiah 61:11)*

God's desire is that our lives thrive in such a remarkable way that they become a display of His goodness before all people. God wants you to arise. He wants His glory to shine on you and through you. I want to make a difference, and I believe that you want to make a difference. Why not start where you are today? It doesn't matter if your life is imperfect or even in disrepair. God will give you the wisdom and the courage to make whatever adjustments need to be made. God will give you the grace to refresh what needs to be refreshed. The story of our lives brings hope and testimony to that of another, giving them the courage to change. When we allow God's glory to shine on us, then we have changed the world! Each of us can be a world-changer!

Do you want to be a world-changer? Where do you need to make some adjustments? God will help you and give you the grace and the strength in the areas over which He has given you charge.

God, make us all world-changers!

# Removing The Mask

*"Wearing a mask wears you out. Faking it is fatiguing.*
*The most exhausting activity is pretending to be*
*what you know you aren't." – Rick Warren*

*You can't keep your true self hidden forever; before long you'll be*
*exposed. You can't hide behind a religious mask forever, sooner or later*
*the mask will slip and your true face will be known. (Luke 12:1-3)*

*I*'ll never forget the first time I "removed my mask." I finally understood the reality that Jesus was actually more attracted to what was under it. He even delights in it. That's what He's after. Removing my pretenses ignited boldness in me to be real for the first time in my life. This revelation brought these questions: "Who am I really? Who was I created to be?" Maybe you struggle to be the same person on Sundays that you are the rest of the week. There are two purposes in wearing a mask. First, it changes your identity. At church, you look like a Christian. Around non-Christians, you blend in very easily. And like a chameleon, you secure your mask in place because you want to blend in with your surroundings. Second, it hides your identity. You don't want anyone to see the "real" you. So, you put on a mask as a way of hiding who you really are. Let me tell you the two truths I've learned about masks. First, none of the masks we wear are remotely close to who we are. And secondly, none of the masks we wear are remotely close to who God created us to be. It's okay to remove the mask today. The sooner we take them off, the sooner we can step into the person God has created us to be!

# Staying In The River

*"Come to the water. Come to the water of life.*
*It will never run dry." – Chris Tomlin*

*Where the river flows everything will live. (Ezekiel 47:9)*

*Jesus said, "If any man thirsts, let him come unto Me, and out*
*of his belly shall flow rivers of living water." (John 7:37)*

Jesus speaks of the Holy Spirit. The Holy Spirit is a life-giving river. The presence of Jesus is a river of living water. If we don't stay in the "river," we wither and lose our life. If the Spirit isn't leading us and directing us, we lose our purpose. It's the "river" of the Spirit that brings all the blessings and the success and the victories of God. Everything comes from the "river." It's much easier to get out of the river than to stay in the river. If you ever step out of the river of Holy Spirit, then everything that you know and have can dry up, leaving you joyless and lifeless. We have to stay in the river. The river leads us. The river restrains us. The river guides us. If you've ever stood in a river, you know it has a current. If it's a real river, you don't just get in and do what you want. The current constrains you. The current pulls you. That's how the river of the Spirit is. Even if you start going in a direction that God doesn't want you to go, if you're in the river, there is a restraining. The current will get you going back in the right direction. That's the power of the Holy Spirit. That's staying in the river!

Jesus, we come to You in our thirst today.

# Set On The Spirit

*"Trying to do the Lord's work in your own strength is the
most confusing, exhausting, and tedious of all work. But
when you are filled with the Holy Spirit, then the ministry
of Jesus just flows out of you." – Corrie Ten Boom*

*Those who live according to the flesh have their minds set on what
the flesh desires; but those who live in accordance with the Spirit
have their minds set on what the Spirit desires. (Romans 8:5)*

*I* pray to be a person who has their mind set on what the Spirit wants.
I don't want to be moving in the wrong direction. I don't want
to get out of the "river" of the Holy Spirit. I want the seeds that have
been planted in my life to bloom and to grow. We need to be men and
women after the Spirit. We need to be sons and daughters and mothers
and fathers and husbands and wives that are after the Spirit. We need
to be like Moses. He was so spirit-led that he said, "I want my words
and my actions to be after You Lord!" He said, "If Your presence does
not go with us, do not bring us up from here." In other words, "God,
if you're not going with me, then I'm staying right here." I have learned
(the hard way) that if the Holy Spirit is not in my plans, then I end up
with a disaster. I need the restraining power of the Holy Spirit in my
words, actions and thoughts. I don't want to do what His Spirit won't
bless. How about you? Maybe today you feel like you've gotten off
course. Right now, you can speak to God and say, "God, if you're not
going with me, then I'm staying right here." Get your mind set on what
the Spirit wants and He will guide you into all things.

# Spirit-Led

*"There is no use in running before you are sent; there is no use in attempting to do God's work without God's power. A man working without this unction, a man working without this anointing, a man working without the Holy Ghost upon him, is losing time after all." – D. L. Moody*

*Are you so foolish? After beginning by means of the Spirit, are you now trying to finish by means of the flesh? (Galatians 3:3)*

In other words, "You began in the Spirit, make sure you finish in the Spirit." Maybe you started your Christian walk in the Spirit. Maybe you started your marriage in the Spirit. Maybe you started your business in the Spirit. But, time and life can pull at us and we can begin to operate in the flesh and not in the Spirit. In the beginning, you're in the Word, you're in your prayer closet, and you call out to God in everything you do. The writer in this text is basically warning us, if we ever think we can finish in the flesh, we are foolish. Without the Spirit, things wither and die and life becomes a shell. Nothing will ever take the place of Jesus. Our lives can look great on the outside, but on the inside be completely barren or in turmoil. On the outside it can look like we are living. But is there a flow on the inside?

Is the Spirit leading you, my friend? Is the restraining power of the Spirit so forceful in your life that you refuse to do anything unless His current is leading you?

# Life-Giver

*"We are all priests before God, there is no such distinction as 'secular or sacred.' In fact, the opposite of sacred is not secular; the opposite of sacred is profane. In short, no follower of Christ does secular work. We all have a sacred calling." – Ravi Zacharias*

*Many of the Samaritans from that town believed in Him because of the woman's testimony... (John 4:39)*

Mary Magdalene is found throughout the New Testament. We know that Jesus cast out seven demons from her. He had a plan. She was at the cross when they hung Him. She was the one that discovered the empty tomb. She was the first one to whom Jesus appeared to at the Garden Tomb. She was mourning His death and He called her by name. "Mary." He loved her. He had a purpose for her. She was called to be a life-giver.

Don't allow anyone to ever make you feel unqualified because of your past or your mistakes. We are all called. And Jesus uses our lives to reach people groups that would otherwise not be reached if not for our testimonies.

Who will you speak life to today?

Jesus, put someone in my path that needs me to speak life to them today.

# At His Feet

*"There is a strain of loneliness infecting many Christians,*
*which only the presence of God can cure."*
*– Aiden Wilson Tozer*

*"Mary has chosen what is better, and it will not*
*be taken away from her." (Luke 10:42)*

We all know the story. Martha was fretting because the house needed to be cleaned. She was running around, huffing and puffing, picking up, polishing and dusting. Then, she sees her sister sitting at the feet of Jesus, seemingly doing nothing. She sees Mary *resting*. Mary was resting in His presence. She was resting and worshiping. And, Martha called her out right in front of Jesus. Honestly, how could she just sit there? But, Jesus said to her, "Your sister has chosen what is better, and it will not be taken away from her."

Even as I write this, I feel a tugging of conviction. Not condemnation. I feel the Father calling to me, telling me the same thing. "Choose what is better, Christy." I may be doing *good* things. I may even be doing them for Him. But I can't forget the most important thing, I can't forget what is "better." Just sitting in His presence. Just resting in His presence. Just worshiping in His presence. That is what is "better." And, what happens as we rest in His presence can never be taken from us. Jesus wants you to rest in Him.

Pardon me while I do just that. I'm going to go sit at the feet of Jesus this morning.

# Pour It Out

*"The unbelieving world should see our testimony lived out daily because it just may point them to the Savior." – Billy Graham*

*"Truly I tell you, wherever this gospel is preached throughout the world, what she has done will also be told, in memory of her." (Matthew 26:13)*

*I* love the story of the woman pouring out her perfume on Jesus' feet. The Bible tells us that the value of that perfume was the equivalent of a year's salary. She gave Him her past in that perfume. And, He wanted her story told for all eternity. I love the fact that despite her past mistakes, she got close enough to Jesus to catch the look in His eyes. I imagine she saw something in His face she had never seen before. His grace captured her! I love this woman. She gives us a living and breathing example of the power of God to change lives. We can see our own journey woven through hers.

My friend, like mine, did your past sins and mistakes cost you greatly? Do you try to cover them up so that no one will see? Here's the truth…like this woman, we need to pour them out at the feet of Jesus. He understands how much your past has cost you. He understands that more than you do. But He wants to make an exchange. He wants to take your past and give you His grace. Will you receive that gift today?

Jesus, we pour it all out at Your feet today.

# What Are You Saying?

*"Remember who you are. Don't compromise for
anyone, for any reason. You are a child of the
Almighty God. Live that truth." – Lysa Terkeurst*

*But David strengthened himself in the
Lord his God. (1 Samuel 30:6)*

*D*avid encouraged himself. He talked to himself. What are you saying when you talk to yourself? You may be talking to yourself, but what you're saying to yourself is not the right thing to say! You may be saying all the negative things. You may be talking about how bad things are. You may be speaking of how troubled you are. Sometimes, you have to speak over yourself. You have to speak life over yourself. You have to speak a Word over yourself. Strengthen yourself! Encourage yourself! That's what David did. He talked to himself. Your friends may not understand what you're going through. The people in your church may not understand your situation. Sometimes YOU have to be the one to speak over yourself. David didn't use his own words. He wasn't arrogant in his speech. No, the Bible says, "He encouraged himself *in the Lord his God."* David used the Word of God to encourage himself. And God says to you today that you must do the same thing. You must use the Word of God to encourage yourself. Instead of beating yourself up about the mistakes you've made or the problems that you have or the challenges you are facing. Instead of reminding yourself about your past, you need to remind yourself about the God that you serve!

JULY 10

# Hostage

*"No matter what evil you have experienced in the past, that experience should not hold you hostage for the rest of your life." – Pastor John Gray*

*"Come to Me, all you who are weary and burdened, and I will give you rest." (Matthew 11:28)*

Jesus invites us to come to Him to get "unburdened." He invites us to come to Him to be set free. But, in order to be set free, you must be aware that you are a hostage. It's hard to set people free who don't know they're in jail. In order to break chains, you must know that you are in chains. In order to be free, you must recognize your slavery condition. God can only help people who are aware that they need help. How can you know that you need help? Jesus came not only to give you rest, but He came that you would have life. He came not only that you would have life. He came that you would have abundant life! Do you have abundant life? If the answer is no, then you may be a hostage - a hostage to burdens that you were never meant to carry. Or you may be a hostage to chains that you were never meant to wear.

The solution is simple. Jesus says, "Come to Me." That's it. If you need rest and freedom and abundant life today, just come to Jesus.

Jesus, we come to You today with our heavy loads and our weariness. Thank you for supernatural rest today.

# It Will Get Done

*"The best time to plant a tree was twenty years ago.*
*The second-best time is now." – Chinese Proverb*

*…being confident of this, that He Who began a good work in you will*
*carry it on to completion until the day of Christ Jesus. (Philippians 1:6)*

God *will* complete what He's started in you. It's not up to you to do that. The completion of the good work He is doing in you is *not* based on your performance. You will fall down over and over and over. Your heart will be broken, multiple times. There will be times that you *will not* be okay. But, you will get up and you will survive. And all of this is part of that "good work" that Jesus is completing in you! Completion will take many twists, turns and broken roads. Completion will include many "start-overs." Grace is undeserved favor and it doesn't have an expiration date.

Be confident! He isn't finished yet, but He will finish what He started in you! Completion of the "good work" that He has begun in you will include every moment, every experience, every failure and every victory.

Lord, we thank you for loving us today. Thank You that there is no limit to how many times we can start over. Thank You for completing in us what You started.

## JULY 12

# Bad Idea!

*"The difficulty lies not so much in developing new ideas as in escaping from old ones."* – *John Maynard Keynes*

<u>*And when the woman saw*</u>*...that the fruit was also desirable for gaining wisdom…she ate. (Genesis 3:6)*

It wasn't Eve's idea to eat the forbidden fruit. But Satan's idea became her idea. The devil told her why she needed to eat the fruit. But she adopted the idea and it became *her* idea. Satan has deceived many of us today because he's told us his ideas for so long that we believe that they are our ideas. And so we say things like, "I can't break this habit." "My marriage can't be saved." "I can't control my temper." "I can't control my cravings." Those are only our ideas by *adoption*, not by origination. God would never give us those ideas. God would never give you the idea that you have to be an addict for the rest of your life. God would never give you the idea that divorce is the only way out. God would never give you the idea that you have to keep going to bed depressed and taking medication for the rest of your life. God would never give you the idea that you are destined to be defeated. The devil takes *his* idea and makes it *your* idea. That is what the Bible calls a stronghold.

Will you let Jesus get inside and take over today? He has great ideas! His ideas give life, not death. His ideas give victory. They don't make victims.

Lord, protect our minds today from the evil one.

# Stop Pushing!

*"The moment of surrender is not when life is over,
it's when it begins." – Marianne Williamson*

*Don't work yourself into the spotlight; don't push your
way into the place of prominence. (Proverbs 25:6)*

I was at a women's conference recently. I was there to attend and not to speak, which was really nice. At least, it should have been. But I found myself critiquing the event in my mind, especially the speaker. Let me be very clear. The speaker was great! And, even in the moment, I couldn't understand what was happening inside of me. I'm not normally *that* person! I actually felt very disturbed in my spirit for several days. I finally had to come face to face with the Holy Spirit and ask Him to show me what was happening. He said, "Christy, you're jealous. You think that it should have been you. And you're upset with Me because you don't see what's next on your journey." Ugh. Busted. At the root of my feelings was insecurity. Something dark that I didn't even know was there rose up inside of me that told me I have no value if I'm not the one in the spotlight. The Holy Spirit reminded me that I've never had to push my way into anything. None of us do. If we're called, and we are all called, then we need to let Him promote us rather than striving to make things happen on our own. Surrender is a beautiful thing. It's really the answer to so many afflictions. In that meeting with the Holy Spirit I did just that. The peace that comes with surrendering your will to Him is indescribable. I highly recommend it! What do you need to surrender today, my friend?

# The Invitation

*"Where there is great love there are always miracles." – Willa Cather*

*On the third day a wedding took place at Cana in Galilee. Jesus' mother was there, and Jesus and His disciples had also been invited to the wedding. When the wine was gone, Jesus' mother said to Him, "They have no more wine." What Jesus did here in Cana of Galilee was the first of the signs through which He revealed His glory... (John 2:1-3, 11)*

*H*ave you ever needed a miracle? Maybe you need one today. What is needed for a miracle or an answer to prayer? Let's look at the miracle in John 2 as an example to us all. There's a wedding where they ran out of wine and Jesus was there. Why was Jesus there? Jesus was there because they invited Him. And Jesus always comes where He's invited. If Jesus is not invited, there will be no miracle.

My friend, where do you need an answer to prayer today? In what area of your life do you need a miracle? Will you invite Jesus into every part today? Invite Him into every part of your heart, every part of your mind and into your family situation.

Jesus ALWAYS comes where He's invited.

Jesus, we invite You into our day. We surrender every conversation and situation that we might encounter today. You are welcome in our hearts.

# It's Okay To Kill

*"The more my trust rests in God, the less I trust myself. If we truly desire to live the crucified life, we must get rid of self-trust and trust only in God." – A. W. Tozer*

*So I say, walk by the Spirit, and you will not gratify the desires of the flesh. (Galatians 5:16)*

As Christians, we have the Holy Spirit living within us. He is separate from Christy. He will never be Christy. Christy will never be Him. The flesh will never be changed. Christy will never be changed because of her flesh. Who I am NEVER changes. It's hopeless. I'm helpless, no matter how hard I try. To change us, God puts His Spirit inside of us. And as we live under His control, we've not only been justified from our past sins, we can also live victoriously because the Spirit is controlling us. But, the flesh hasn't disappeared. And because the flesh controlled us for so many years, it's always looking to reassert itself. Christy is always looking to get back in the game. "I don't want the Holy Spirit leading. I want Christy leading. I don't want the Father, Son and Holy Spirit. I want me, myself and I."

I would love it if I only had to crucify my flesh once, never to be resurrected. But sadly, I have to kill it on a regular basis, sometimes more than once each day. It is crucial that we walk by the Spirit.

How about you? Do you need to kill your flesh today like I do? Living life being led by the Spirit is far better than living life being led by Christy.

# JULY 16

# Spread Out

*"It's important to understand that God's dream for your*
*life is so much bigger than your dream for your life."*
*– Christy Sawyer*

*No man shall be able to stand against you all the days of your*
*life… You will go on to have success. (Joshua 1:5, 9)*

*D*o you believe that God is for you? If you don't believe that, you'll never see His promises. It's important to get your thinking right and understand that God said, "No man can stand before you and stop you." He promises to deal with your opposition. What is your dream for your life? Whatever that is, God's dream for your life is so much bigger. In the Old Testament book of Zechariah, it starts out with God blessing and prospering His people. And, when He began to prosper them, they began to spread out. When God begins to prosper your life spiritually, physically and emotionally, you begin to spread out and go places that you've never gone. When God begins to put His favor on your life, it begins to take you beyond anything you ever imagined. God wants you to have a vision bigger than where you are now and what you are doing now.

What's holding you back? There's nothing to fear! God says, "No man shall be able to stand against you all the days of your life!" Dream big!

Father, forgive our unbelief!

# Look Up Child!

*"Never let your head hang down. Never give up and sit
down and grieve. Find another way. And don't pray when
it rains if you don't pray when the sun shines."*
– *Richard Nixon*

*…They could not lift up their heads. (Zechariah 1:21)*

*H*ave you ever felt so oppressed that just lifting your head seemed an impossible task? In this scripture, the people were so oppressed that they walked around with their heads down, not looking up and not looking out. They had lost their confidence. What's interesting is that God had just spoken blessing and success over them. Immediately the enemy came to oppress them so that they couldn't even lift their heads. They felt defeated. Has the enemy tried to hold you down? Is he trying to stop you from fulfilling what God has called you to do? Listen, you have the Spirit of God on your side! He comes to raise you up and to lift your head today! No one can stand against you! No voice in your past or in your future!

Father, we give you thanks that You are the Lifter of our heads! I pray protection against the attempts of the enemy to oppress, and I pray silence over the assaults of his whispers. I thank you for the power of the Holy Spirit that is with us always. Jesus, may we keep our eyes fixed on you today.

# Hidden Treasure

*"God wants to open your eyes to things that would
otherwise remain unseen, so that you can claim what would
otherwise remain unclaimed." – Christy Sawyer*

*I will give you hidden treasures, riches stored in secret
places, so that you may know that I am the Lord, the God
of Israel, Who calls you by name. (Isaiah 45:3)*

Nothing God does is without significance. God knew you before your birth. He recorded your existence before time began. He knew before there was land and sea that you would be reading this today. He has a plan for your life. And, that means that He has "treasures in darkness and riches stored in secret places" for you. But, you must specifically and deliberately ask God to reveal them to you. You need the Lord to open your eyes to see things that you can't normally see, so that you can claim things that would otherwise be unclaimed. God doesn't usually place His storehouse of treasures in open and obvious places. God has "secret places" where most treasures can be found. And to find the treasure that He has for you, your eyes have to be open to them. That is why it is so important to be led by the Spirit. The Holy Spirit will give us spiritual eyes to see things that we could never see with our human eyes.

Father, will you open our eyes today to see the hidden treasures that you have for us in secret places. Holy Spirit, lead us today. Give us eyes to see and ears to hear. Even in, and especially in, the darkest times, You have treasures for us to claim.

# Follow The Leader

*"You are never left alone when you are alone with God."*
*— Woodrow Kroll*

*I will go before you…(Isaiah 45:2)*

"I will go before you." This is one of God's promises to us. Now, if you've never encountered trials or difficulties and have found this life easy and smooth, then you may not feel the need for the Lord to go before you. But, if you know what it is to be surrounded by difficulties that you can't solve by any strength or wisdom of your own, then you understand the need for the Lord "to go before you." I don't know anyone who likes trials and difficulties. But the truth is, we never receive any real blessing without them. The Lord makes Himself most known in our trials.

Can I help you today? To save you some heartache, even in the times when there isn't a struggle, you STILL need to let Him go before you. Let the Holy Spirit lead you every step of the way, even in the good times. If you don't, I can promise that you will go down the wrong road.

What are you facing today? Invite the Holy Spirit to go before you and lead you. He may take you around it, remove it completely, or lead you through it. But He WILL go before you.

Holy Spirit, thank You that we are never alone. Go before us this day. We surrender every minute to You.

## JULY 20

# The Broken Road

*"I set out on a narrow way many years ago. Hopin' I would find true love along the broken road. But I got lost a time or two. I wiped my brow and kept pushin' through. I couldn't see how every sign pointed straight to you."*
*– lyrics/Bless the Broken Road*

*"I will go before you and make the crooked places straight…" (Isaiah 45:2)*

We are all on a path in this Christian walk. Some paths are crooked. They are bent and curved because of sin. Somewhere on the journey, sin bent crooked what was originally straight. There are crooked tempers, crooked attitudes, crooked wills and crooked lusts. Some of our paths were bent out of their original state by sin and now don't lie level with God's will and God's Word. But, there are also crooked places in our paths in which we had no hand in creating. Things like afflictions in our bodies or minds, financial situations, trials in our families, persecution at work, losses in businesses, or bereavement of children. Nonetheless, God has promised to make our crooked paths straight. So no matter why or how they are crooked, He promises to straighten our crooked places. Sometimes He removes them. Sometimes, He takes us out of them. Sometimes, He gives us peace as we encounter them. And sometimes, He bends our will to submit to them.

Lord, we thank you that this day You will make our crooked places straight. No matter how You do it, we will let You lead us.

JULY 21

# The Treasure Hunt

*"May we never lose our wonder…wide-eyed and mystified, may we be just like a child, staring at the beauty of our King." – Amanda Cook*

*…Having made known to us the mystery of His will, according to His good pleasure which he purposed in Himself, that in the dispensation of the fullness of the times He might gather together in one all things in Christ, both which are in heaven and which are on earth – in Him. (Ephesians 1:9-10)*

This very day, just a few hours ago, I had a Bible placed in my hands that was placed in my grandfather's hands in 1966, ten years after he became a minister. I never met my grandfather, Brooklin. He was my birth father's father. I was put up for adoption and spent much of my adult life trying to piece my history together. If you had asked me twenty years ago if I wanted to know everything, I would have grabbed at it eagerly. But, my true Father always knows what's best for His girl. "Having made known to us the mystery of His will *according to His good pleasure…* "Twenty years ago, my grandfather's bible and the knowledge that he was a pastor would not have meant to me then, what it means to me now. God meant for me to find this treasure today. I have been searching for answers and treasure that I needed right now, and right now was when He "made known to me the mystery…" Do you have questions today? If you will seek His treasure, you WILL find it.

# He Loves Them More

*"I don't believe there are devils enough in hell to pull a boy out of the arms of a godly mother."* – Billy Sunday

*"Therefore I tell you, whatever you ask for in prayer, believe that you have received it, and it will be yours."* (Mark 11:24)

Today is the wedding anniversary of my oldest daughter Ashley and her husband Herman. It is cause for celebration for this mother because it is proof that God answers prayer, and He loves our children more than we could ever love them. After years of many different kinds of struggles, and after countless sleepless nights and sometimes hour-by-hour prayers, I see the fruit of those prayers. I admit, there were many times that I wondered if God was listening and if He was doing anything at all. I prayed many prayers for my daughter and God has answered many of those. However, one very specific prayer I prayed was that He would send her someone that loved Jesus, someone that would cherish my daughter and lead her the way that God intended. And did He ever! More than I could have ever imagined!

Parents and grandparents, I know what it's like to go to hell and back with your children. Don't give up! Keep praying. God is working it all out! And as much as you love those babies, He loves them more!

Father, we trust you today with our children. We place them in Your hands. We thank You in advance for getting them where You want them to go!

JULY 23

# Shaking And Pressing

*"Before God could bring me to this place He has broken me a thousand times." – Smith Wigglesworth*

*"But we have this treasure in earthen vessels, so that the surpassing greatness of the power will be of God not from ourselves; we are afflicted in every way, but not crushed; perplexed, but not despairing; persecuted, but not forsaken; struck down, but not destroyed…" (2 Corinthians 4:7-9)*

You have a calling. God has called you to fulfill a purpose. Sometimes, we go through hardships that can distract us from the work we are called to. Hardships and trials can even be paralyzing. The enemy of your soul would love for you to get your eyes on your problems and off of what God has for you. We must keep our focus on Jesus through everything. When we stay diligent with what He's given us, God will fill us to overflowing. Think about this example: If you went into a specialty store to purchase rice, the person behind the counter would pour the rice into a measuring scale. But they wouldn't fill it all the way up. They would only go three-quarters of the way up and then shake the scale and press on the rice. The reason for shaking is to both level out the rice and fill in any gaps that formed underneath. In other words, because of the shaking and pressing, you get more rice. That's what God can do in the middle of your trouble. He lets life press us down so He can "fill in the gaps."

God, we need Your sustaining power today. Help us to stay diligent in what You want us to do. Thank you for "filling in the gaps."

# JULY 24

# Good, Good Father

*"God attaches no strings to His love. None. His love for us does not depend on our loveliness. It goes one way. As far as our sin may extend, the grace of our Father extends further." – Tullian Tchividjian*

*"When he came to his senses…" (Luke 15:17)*

There was a father who was a businessman who had a plan for his sons. He trained them. He provided for them. He prepared them to take over the family business. But, one of the sons decided to go his own way. He asked his father to give him his inheritance now, rather than later. So, while his brother continued following the father's rules and working alongside him, the prodigal son took all his father had given him, left town, and squandered it all away with wild living. Prodigal actually means, "to be wasteful in a reckless way." By the time it was all said and done, things had gotten so bad that he ended up with a job feeding pigs, and the pigs were eating better than he was! It was at about this point that "he came to his senses." Other translations say, "When he came to himself." Do you remember when you came to your senses? Or, are you still living below your inheritance? The prodigal had convinced himself that he was no longer worthy to be called his father's son. Have you ever felt that you were not worthy to be called God's child? If you feel that way today, you need to come to your senses! Quit settling for crumbs when your Father has a feast prepared for you!

God, You are a good, good Father. Thank you for the banquet that You have prepared for us.

# Don't Miss The Point!

*"Grace is the gift of feeling sure that our future, even our dying, is going to turn out more splendidly than we dare imagine." – Lewis Smedes*

*The older brother stalked off in an angry sulk and refused to join in. His father came out and tried to talk to him, but he wouldn't listen. The son said, "Look how many years I've stayed here serving you, never giving you one moment of grief, but have you ever thrown a party for me and my friends? Then this son of yours who has thrown away your money on whores shows up and you go all out with a feast!" His Father said, "Son, you don't understand. You're with me all the time, and everything that is mine is yours – but this is a wonderful time and we had to celebrate. This brother of yours was dead and he's alive! He was lost and now he's found!" (Luke 15:28-32)*

*B*oth sons missed the point. Neither really understood the depth of the father's grace. There are two ways to miss it. It's easiest to see in the prodigal son who ran in rebellion, satisfying his own selfish desires. It's harder to see it in those who run headlong into religious activities thinking they can impress God with their commitment. Like the Pharisees, they feel justified by their anger at the more obvious sins of others. But, in neither case do they fully understand the abundance of God's love and grace. The notion of God's love and grace coming to us free of charge, no strings attached, seems to go against every instinct that we have.

# Grace And More Grace

*"Amazing grace! How sweet the sound, that saved a wretch like me! I once was lost but now am found, was blind but now I see." – John Newton*

*But God's not finished. He's waiting to be gracious to you. Cry for help and you'll find that it's grace and more grace.*
*(Isaiah 30:18-19)*

The disciple John was an apostle, an evangelist, and an author. But if John were asked, "What is your primary identity in life," he wouldn't list any of those titles. He would answer, "I'm the one that Jesus loves." What would it mean, if we too came to the place where we saw our primary identity in life as "the one Jesus loves"? How differently would we view ourselves at the end of the day? How differently would that affect how much grace we accepted each day? Grace means there is nothing we can do to make God love us more. And, grace means there is nothing we can do to make God love us less. Grace is crazy math. Grace can redeem something that you've lost and give it back to you multiplied to the one hundredth. It can take years that you've lost and, in an hour, restore it all back to you.

God is waiting to be gracious to you. Cry for help! And when you do, you'll find that it's grace and more grace!

Father, we are thankful that you are not finished with us. We ask for your grace today.

# He Stooped Down

*"He stoops down to make us great. That's God's grace."*
*– Billy Graham*

*We can understand someone dying for a person worth dying*
*for, and we can understand how someone good and noble*
*could inspire us to selfless sacrifice. But God put His love on*
*the line for us by offering His Son in sacrificial death while*
*we were of no use whatever to Him. (Romans 5:7-8)*

God put His love on the line for us "while we were of no use whatever to Him." Notice that God didn't say, "When those scoundrels show the least bit of interest in cleaning up their act, then I'll meet them more than halfway." No, it was while we were sinning and loving it, the Father stooped down and extended supreme grace in the person of His Son. He didn't ignore our sin. He didn't excuse our sin. He *looked past our sin* and He accepted us in spite of it. Isaiah said, "The Lord longs to be gracious to you, and therefore He waits on high to have compassion on you."

It doesn't matter how far you've fallen. God will stoop down to where you are. He yearns to have compassion on you. He longs to extend grace to you. He looks past every sin and accepts you in spite of them. Just cry out to Him today. He's been waiting for you.

Lord, Your love for us leaves us breathless. It makes no sense. It is the greatest gift we've ever received. Thank you.

# The Heart Surgeon

*"I do not at all understand the mystery of grace – only that it meets us where we are but does not leave us where it found us." – Anne Lamott*

*I will give you a new heart and put a new spirit in you; I will remove from you your heart of stone and give you a heart of flesh. (Ezekiel 36:26)*

Max Lucado writes: "Grace is God as a heart surgeon, cracking open your chest, removing your heart; poisoned as it is with pride and pain, and replacing it with His own. Rather than tell you to change, He creates the change. We don't have to clean up so He will accept us. He accepts us and begins cleaning us up." God doesn't stand on a high hill and tell you to climb out of the valley. He bungees down to where you are and carries you out. God doesn't build a bridge and command you to cross it. He crosses the bridge, throws you across His shoulders and carries you over.

How is your heart today? Bit by bit, trial by trial, life can begin to harden our hearts. But God has a new heart and a new spirit for you. He will do all the work. Will you trust The Surgeon with your heart today?

Father, we thank you that you are always willing to replace our hearts of stone with hearts of flesh. Thank you for accepting us as we are.

# Outlandish Grace

*"The law works fear and wrath; grace works
hope and mercy." – Martin Luther*

*You did not save yourselves; it was a gift from God. (Ephesians 2:8)*

There is no word sweeter to the sinner's ears than the word grace. Being the "chief of sinners" I know this without a doubt. Your sin will never be bigger than God's love. The prodigal can never outrun the Father. Being lost is not a necessary condition to being found. God doesn't measure you by the good you do. God measures you by the grace you accept. God's grace for you is extraordinary grace. As Brennan Manning writes: "It's grace that pays the eager worker who works all day long the same wages as the lazy worker who shows up at ten minutes till five. It's grace that hikes up the robe and runs at breakneck speed toward the prodigal reeking of sin and wraps him up and decides to throw a party, no ifs, ands, or buts. It's grace that raises bloodshot eyes to a dying thief's request – 'Please, remember me' and assures him, 'You bet I will!'" It's grace that works without asking anything of us. Grace calls us to change and then gives us the power to do it. Grace is sufficient even though we try with all our might to find something or someone it can't cover.

Isn't it wonderful? Isn't it too much to take in? Will you believe that this outlandish grace is for you today? You can't do this by yourself. You can't save yourself. This is a gift from God.

## JULY 30

# Quit Being Contrary!

*"The Spirit-filled life is not a special, deluxe edition of Christianity. It is part and parcel of the total plan of God for His people." – A. W. Tozer*

*For the flesh desires what is contrary to the Spirit, and the Spirit what is contrary to the flesh. They are in conflict with each other, so that you are not to do whatever you want. (Galatians 5:17)*

The Spirit of God inside of me always desires what is contrary to my flesh, my human nature. The Spirit desires to make me like Christ. The Spirit desires that I serve other people humbly in love. The self, Christy, says, "Forget about others. I don't care about anyone else. I care about me." That's how flesh is. The flesh is always fighting the moving of the Spirit. Whenever the Spirit working inside of me begins to crave the Word of God or to crave Christian fellowship, my flesh says, "No, you're too tired." When the Spirit is speaking and leading, the flesh says, "No, you're too busy." And so there's an inner conflict happening. Flesh and Spirit fight against one another.

Father, save us from ourselves. Thank you that You provided a way that our flesh doesn't have to rule over us. For greater is He that is in us than He that is in the world. Teach us how to follow the leading of the Spirit day-by-day and even minute-by-minute.

# 70 x 7

*"The weak can never forgive. Forgiveness is the*
*attribute of the strong." – Mahatma Gandhi*

*Then Peter came to Him and said, "Lord, how often shall my*
*brother sin against me, and I forgive him? Up to seven times?"*
*Jesus said to him, "I do not say to you, up to seven times,*
*but up to seventy times seven." (Matthew 18:21-22)*

Peter asks Jesus a question. And as Jesus did often, He answers the question with a parable. But Jesus tells a shocking story to illustrate to us what unforgiveness looks like from God's perspective. "So, My heavenly Father also will do to you if each of you, from his heart, does not forgive his brother his trespasses." (v. 35) God doesn't play around when it comes to forgiveness. There is never a situation where God will allow us *not* to forgive. And Jesus said, "If you don't forgive your brother or sister from your heart, My Father will turn you over to torture." Well, unforgiveness is literally torture. It shows up physically in stress, ulcers, nervous disorders, headaches, high blood pressure, and depression. So many physical problems are caused by the lack of forgiveness. The stress and the anxiety of living with the weight of unforgiveness is like a death sentence. God never created us to be storage containers for hatred.

Are you struggling with unforgiveness today, my friend? Are you experiencing the physical manifestations of holding that inside of you? Will you forgive today *from your heart*? Not for *their* sake, but for yours! God wants you to be free and well!

## AUGUST 1

# Don't You Remember?

*Do not fret, for God did not create us to abandon us.*
*– Michelangelo Buonarotti*

*Now Peter sat outside in the courtyard. And a servant girl came to him,*
*saying, "You also were Jesus of Galilee." But he denied it before them*
*all, saying, "I do not know what you are saying." (Matthew 26:69-70)*

*H*ave you ever felt like everything in your life was falling apart, just like Peter did so long ago? Sometimes it's hard to even remember a time when you were REALLY with Jesus. A time when you actually woke up early in the mornings to pray, and worship, and just spend time with Him. Was there a time when I really woke up so full of the joy of the Lord, thanking Him that I had another chance to lift my hands and worship Him?

This girl reminds Peter in the midst of his broken moment, "Don't you remember when you used to have faith?" "Don't you remember when you were walking with Jesus?" And, Peter says, "I don't even know what you're saying." But, God chased Peter down and triggered a time in Peter's mind when he used to walk with Him. "Maybe if Peter can remember what it was like to hear from Me, then, perhaps, he can reach even further back and remember that I have a plan for his life."

During this time of brokenness and what may seem like the end, God said to Peter, and He says to you, "I still have a plan for you."

# No Schemes!

*"Is prayer your steering wheel, or your spare tire?"*
*— Corrie ten Boom*

*"I find rest in God; only He can save me." (Psalm 62:1)*

Many years ago, I went through a devastating financial loss. I was a wreck. I lost almost everything. I lived in fear and anxiety. I was desperate to turn my situation around. I had friends who were very successful in business, so I went to them for advice. They shared with me an "investment opportunity" which they guaranteed would help me not only get back on my feet quickly, but would also give me financial security for years to come. Did I mention I was desperate? So, I borrowed money from my parents, and with great hope, gave the check to my friends. Sixty days later, I received the terrible news that all the money was gone. The so-called "investment opportunity" turned out to be a Ponzi scheme. So, on top of everything else, my parents' money was lost, as well.

When we get into trouble, we want out, and we want out fast. Our desperation can cause us to neglect the only One who can save us. The end result: we end up in a worse situation than we started.

Are you in trouble today? Are you in a desperate situation? Take it from someone who has been there a few times, turn to God first! He is the only One who can save you. You will find rest in Him.

## AUGUST 3

# Lord Have Mercy!

*"Our Savior kneels down and gazes upon the darkest acts of our lives.*
*But rather than recoil in horror, He reaches out in kindness and says,*
*'I can clean that if you want.' And from the basin of His grace, He*
*scoops a palm full of mercy and washes away our sin." – Max Lucado*

*Therefore, let us then approach God's throne of grace with*
*confidence, so that we may receive mercy and find grace*
*to help us in our time of need. (Hebrews 4:16)*

"*Let* us approach with confidence." *Confidence* in this text means *freely and with boldness.* In other words, we can speak freely and boldly to God. He says, "Come to Me and hold back nothing!" What Jesus has done on the cross has given us access to God's presence. The end of the verse says, "…so that we may receive mercy and find grace to help us in our time of need." Some literal translations say it like this: "So that you'll find God's grace, help or strength given to you…just in the nick of time." He'll give you what you need, just when you need it, when you come to the throne of grace.

What do you need today? Go to the throne of grace freely and boldly, holding back nothing!

Father, thank You that there is nothing that we have ever done that would cause you to recoil from us. Thank you for grace and mercy given to us just in the nick of time.

## AUGUST 4

# I'm Supposed To Be Jesus

*"If God calls you to be a missionary, don't stoop
to be a king." – Jordan Grooms*

*"As You sent Me into the world, I have sent
them into the world." (John 17:18)*

One of my favorite places to go is the dog park. It's become a "happy
place" for me. I love to watch the dogs socialize. Besides the "sniffing"
process, we could learn a lot from dogs! While there the other day, my
one-year-old goldendoodle, Daisy, happily approached a lady sitting on
a bench alone. I was just about to call Daisy, but then the lady began
hugging her and petting her. It was then that I noticed the lady was
crying. She looked at me and said, "It's just that I miss my dogs." I wish
that I could tell you that I walked over, sat on the bench and talked with
her. But I can't. I actually didn't respond at all and pretended to be busy
with my older dog, Dusty. I counsel people almost every day. I listen to
people's problems almost every day. I "spend" all of my energy on others
most of the time. So, of course, I should "conserve" what little I have
left. Right? Wrong. I am so ashamed that I missed the opportunity to
show love and compassion to that lonely woman. I have thought of her
constantly. The Holy Spirit "gently" reminded me that I promised Him
to make myself available at all times. I've asked Him to place people in
my path so that I could point them to Jesus. I blew it. I really blew it.

As God sent Jesus into the world, Jesus sends us into the world. For
everybody. Even strangers at a dog park.

# Open The Door!

*"Secret sins commonly lie nearest the heart." — Thomas Brooks*

*In the first year of his reign, in the first month, he opened
the doors of the house of the Lord and repaired them.
(2 Chronicles 29:3)*

*I*n 2 Chronicles 29, Hezekiah had just become king. Scripture tells
us that his first order of business was to get the temple back in order.
Because the people began worshiping idols, the temple was no longer
God's dwelling place. Since it wasn't being used as a place of worship,
some of the temple doors were permanently shut. What is an idol? An
idol is anything that we give more attention than we give God. Just like
the people of Israel, if you allow idols to take over in your life, the doors
to the "temple" will be shut. In other words, instead of God being at
your center, you move Him off to the side. And as a result, the "door"
that was always open to Him, gets shut. That's why it can sometimes
be hard to hear God's voice. Hezekiah was a smart man. He knew the
first thing he needed to do as king was to open the doors to the temple.

Have the doors of your heart closed to the voice of God? Have you
allowed "idols" to move in and take His rightful place in your life? Friend,
I invite you to do, like Hezekiah, open the doors of the house of the
Lord today! Invite Him back in. He longs to be in the center of your life.

# The Most Dangerous Weapon

*"When the world beats you down, open up your Bible."*
*– Lysa TerKeurst*

*…and the sword of the Spirit, which is the*
*Word of God. (Ephesians 6:17)*

Not long ago, while going through security at the airport, my bag was pulled for a security check. The gloved TSA officer handled my backpack as though it carried weapons of mass destruction. As I travel frequently, I'm always careful about what I pack in my carry-on luggage, so I was confused about what could have triggered a security check. Finally, she said, "Here's the problem." I watched with fascination as she pulled my Bible out of my backpack! I said, "Are you telling me that my Bible is what flagged my bag?" She said, "Yes ma'am." To which I replied, "Well, the Bible is the most dangerous weapon a person can have." She looked at me as though I had grown a horn out of my forehead. I started laughing and said, "I LOVE that my Bible caused such a scene!" She gave me a small grin, closed my bag, and sent me on my way. I think I smiled for the duration of my flight.

But, it's the truth! The Word of God IS your greatest weapon. Do you feel unsafe or unprotected? Are you unsure about your future? Draw your "sword" mighty warrior!

# Sacrifices

*"Whatever troubles are weighing you down are not chains. They are featherweight when compared to the glory yet to come. With a sweep of a prayer and the praise of a child's heart, God can strip away any cobweb."*
*– Joni Eareckson Tada*

*And now my head will be lifted up above my enemies around me, in His tent I will offer sacrifices with shouts of joy; I will sing, yes, I will sing praises to the Lord. (Psalm 27:6)*

When everything seems to be going wrong, when darts of despair are coming at you from every direction, the idea of lifting your voice in praise to the Lord seems exhausting. "I will offer *sacrifices* with shouts of joy." The definition of sacrifice is: "surrendering a possession as an offering to God." When you *choose* to praise the Lord in the middle of your tragedy, it is truly a sacrifice. That means that you are surrendering your situation, your grief, your anxiety, your fear and your thoughts, as an offering to God. When you *choose* to "offer shouts of joy" and to "sing praises to the Lord" despite how you feel, scripture says that "your head will be lifted up above your enemies."

If you are struggling with a seemingly impossible situation, or you feel surrounded on every side, begin to give God your sacrificial praise and shouts of joy. Before you know it, He will lift your head up above your enemies!

# Into His Wonderful Light

*"We can easily forgive a child who is afraid of the dark; the real tragedy of life is when men are afraid of the light."*
*– Plato*

*"…that you may declare the praises of Him Who called you out of darkness into His wonderful light." (1 Peter 2:9)*

*I* had coffee with a friend this morning. Driving there, I felt anxiety rising in me. There had been an awkwardness between us for some time. Little comments, here and there, had rubbed me the wrong way. Then, in private, I would replay those comments in my mind and, inadvertently, put my own spin on them. Looking back, most of what I was I feeling was a result of my own imagination!

Thoughts can be dangerous things. If you don't bring them into the light, they can begin to take the shape of ominous and dangerous things. Facts quickly turn to fiction. No matter how upsetting or uncomfortable your thoughts, bringing them into the light, shines truth on them.

And, that's exactly what happened with my friend. We brought our concerns "out of darkness into His wonderful light." I sure wish we hadn't waited so long!

Do you have some thoughts that need to be brought into the light? The enemy would love nothing more than for you to keep them in the dark.

## AUGUST 9

# A Well-Loved Woman

*"All girls are princesses. Didn't your father tell you that?"*
*– Sarah (A Little Princess)*

*The King's daughter is all-glorious within... She*
*is lovely and stunning... (Psalm 45:13)*

There is something heartbreakingly beautiful about a well-loved woman. She can be skinny, fat, old, young, handicapped, rich or poor. She can be scarred, have acne, or arthritis. A well-loved woman radiates beauty on the outside, because of what is on the inside of her. It has nothing to do with her looks, her intelligence, her upbringing, her sex appeal, or her bank account. It has nothing to do with how many, or if there are any, beauty contest trophies are on her shelf. It has nothing to do with her age or her career. *It has everything to do with WHO it is that loves her.*

Maybe you've never felt like a well-loved woman. Maybe your earthly father never told you that you are a princess. Your Heavenly Father wants to remind you that you are the King's Daughter, and that you are all glorious within. You are lovely and stunning.

You *ARE* a well-loved woman.

AUGUST 10

# Bad Roots

*"When the root is bitterness, imagine what the fruit might be." – Woodrow Kroll*

*See to it that no one falls short of the grace of God and that no bitter root grows up to cause trouble and defile many. (Hebrews 12:15)*

I opened a business several years ago. For our grand-opening, we had an elegant evening party with violins, and fountains and twinkle lights. Everyone was dressed up. It was lovely. I was so proud. We had remodeled a historic house and it was breathtakingly beautiful. I had some of our employees walking around with drinks and hors d'oeuvres, while others were giving tours of our beautiful business. One of them approached me and said, "We have a problem." All of the bathtubs, sinks and toilets were posing as chocolate fountains! They were literally spewing up brown water. We called a plumber. The plumber had to call a "special team" plumber. They had to dig down ten feet to find the problem. A tree had been cut down a long time ago, but even though the tree was nowhere to be seen, the root remained. The water pipes were filled with these very large roots. We had made everything so beautiful. We covered up the past with paint and wallpaper. But we hadn't dealt with the roots. We thought the remodel was complete, but we hadn't dug deep enough.

Are there bitter roots that you've tried to cover? You can hide them for a while, but eventually they have to be dealt with. The longer you wait, the more "expensive" it is to repair the damage that bad roots cause.

# Mara

*"The medical evidence is clear and mounting. It's no exaggeration to say that bitterness is a dangerous drug in any dosage and that your very health is at risk if you stubbornly persist in being unforgiving." – Lee Strobel*

*But she said to them, "Do not call me Naomi; call me Mara, for the Almighty has dealt very bitterly with me." (Ruth 1:20)*

Naomi's husband and her sons had been killed. She was devastated and blamed God for it. She asked to be renamed because of her bitterness. Mara means bitter. Often, our resentment isn't as much towards people in our lives as it is towards God. "Why didn't God stop this?" "Why did God allow me to go through this?" "Maybe God didn't cause it, but He could have stopped it." "Why didn't God stop the abuse?" "Isn't God Sovereign?" But that's not what sovereign means. Yes, God is the Supreme Ruler of the Universe, but God will never act outside of His character. He doesn't want robots. He created us in His image, and He gave us a will. And because He gave us a will, we messed it all up in the beginning. Now, we live in a fallen world, where there is sickness, tragedy, and a very real enemy that would like nothing more than for us to have a root of bitterness towards God. Your enemy would love for you to begin blaming God for your situation.

Don't be deceived. If you feel bitterness towards God, tell Him about it right now. Let Him help you remove that root of bitterness.

# He SO Loves You

*"One who has been touched by grace will no longer look on those who stray as "those evil people" or "those poor people who need our help." Nor must we search for signs of 'love-worthiness.' Grace teaches us that God loves because of who God is, not because of who we are." – Philip Yancey*

*God said, "I have loved you with a love that lasts forever. I have kept on loving you with a kindness that never fails." (Jeremiah 31:3)*

The Message translation (Jeremiah 31:3) says it this way, "I've never quit loving you and never will." He just can't help Himself from loving you. He literally can't help Himself, because God doesn't *have* love. God doesn't *do* love. God *is* love. John 3:16 doesn't say, "He loves the world." It says, "He SO loves the world." It makes me think of my kids. I'm crazy about them. I don't just love them. I SO love them. And I'm a mere human. My love for my kids is miniscule compared to the love that your Father has for you!

You may say, "To tell you the truth, Christy, I don't know if I believe that God loves me like that." He can't help it! He does love you like that, because He IS love. You are the object of His obsession! Just like I used to watch my kids sleep, just because I couldn't get enough of watching them, God watches you while you sleep. He can't get enough of watching you.

He loves you with a love that lasts forever. He's never quit loving you, and He never will. He SO loves you.

## AUGUST 13

# Planted

*"Someone's sitting in the shade today because someone planted a tree a long time ago." – Warren Buffett*

*To all who mourn in Israel, He will give a crown of beauty for ashes, a joyous blessing instead of mourning, festive praise instead of despair. In their righteousness, they will be like great oaks that the Lord has planted for His own glory. (Isaiah 61:3)*

Only God can take a tangled mess of a life, ashes and all, turn it around, and transform it in such a way that will give hope to others who have abandoned all hope.

I love oak trees, most likely because my dad (a West Virginian timber man) has taught me so much about them. An oak grows slowly, but surely, at its own rate. The oak is a symbol of strength and is often associated with honor and wisdom. It is a giving-tree with multiple uses: medicinal, food and refuge. I love that Isaiah compares the righteous to a "great oak that the Lord has planted for His own glory." Only God can exchange your mourning for joy and your despair for praise. He will take your weaknesses and turn them into strengths. Only God can plant you like an oak tree and use you to provide hope for others.

# Reign

*"Once a king or queen of Narnia, always a king
or queen of Narnia." – C.S. Lewis*

*...How much more will those who receive the overflow
of grace and the gift of righteousness reign in life through
the One Man, Jesus Christ. (Romans 5:16)*

You are royal by blood – the blood of Jesus Christ. You don't become a child of the King by working for it. It's your position. The enemy would try to tell you that you've been disqualified for this position. But your Father has called you to reign. You have a title and a position. And with that title and position, you are entitled to some things. "How much MORE will those who receive the overflow of grace REIGN in life through Jesus Christ." Some of God's children walk around like raggedy orphans. But your Father paid the highest price for you and recreated you into His righteous and reigning child. You are no longer an orphan striving for meaning and purpose. He is already pleased with you without you ever having to perform!

Thank You, Father, for Your overflow of grace and the gift of righteousness. Help us to live and reign from our positions of royalty.

# Delight In Him

*"When I trust deeply that today God is truly with me and holds
me safe in a divine embrace, guiding every one of my steps
I can let go of my anxious need to know how tomorrow will
look, or what will happen next month or next year. I can be
fully where I am and pay attention to the many signs of God's
love within me and around me." – Henri J.M. Nouwen*

*Take delight in the Lord, and He will give you
the desires of your heart. (Psalms 37:4)*

God gives wonderful gifts. But the reality is, the best thing about God is God, and the best thing about Jesus is Jesus. When we come to Him with nothing but requests, He is gracious and often answers our requests. But that ends up being the extent of the relationship. When we come to Him just to be with Him, His heart bonds with our heart and our desires blend with His. He loves to give you the desires of your heart. That's what happens in intimate relationships. Connected hearts seek to meet the needs and desires of the other.

What are the desires of your heart? Are you willing to take the emphasis off the desires and take delight in the Lord first? He wants, first and foremost, to be in relationship with you. The desires of your heart come naturally after that.

# Like A Tree

*"Someone's sitting in the shade today because someone planted a tree a long time ago." – Warren Buffett*

*He shall be like a tree planted by the rivers of water, that brings forth its fruit in its season, whose leaf also shall not wither; and whatever he does shall prosper. (Psalm 1:3)*

Psalm 1:3 is a beautiful promise that is for you. It speaks of being planted, fruitful and prosperous. You need to get "planted" in the Body of Christ. The value of fellowship with other believers is immeasurable. There is value in the good times, but also in the bad times. It is a priceless gift to have a man or woman of God that you can call on when you're in trouble. You get "watered" by the Word of God which will make you fruitful. You need to read, study and meditate on God's Word. And there is power in praying God's Word. Whatever area of your life that you may be struggling in, see what the Word of God says about it. If you're having marital problems, what does God's Word say about it? If you're having financial struggles, what does the Bible have to say about that? When you do these things, scripture says that you will be fruitful and that whatever you do shall prosper.

Are you connected to a church? If not, visit one this Sunday. In the meantime, get into the Word of God so that He can "water" you and refresh you today.

# Old Yet Ever New

*"The gospel is ever new." – Brooklin Walker, my grandfather*

*"Because I am God, your personal God…your Savior. I
paid a huge price for you… That's how much you mean to
Me! That's how much I love you!" (Isaiah 43:3-4)*

I was looking through my grandfather's old Bible this morning. I found a note that said, "The gospel is ever new." I had to chew on that for a while because the verse, "Jesus is the same yesterday, today and forever" kept going through my mind. But then I began to recall the many comments that I get after I preach a sermon, "That was just for me!" or "I've never seen that Scripture like that before." I know that God never changes. But I also know Him to be a personal God. I believe He gives us fresh eyes and minds to see things in a fresh and new way. I believe He can take a sermon or a message, divide it up for exactly the amount of people receiving it, and then multiply it by sending them out to share that message with someone else. It comforts me to imagine my grandfather reading his Bible. I imagine that on the day he wrote, "The gospel is ever new," that he read something that he had read hundreds of times before, but the Holy Spirit showed him something new that day.

Do you know God to be your personal God? He has a fresh new word for you today.

Father, thank You that you are the same yesterday, today and forever. But, thank You for a fresh new word every day. Thank You for being a personal God.

# "Honey, Did You Take Out The Trash?"

*"I do not preach any new truth. I do not have any new
doctrine… We must have a revival that will mean purity of
heart as a normal standard for everybody. We must be clean
people, and not only clean outside." – A. W. Tozer*

*He brought in the priests and the Levites, and assembled them in
the East Square, and said to them, "Hear me, Levites! Now sanctify
yourselves and sanctify the house of the Lord God of your fathers and
carry out the rubbish from the holy place." (2 Chronicles 29:4-5)*

"*C*arry out the rubbish from the holy place." How can there be trash
in the temple of God? Israel had fallen away from God and began
worshiping idols. They abandoned the temple of God. They quit caring
about the things of God, including His temple. As a result, the doors
fell off the hinges and rubbish began to accumulate. A temple has to
be maintained. It has to be cleaned. When Hezekiah became king, He
made the temple of God a priority. He ordered that all the trash be
taken out. It took the priests eight days to remove all the garbage that
had piled up in the temple. But the Bible says that after all the garbage
had been removed, "the song of the Lord began…and the king and all
who were present with him bowed and worshiped." You and I are the
temple of God. And like the Israelites, we let trash accumulate in us.
Anything that is not of God or that offends Him is garbage. If we will
take out the trash, His Word says that, "the song of the Lord will begin."
If you have felt disconnected from God or can't find your peace or joy,
perhaps you need to take out the trash.

Father, we confess that we allow the things of this world to accumulate in Your temple sometimes. Help us to take the trash out today.

# AUGUST 19

# Knowing Him

*"You don't realize Jesus is all you need until*
*Jesus is all you have." – Tim Keller*

*"More than that, I count all things to be loss in view of the surpassing*
*value of knowing Christ Jesus my Lord..." (Philippians 3:8)*

*Y*ou can actually celebrate God's goodness and yet never behold Him. It would be like going to a party, and the host is over in the corner, and you may wave or make eye contact, but you never actually meet. At some point, all the food, the wonderful music and all the people you meet, should actually draw you to the person who is hosting the party.

You can go to church every Sunday, clap your hands during worship, raise your arms during prayer and drop your money in the offering plate yet never know the "person who is hosting the party." He *wants* you to behold Him. He wants you to know Him. Knowing Him is the most important thing in this life.

Do you really know Him? Are you talking to Him throughout the day? Is He talking back to you? If not, start now! Just begin by saying, "Jesus..."

## AUGUST 20

# Better Than Blue-Ribbon Bulls

*"In happy moments, praise God. In difficult moments, seek
God. In quiet moments, worship God. In painful moments,
trust God. Every moment, thank God." – Rick Warren*

*"I'm hurt and in pain; give me space for healing, and mountain
air. Let me shout God's name with a praising song, let me tell of His
greatness in a prayer of thanks. For God, this is better than oxen on
the altar, far better than blue-ribbon bulls. The poor in spirit see and
are glad – Oh, you God-seekers, take heart!" (Psalm 69:29-33)*

*I* went through a very dark time in my life several years ago. It was
painful and depressing. I lived in fear, just waiting for the *next* thing
to go wrong. Things were so dire, that my anxiety began to affect me
physically. No matter how hard *I* tried to keep myself from slipping
into the darkness, I still fell into a dark pit. And despite *my* best effort
to turn my situation around, things only got worse. At the very lowest
point, I made a choice. I chose to praise and worship the Lord anyway. I
felt nothing. But I told Him, "If you never bless me again, if nothing in
my life gets better, I will still praise You." I lifted my heavy-as-lead arms
towards Heaven and I praised Him. He was happier with my sacrifice
(and it was a sacrifice) of praise than He would have been with anything
else. That was a turning point for me. My situation didn't change for
quite some time. But I changed.

Are you hurting or in a painful situation? Lift your hand to God
in thanks and praise. "For God, this is better than "blue-ribbon bulls."

## AUGUST 21

# This Is A Fight

*"Where there is only a choice between cowardice and violence,
I would advise violence." – Mahatma Gandhi*

*Be strong in the Lord and in His mighty power. Put on the full armor
of God, so that you can take your stand against the devil's schemes. For
our struggle is not against flesh and blood… (Ephesians 6:10-12)*

People are not your problem! If you are a believer in Christ, then you are in a fight. It's called spiritual warfare, and it begins the moment you become a Christian. It doesn't end until we leave this world. At first glance, it's easy to believe that your struggles are with people, but scripture makes it clear that your struggle is with the powers of darkness. Satan will use people to tempt, torment and attack you. But, they're just pawns. They're not the problem. The devil is just using that person to hold you back. The Apostle Paul warns us, "to stay alert." And, 1 John 4:4 reminds us, "You, dear children, are from God and have overcome them, because the One Who is in you is greater than the one who is in the world."

This is a fight, my friend. You can't fight this fight in your own strength. You need to Jesus fight for you and with you!

Lord, in Your power and with our armor in place, we take our stand against the devil's schemes. Your power in us is greater than our enemy that is in the world.

# You Can Take Root Again

*"A journey of a thousand miles begins with a single step."*
*— Lao Tzu*

*And the surviving remnant of the house of Judah shall*
*again take root downward bear fruit upward.*
*(2 Kings 19:30)*

"*S*hall AGAIN take root downward and bear fruit upward." I love the word "AGAIN" in this verse. Judah had messed up, but it said that Judah would "again" take root downward. Have you ever messed up? (My hands and feet are raised!) The Word of God says that if you've messed up, you can take root again. I'm sure that you have many areas in your life that have good fruit. But maybe you have areas in your life where there is some not-so-good fruit. The Bible says, in those areas, take root *again*. In other words, if you're having problems in your marriage, commit to praying with your spouse every day or go to a marriage conference. If you're having problems with your finances, take a Dave Ramsey class. Get in a small group that deals with the area in which you are struggling. Where there is bad fruit, take root AGAIN. You may have made mistakes, but don't get discouraged. Take root AGAIN.

Father, we thank you that we can always start over. Nothing is impossible with You. Help us to identify the areas where we have bad fruit and help us to take root again.

## AUGUST 23

# Lay Hold

*"You can never cross the ocean until you have the courage
to lose sight of the shore." – Christopher Columbus*

*Through acts of faith, they toppled kingdoms, made
justice work, and took the promises for themselves.
(Hebrews 11:33)*

The promises of God aren't going to just fall out of the sky and onto
your head. You have to lay hold of every promise in God's Word.
When you read something in His Word and you feel something begin
to stir inside of you, you need to say, "That Word is for me!" God has
called you to be fierce and dangerous. He has called you to "topple
kingdoms" and to "make justice work." But this can only happen when
we take action. Faith requires action. Our faith is built by laying hold
of the promises of God.

Maybe you've been sitting passively for a long time. Perhaps you've
even been hoping, but nothing has happened. It's time to take action.
Lay hold of God's promises today. You need to take hold of whatever
you need…whatever God has for you. He offers you ALL the promises
in His Word to equip you for this time for which He created you.

Lord, speak to us today through Your Word. Cause the words to
jump off the page and stir our hearts.

# Invincible

*"Inaction breeds doubt and fear. Action breeds confidence and courage. If you want to conquer fear, do not sit home and think about it. Go out and get busy." – Dale Carnegie*

*On your feet, Daughter of Zion! Be threshed of chaff, be refined of dross. I'm remaking you into a people invincible. (Micah 4:13)*

*G*rowing up, my grandparents and my parents always talked about Jesus coming back! And I believe that there are many people that just sit around waiting for that glorious moment. But as He tarries, you were not created to just sit around doing nothing. You were created to rise up in these last days invincible. As a child of the King, you were created for more than you can even see with your natural eyes. You are positioned in a place of authority and power. Where generations before only dared to whisper, you will speak out loud.

All that God has laid on your heart, do it with fierce joy, strength and faith. He is remaking you into a "people invincible," in Jesus' Name.

Jesus, come quickly! But, in the meantime, we stand to our feet to be threshed of chaff and refined of dross. Make us invincible!

# You Are A Carrier

*"The breaking of the alabaster box and the anointing of the Lord filled the house with the odor, with the sweetest odor. Everyone could smell it. Whenever you meet someone who has really suffered; been limited, gone through things for the Lord, willing to be imprisoned by the Lord, just being satisfied with Him and nothing else, immediately you scent the fragrance. There is a savor of the Lord. Something has been crushed, something has been broken, and there is a resulting odor of sweetness." – Watchman Nee*

*"This is why I remind you to fan into flame the spiritual gift God gave you when I laid my hands on you. For God has not given you a spirit of fear and timidity, but of power, love, and a sound mind." (2 Timothy 1:6-7)*

Jesus spoke as one Who had authority and people recognized that. He didn't just say "words," He actually knew and lived what He spoke. So many people study the Bible and they know *about* the Word of God. But there is an area of your life that actually *carries* the Word of God. It's an area that you haven't just read about. You KNOW Him in that area. And whatever that area is, that is where you carry the anointing of God. Do you know Jesus as Healer? Do you know Him as Friend? Do you know the Lord as the Prince of Peace? Or, do you know Him as Provider? Whatever He has been to you, it is in that area that you are a carrier of the Word of God.

Jesus, we are honored to be carriers of Your Word.

# Face It!

*"You gain strength, courage and confidence by every experience in which you really stop to look fear in the face. You are able to say to yourself, 'I have lived through this horror. I can take the next thing that comes along.' You must do the thing you think you cannot do." – Eleanor Roosevelt*

*Don't become so well-adjusted to your culture that you fit into it without even thinking. Instead, fix your attention on God. You'll be changed from the inside out. Readily recognize what He wants from you, and quickly respond to it. Unlike the culture around you, always dragging you down to its level of immaturity, God brings the best out of you, develops well-formed maturity in you. (Romans 12:1-2)*

What do you fear? Rejection? Failure? Success? That you'll be laughed at? God says, "I will make you face the things that you fear." When you face what you fear, you become fearless. So, God will intentionally position your life, to face off with that one thing that you're afraid of. And then He'll bring you through it. God doesn't just use areas of your life where you are strong and see Him unnecessary. God anoints the areas of your life where you are weak, so He can show Himself strong.

God wants to bring you face-to-face with your fears so that you will become fearless. He will show His strength in your weakness.

# AUGUST 27

# Threshed

*"Truth, like gold, is to be obtained not by its growth, but by washing away from it all that is not gold." – Leo Tolstoy*

*These blasphemers have no idea what God is thinking and doing in this. They don't know that this is the making of God's people, that they are wheat being threshed, gold being refined. (Micah 4:11-12)*

Threshing is the process of loosening the edible part of the grain and separating it from the worthless part of the grain. How does wheat get threshed? By beatings and getting walked on. So, the next time somebody treats you badly, just say, "Why, thank you for helping me get threshed!" "Thank you for helping the good parts of me to rise up and the bad parts to fall off onto the ground where you are!" (Just kidding. Well, maybe not.) Hardship is what refines you. Hardship is when you find out what you're made of. Hardship is where you find out where you are strong, and where you are weak. The enemy will always try to distract you and diminish you, because he knows you are being refined. He couldn't care less about your past, even though he loves to bring it up to distract you. Every single attack on your life is actually about who God is refining you to be in the future.

Whatever you're going through, know that God is refining you as gold.

# A More Opportune Time

*"Hell is empty, and all the devils are here." – William Shakespeare*

*That completed the testing. The devil retreated temporarily,
lying in wait for another opportunity. (Luke 4:13)*

The devil always waits for another opportunity. He's looking for another way to tempt. He's waiting for a better time. "It didn't work today, but I'll try something else tomorrow." "I know more about her now. I see her weaknesses." "I know what pushes her buttons and how to push her over the edge." Know that even after a victory and while we celebrate that we've made it through this time, the devil is already looking for a more opportune time. When there's more talk than prayer, that's a more opportune time. When there's gossip and trash-talking, that's a more opportune time. When there's unforgiveness, that's a more opportune time. You can't ever take your spiritual armor off, because your enemy is always lying in wait for another opportunity.

Jesus, protect us from our enemy. Help us to stay alert at all times. Guard our hearts, our minds, our bodies, our homes, our families and our churches.

# Do You Want To Be Made Well?

*"Healing is a matter of time, but it is sometimes also
a matter of opportunity." – Hippocrates*

*Now a certain man was there who had an infirmity thirty-
eight years. When Jesus saw him lying there, and knew that
he had already been in that condition a long time, He said
to him, "Do you want to be made well?" (John 5:5-6)*

The Bible says that this crippled man had been doing the same thing for thirty-eight years. For all those years, he went to a pool, sat and waited for something to happen. Year one, no breakthrough. Year two, still no breakthrough. Year three, four, five…all the way through thirty-eight years, believing for something to happen, but never receiving healing. Jesus saw him lying there and asks him a question. By the way, when Jesus asks a question, it's not because He doesn't know the answer. By asking the crippled man the question, Jesus was trying to invoke a level of faith within the man that was so great, that he would declare out loud what he believed he would receive. Jesus asked, "Do you want to be made well?"

Maybe you have had a "condition" for a long time. Perhaps a situation that never changes. Jesus asks you the same question. He doesn't ask you the question because He doesn't know the answer. He wants you to answer the question, so that *you* know the answer. He wants to know what you believe He will do. Do you *want* to be made well?

# Crippled

*"All my heroes walk with a limp. They limp because their faith was forged in the fires of pain, suffering, and doubt."*
*– C.S. Lewis*

*And Mephibosheth ate at David's table, just like one of the royal family. Mephibosheth lived in Jerusalem, taking all his meals at the king's table. He was lame in both feet.*
*(2 Samuel 9:12-13)*

Mephibosheth was the son of Jonathan and the grandson of Saul. He had been crippled as a young boy. Both Mephibosheth's father and grandfather had been killed in battle. King David and Mephibosheth's father, Jonathan, had been best friends. They were like brothers. David had made an oath to Jonathan and wanted to honor it by finding and caring for Mephibosheth. When summoned by King David, he was terrified, not knowing if he would be killed. He was a cripple and he had lost his heritage. He didn't belong. But the king showed kindness to him. Mephibosheth bowed and asked why David would "notice a stray dog like me?" But the king restored all that had been lost to Mephibosheth and invited him to dine at his table for life.

Sometimes we allow our fear to make us an exile, an outsider, a spectator. We don't believe that God would ever want to have us because of our lameness. We get comfortable with our old crippled life. Yet, despite our lameness, we are invited to the King's table. Once we get our crippled feet, our humanity, our sin under God's table, we can function as royalty. There is not a place low enough that the table will not cover.

## AUGUST 31

# Dead Branches

*"Sometimes we just have to cut off the dead branches in
our life. Sometimes that's the only way we can keep the
tree alive. It's hard and it hurts, but it's what's best."
– Nicole Williams*

*He cuts off every branch in me that bears no fruit,
while every branch that does bear fruit, He prunes so
that it will be even more fruitful. (John 15:2)*

There was a season in my life where I felt I was dragging around "dead branches." I had lost my peace, my joy, and my trust. I was mad at God. Everything in my world was crumbling around me. I was so bitter. And I was trying to "handle" everything myself. I was trying to "hustle" money so I could pay my bills. Everything in my life seemed to be dead and bearing no fruit. God began to do some cutting.

Do you have dead branches that you are dragging around? Maybe it's a bad relationship. Maybe it's guilt and shame. Or maybe it's an old wound from your past. It would be wonderful if we had God's perspective. Then, we could agree with Him and say, "Yes, God. Let's get rid of that dead branch." But usually we're too afraid to give up what we know for something new that we just can't see or understand.

You have two choices. You can either continue dragging dead branches around for the rest of your life. Or, you can let Him cut them away. Both choices are painful. But the latter guarantees a fruitful life.

SEPTEMBER 1

# Led Astray

*"All deception in the course of life is indeed nothing
else but a lie reduced to practice, and falsehood passing
from words into things." – Robert Southey*

*"But I am afraid that just as Eve was deceived by the
serpent's cunning, your minds may somehow be led astray
from your sincere and pure devotion to Christ."*
(2 Corinthians 11:3)

*P*aul is concerned that these Christians living in Corinth have been tricked, duped, and deceived. He says, "I am concerned that the serpent has coiled itself around your mind." Why do you suppose Paul is concerned that the serpent has taken control of their minds? Many people try to fix their problems by addressing their problems, but all the while, the enemy has his grip on their minds. So, if you don't get him off and out of your mind, you're not addressing what's causing the problems. Many try to change their circumstances, improve their marriages, and solve their problems without first fixing their minds. The enemy will stop at NOTHING to mess with your mind. Satan's method of deception is to give you *his* thoughts in *your* mind until you adopt them as your thoughts. He pumps your mind with *his* ideas until you think they are *your* ideas.

How is your mind today? Is it fixed on Jesus or has it been led astray? Do you have peace or are you in turmoil? My friend, let's take every thought captive to the obedience of Christ today. Let's fix our eyes and our minds on the One Who has ALL power in His hands.

# Lead

*"A happy family is but an earlier Heaven." – George Bernard Shaw*

*He must manage his own family well and see that his children obey him,
and he must do so in a manner worthy of full respect. (1 Timothy 3:4)*

You are a leader! You may be a leader in your home, at work or in ministry. In First Timothy 3:4, Paul was describing to Timothy the qualifications he should look for in a church leader. At the top of the list, "He must manage his own family well." His home life, like his personal life must be a good example. His walk should match his talk. He or she should be a spiritual leader in their home. If someone can't manage their home life well, how can they help other families in the church lead others to salvation? This is one of the reasons that the enemy targets our families. He tries to keep us stuck in cycles by creating chaos and confusion in our homes. If he succeeds, then he's kept us from reaching the lost outside our homes.

Is there confusion and chaos in your home? You can stop that cycle today by humbling and submitting yourself to your Master. You are the leader! He will give you the grace to lead.

# What Is That Smell?

*"The Holy Scriptures are our letters from home." – Augustine of Hippo*

*To the one, we are an aroma that brings death; to the other,*
*an aroma that brings life. (2 Corinthians 2:16)*

There are some people who, when they hear the Gospel, breathe it in as life. And as a result, their lives are blessed, and their families are blessed. They grow and get stronger in the Lord. But then there are other people, who will hear the same truth, the same Gospel, and it does nothing for them. Those same two people can go through the most unspeakable circumstances, such as the loss of a child, the end of a marriage, a bankruptcy, or a bad report from the doctor. The person who breathes the Gospel in as life will get better. The person who breathes it in as death will get bitter. This outcome is completely determined by what you breathe in.

The Word of God *is* life. It is our life-source and our life-line. It is the answer to every question and the solution to every problem.

Do you need a fresh breath of life today? Does your marriage need new life? How about your children?

Lord, give us fresh eyes and fresh ears to see and hear Your Word. Let the Gospel be an aroma that brings life to us and to our families.

SEPTEMBER 4

# Stand Up and Stand Out

*"Nothing can dim the light that shines from within."*
*– Maya Angelou*

*Arise, shine; for your light has come! And the glory of the Lord is*
*risen upon you. For behold, the darkness shall cover the earth, and*
*deep darkness the people; but the Lord will arise over you, and*
*His glory will be seen upon you. The lost shall come to your light,*
*and kings to the brightness of your rising. (Isaiah 60:1-3)*

*G*od does not want you hidden, nor does He want you to hide the light that is in you. God has put a light in you that the world is longing to see. How do you shine that light? Do what it is that you do *well*. And, do what you do well with a good attitude. Is this too simple an answer? Think about encounters you've had lately. Sadly, far less often do I find people who do what they do well and with a good attitude than I do folks that are satisfied with mediocrity and an "I couldn't care less" attitude. When you do your best, combined with a good attitude, the light that God has put in you will begin to shine through you in a very dark world.

Today, stand up and stand out! Arise! Shine! For your light has come! And the glory of the Lord is risen upon you!

# Into The Light

*"Darkness cannot drive out darkness; only light can do that.*
*Hate cannot drive out hate; only love can do that."*
*– Martin Luther King, Jr.*

*But you are chosen…God's special possession…that you*
*may declare the praises of Him who called you out of*
*darkness and into His wonderful light. (1 Peter 2:9)*

The devil trembles at the idea of you going into the world and declaring the praises of God. That's why he tries to keep you in darkness because you can't see clearly in the dark. Everything looks distorted in the dark. Shadows always look like monsters. But, as soon as you flip the switch and turn the light on, the shadows are gone and you see the truth. You begin to quickly see that you really had nothing to fear in the first place. How do you get out from the darkness and into His wonderful light?

First, you must saturate your mind with the Word of God. The Word is a light that will light up any darkness in our minds. And secondly, if you find yourself in darkness, get up. Literally. Get out of bed. Get dressed. Take a shower. Brush your teeth. Surround yourself with Godly people who will speak truth into your life and will fight in prayer with you and for you. Find a church. Find a small group. Get and stay connected to the Body of Christ.

You are chosen, you are His, and He calls you into the light.

# Build Your House

*"If we have built on the fragile cornerstones of human wisdom, pride, and conditional love, things may look good for a while, but a weak foundation causes collapse when storms hit." – Charles Stanley*

*Through wisdom a house is built... (Proverbs 24:3)*

How does your house look? I'm not talking about the square footage or the paint color. I'm talking about those under your authority. How are they doing? If your "house" is built with wisdom, the people under your covering will prosper. That includes your children, your grandchildren, your employees, etc. Of course, those under your authority will go through things, but because of your prayer and leadership, they will make it! When the Queen of Sheba went to visit King Solomon, the first things she noticed was the grounds and buildings, and especially the servants. She was struck by how sharp and friendly they were. They served with class and excellence and did their jobs with joyful and enthusiastic attitudes. Maybe sometimes, instead of searching for devils to fight in our homes and businesses, we just need to be kind to people. Perhaps, we just need to smile once in a while. Maybe we need to start taking pride in what we do and do it with excellence. There are some folks who may never see or hear a preacher, but they are watching and listening to you.

Father, like Solomon, we ask for Your wisdom today.

# What Are You Thinking?

*"The glow of one warm thought is to me worth*
*more than money." – Thomas Jefferson*

*It shall be done for you as you have believed.*
*(Matthew 8:13)*

Positive minds produce positive lives. Negative minds produce negative lives. Positive thoughts are always full of faith and hope. Negative thoughts are always full of fear and doubt. Some people are afraid to hope because they've been hurt so much in life. They've had so many disappointments that they don't think they can face the pain of another one. So, rather than risk being hurt again, some people simply refuse to hope or believe anything good can ever happen to them. This kind of negative thinking sets up a negative lifestyle. "For as he thinks in his heart, so is he."

I pray that you have a positive mind with positive thoughts and are living a positive life! But, if you're struggling, I would ask, "What is it that you believe? What are you thinking?" Fill your mind so full of the Word of God that there is no room left for anything else.

Jesus, heal our minds and hearts today. Give us the courage to hope again, believe again and love again! Protect our minds from negative thoughts, and fill our minds with Your Truth.

# Salt Is Good

*"Where would we be without salt?" – James Beard*

*We know that God works all things together for good for the ones who love God, for those who are called according to His purpose. (Romans 8:28)*

Romans 8:28 does not say that all things *are* good. It says that all things *work together for our good.* Do you like salt with your meals? I love salt. Table salt is made up of both sodium and chloride. By itself, sodium is a deadly poison, and so is chloride. But, put them together and you have table salt. Salt flavors food, and a certain amount of salt is necessary for health and life. We can't live without at least some salt in our systems.

God can take things that are bad, mix them with His love and wisdom, and work all things together for good. This is a promise!

Are there things in your life that cause you to be ashamed? Maybe something you wish had never happened? Are there regrets and bad decisions? God says, that He will work *all those things* together for your good.

God, we love You. Thank you that You have called us according to Your purpose. We trust that, today, You are working all things together for our good.

# Unusual Calling

*"The placed God calls you to, is the place where your
deep gladness and the world's deep hunger meet."*
*— Frederick Buechner*

*So Pharaoh asked them, "Can we find anyone like this man,
one in whom is the spirit of God?" Then Pharaoh said to Joseph,
"Since God has made all this know to you, there is no one so
discerning and wise as you. You shall be in charge of my palace,
and all my people are to submit to your orders. Only with respect
to the throne will I be greater than you." (Genesis 41:39-40)*

God gave Joseph an unusual assignment. He called him to serve in an unusual setting. But what a powerful calling it was! There is a call on your life, my friend. Often, in our limited thinking, we expect that God's calling has to be accomplished only in a church setting. But God is too wise to put the most lights where there are already lights. God wants to put lights in the marketplace, in corporations, in banks, in the public school systems, in local government, in the hospital systems and in the service industry. Throughout biblical history, and today, God strategically places His representatives in positions of public influence. If you are breathing today, then God has left you on this earth because He has work for you to do.

When you wake up on a Monday morning, where do you go? That is your assignment! It could be in your home, the place you volunteer or where you go to work. "Can we find anyone like this man in whom is the spirit of God?" Yes. You!

# Do Not Fear To Go Down To Egypt

*"God never made a promise that was too good to be true."*
*– D.L. Moody*

*Then God spoke to Israel in the visions of the night, and said, "Jacob, Jacob!" And he said, "Here I am." So He said, "I am God, the God of your father, do not fear to go down to Egypt..." (Genesis 46:2-3)*

God said to Jacob, and He says to you, "Do not fear to go down to Egypt." "*Down* is where I'm going to achieve greatness in you. Not up here where things are easy, but down in Egypt, where things are a bit tough. You don't go anywhere that the Lord doesn't allow you to go. He's the one forming, fashioning, growing and preparing you. So, if God sees that your formation will be enhanced "down in Egypt," then that may be where you are headed. It's "down in Egypt" where He works the "kinks" out of us, and where we begin to look like Jesus. But, here's the good news – it's never a one-way trip to Egypt. Because Genesis 46:4 says, "I will go down with you to Egypt, and *I will also surely bring you up again!*"

If you are in down in "Egypt" today, be encouraged. God is with you and He is forming, fashioning, growing and preparing you. And, He will surely bring you up again!

# Ask Me

*"Prayer delights God's ear; it melts His heart; and opens His hand. God cannot deny a praying soul." – Thomas Watson*

*"Ask Me…" (Psalm 2:8)*

This morning in my devotion time, I found myself unable to focus. My mind was buzzing with burdens, questions, and all the things that are creating chaos in my life. I finally opened my Bible, and went to Psalm 2. Two words "jumped" off the page. "Ask Me." I sensed that God had been watching and waiting as my mind ran in circles until the moment I finally looked to Him. "Ask Me." So, I did! In my prayer journal, I filled a page with all of my questions, troubles, fears and burdens. That was about four hours ago. Not one of my problems has been resolved. But, I felt peace and the impression that He took them from me and, better yet, I know that He's working them out for me. I can rest in the fact that I know He will show me what my next move needs to be.

Do you have questions? Are there thoughts that are racing in circles in your mind and creating chaos? Your Father is not the author of confusion, but of peace! He said to me, and He says to you, "Ask Me."

Father, we thank you that we can ask You anything! You wait for us to bring to You all of our burdens.

## SEPTEMBER 12

# Jesus Turned Around

*"Jesus is the God whom we can approach without pride and*
*before whom we can humble ourselves without despair."*
*– Blaise Pascal*

*Jesus turned around… (Matthew 9:22)*

*H*ave you ever been in a desperate situation? In Matthew, we read about a woman in a very desperate situation. She had a health issue that was consuming her thoughts, her resources, and her life. She was considered an outcast because of her issue. She had no support. Her friends left her. Her family couldn't be near her. She had spent every dime she had, going to every doctor in town. She was completely isolated, depressed and desperate. But then, one day, she heard about a man that made the blind to see and the lame to walk. A man who, with just one word, could cause a dead man to live again. I believe when she heard about this man, she began to have a tiny spark of hope. It was just enough hope to give her the courage to take a step towards Him. And with every step she took, faith began to rise. So, she crawled through the crowd and reached for Jesus from behind. And when she touched the hem of His robe, the Bible says that, "Jesus turned around."

If you are in a desperate situation, begin to make your way to Jesus. With each step you take, faith will begin to rise. As you draw near to Him, Jesus will turn around.

SEPTEMBER 13

# God Meant It For Good

*"One small crack doesn't mean that you're broken, it means
that you were put to the test and you didn't fall apart."*
*– Linda Poindexer*

*But as for you, you meant evil against me; but God
meant it for good... (Genesis 50:20)*

*I*n Genesis 50:20, Joseph is talking to his brothers. This is after they tried to kill him. This is after they stripped him of the robe given to him by their father. This is after they threw him into a pit. This is after they sold him into slavery. Their actions led to Joseph living as a slave. It led to him being accused of rape and thrown into prison. "But as for you, you meant evil against me…"

Have you ever felt that way? Maybe someone has done you wrong. Maybe you've been treated unfairly. Maybe you've been cheated on or lied about. Maybe you've been unjustly accused of something. Or, maybe you've been left out. Just like in Joseph's case, God will never leave you nor forsake you. He will take every wrong and use it, not just for your good, but perhaps for the good of the one that intended evil for you.

"But as for you, you meant evil against me, *but God meant it for good.*"

# Devil, You Have No Portion Here

*"The strength of a nation derives from the*
*integrity of the home." – Confucius*

*"Do not be afraid of them. Remember the Lord, great and*
*awesome, and fight for your brothers, your sons, your daughters,*
*your wives, and your houses." (Nehemiah 4:14)*

After much opposition, and with the help of the leaders of each family, Nehemiah rebuilt the walls in his city. The wall was to protect the people from the attacks of their enemies. In the same chapter, Nehemiah said to their enemies, "You'll have no portion here." In other words, "Satan, my home does not belong to you. My marriage doesn't belong to you. My children and grandchildren do not belong to you." If there was ever a time that you needed to fight for your family, that time is now. If you leave even a crack, the enemy will move in, divide, and conquer. Destroying your family is the devil's number one priority. So, if your family is his number one priority, it needs to be your number one priority. The Word says, "Fight for your brothers, fight for your sons, fight for your daughters, fight for your wives, fight for your husbands, and fight for your families!" If you will fight for your family, then God will fight for you.

Maybe, like Nehemiah's people, there are some cracks in the walls at your house. The Lord will help you rebuild those walls. The enemy has no portion in your family! Fight for them, and the Lord will fight for you!

SEPTEMBER 15

# You Are Mighty

*"When a man has no strength, if he leans on God,*
*he becomes powerful." – D.L. Moody*

*The angel of God appeared to Gideon and said, "God is with you,*
*O mighty warrior. Gideon said to Him, "Me, my master? How and*
*with what could I ever save Israel? Look at me. My clan's the weakest*
*in Manasseh and I'm the runt of the litter." (Judges 6:12, 15)*

Gideon considered his family to be the weakest in their tribe. I wonder why? Were they known for not paying their bills? Did they have a history of being lazy and unemployable? And, why did Gideon consider himself a runt? Did his parents call him a runt because he was small? Was he compared to his other brothers who were stronger? Was he the last to be picked for games growing up? We find Gideon in Judges 6, all grown up, but still considering himself a runt and his family of no value. When the angel of God appeared to Gideon with an assignment, he was actually hiding in fear from his enemy. But notice how the Lord addressed him: "Rise up, mighty man of valor! I have chosen you for this exact thing."

It does not matter what label has been given to you. It does not matter what your family background looks like. What matters is how God addresses you. God has an assignment for you, my friend. And He says to you today, "Rise up mighty one! I have chosen you for this exact thing."

# You Are Who And What You Think You Are

*"Change your thoughts and you change your world."*
*– Norman Vincent Peale*

*For as a man thinks in his heart, so he is. (Proverbs 23:7)*

My son and I traveled to Scotland not long ago. One of our favorite things to do together is hike. I love to hike and could fill an entire book with hiking stories. I have been "stupid brave" through the years – putting myself in some pretty dangerous situations. I had a car accident a few years ago, and because of an injury, I've been timid about doing things that I used to do. One of those things is hiking. It's not that the doctor said I couldn't, it's just been the fear of falling down and hurting myself. So, while on this trip to Scotland with my son, we had several days of hiking planned. And sure enough, on the first day of hiking, I froze on a narrow, rocky cliff. My son turned around to see what was happening. He saw my fear and said, "Mom, this is not who you are." I had allowed my thoughts to convince me, "You are a weak person, now. You can't do this anymore." But my son reminded me that my thoughts were not true.

We see that same thing happen to Gideon in the Old Testament. He grew up believing that he was a runt. That he was weak and a coward. But the angel of the Lord called the lie a lie and replaced it with the truth. He called Gideon a "mighty man of valor."

Who do you think you are in your heart? I pray that you believe you are who God says you are.

# In Want

*"The farther I run away from the place where God dwells,*
*the less I am able to hear the voice that calls me the Beloved,*
*and the less I hear that voice, the more entangled I become*
*in the manipulations and power games of the world."*
*– Henri J.M. Nouwen, Return of the Prodigal Son*

*And not many days after, the younger son gathered all together,*
*journeyed to a far country, and there wasted his possessions with*
*prodigal living. But when he had spent all, there arose a severe famine*
*in that land, and he began to be in want. (Luke 15:14-15)*

*Y*ou always run out when you're not doing what God wants you to do. You can be wealthy, with plenty of money in the bank, but still be busted. The prodigal son had it all. He had a father that adored him, food on his table, clothes on his back and a bright future ahead of him. But, he decided to leave his father and go his own way and do his own thing. God has a plan for your life. His way is always best. If you don't have God, you don't have anything.

Maybe you feel empty today. Perhaps all your choices have led to an empty life with no meaning. The good news is that, not only will the Father welcome you back home with open arms, He will meet you where you are. He wants to restore to you the inheritance that is rightfully yours.

# Fresh Oil

*"The old saying is true: If you have only the Word, you
dry up. If you have only the Spirit, you blow up. But
if you have both, you grow up. – Jim Cymbala*

*But my horn You have exalted like a wild ox; I have
been anointed with fresh oil. (Psalm 92:10)*

My family loves to talk about "the good ole days", especially as it
relates to church. But God doesn't want you to stay in the past. He
has something new for you every day. In Psalm 92:10, David is thanking
God that he's been anointed with "fresh oil." God wants to give you a
fresh anointing. There's no such thing as operating in the power of an
old anointing. Spiritual experiences from ten or twenty years ago, or
even yesterday, won't do! It has to be fresh. The Bible talks about how
flies would get into old oil because they are attracted to stagnant things.
Remember, when the Israelites tries to save up their manna in the desert?
It rotted and was covered in maggots! You have to have a fresh anointing
from the Holy Spirit, and God has plenty for you each day!

Do you need a fresh start? Make yourself available to the Holy Spirit.
Anointing happens in private. If you want "fresh oil", it starts in the
secret place. It happens when no one else is watching.

Holy Spirit, anoint us with fresh oil.

# It Doesn't Matter How You Look

*"All that glitters is not gold…"*
*– William Shakespeare, The Merchant of Venice*

*So it was, when they came, that he looked at Eliab and said, "surely the Lord's anointed is before Him!" But the Lord said to Samuel, "Do not look at his appearance or his physical stature, because I have refused him. For the Lord does not see as man sees; for man looks at the outward appearance, but the Lord looks at the heart." (1 Samuel 16:6-7)*

When God chooses who He will anoint, He looks not at the appearance of a person, but at the heart. How many times have you assumed a person would be the best choice for something based on how they looked, sounded, or spoke? The prophet Samuel assumed that Jesse's son Eliab would be the Lord's choice for king based on his appearance. Instead of the "kingly-looking" son, God had other plans. He chose the scrawny one! While his brothers were all vying for position, David was in the fields tending sheep and writing psalms and praising God. David was not in public. He was worshiping in private. This is how anointing comes. If you only worship God when you're in a church service but not the other days of the week, you're missing it! God is interested in what we do when no one is looking.

Private worship and making yourself available to Him will bring anointing.

# Misery Loves Company

*"The devil is very busy, and no one knows better than he
that nothing is stronger than its weakest part."*
*– C. Kingley*

*When Jesus saw him and knew he had been ill for a long time, He
asked him, "Would you like to get well?" "I can't, sir," the sick man
said, "for I have no one to put me into the pool when the water bubbles
up. Someone else always gets there ahead of me." (John 5:6-7)*

Why is it that gossips naturally find other gossips? Why is it that bitter people naturally attract bitter people? In John 5, there are lame people hanging out with other lame people. Worse yet, the lame people are depending on the other lame people to help them. With whom are you surrounding yourself? If the company that you are keeping today is keeping you in a place of dysfunction, you need to find yourself some new friends! You need friends that will lift you up, not pull you down.

If you need to get into the "pool" of living water, don't look to "lame" people to help you get there. Dysfunctional friends often feel more comfortable when their friends are also dysfunctional. Ask God to bring you strong, smart, Spirit-filled friends who will cheer you on and pray the best for your life.

# Set Your Mind

*"There are two equal and opposite errors into which our race can fall about the devils. One is to disbelieve in their existence. The other is to believe, and to feel an excessive and unhealthy interest in them."*
*– C.S. Lewis, The Screwtape Letters*

*If then you have been raised with Christ, seek the things that are above, where Christ is, seated at the right hand of God. Set your minds on things that are above, not on things that are on earth. For you have died, and your life is hidden with Christ in God. (Colossians 3:1-3)*

You have a very real enemy that seeks to steal, kill and destroy. We should acknowledge the presence of the enemy, but never allow his existence to overshadow our reverence for God. Whatever we focus on is what we become. The devil doesn't care what you believe just as long as it interferes with your relationship with God. He will do anything to get your focus on him and off of Jesus. Though we are in a real war, we have to remember that we are seated with Christ in the Heavenly places. This position is above every rule, authority, power, and dominion. As a believer, we never need to live in fear. The truth is, hell cringes at the Spirit of God that is in us. Test your thoughts and feelings. When God is speaking, even when He confronts you, you will feel His love. Anything that does not lead you closer to Jesus is from another kingdom.

# Confusing The Enemy

*"Supreme excellence consists of breaking the enemy's resistance without fighting." – Sun Tzu (The Art of War)*

*… Jehoshaphat appointed men to sing to the Lord and to praise Him for the splendor of His holiness as they went out at the head of the army, saying: "Give thanks to the Lord, for His love endures forever." As they began to sing and praise, the Lord set ambushes against the men…who were invading Judah, and they were defeated. (2 Chronicles 20:21-22)*

There is a king, King Jehoshaphat who is surrounded on every side by his enemies. The enemy far outnumbers Jehoshaphat's people. There is no way they can come out of this battle alive, but the king calls out to God. He reminds God of Who He is and what He's done in the past. And then, after he's surrendered the situation to the Lord, Jehoshaphat appoints people to sing to the Lord and praise Him. And the Bible says that when they began to sing and to praise, the enemy is defeated. Your enemy is expecting you to fight in your flesh. And if you do, he will win every time. But when you praise, the enemy gets confused. The more Jehoshaphat's people sang and praised, the more confused the enemy became. They actually turned on each other and killed their fellow soldiers. God will cause your enemies to get confused and be wiped out without you ever lifting a finger. God doesn't need our help to fight the battles. He just wants our praise and our worship.

# Sing

*"Satan so hates the genuine praise of Christ that his
fiery darts of discouragement are not effective against us
when we respond in praise." – William Thrasher*

*"I will sing to the Lord, for He has triumphed gloriously!" (Exodus 15:1)*

In Exodus 15:1, the children of Israel are getting their praise on. They've just been delivered from Egypt. And then with Pharaoh's army behind them, God parted the Red Sea and they walked across on dry land. They had a lot to sing praises about. You know how it is. The check finally came. Your kids went to church. You got approved for the mortgage. You're in the zone. "God is good, all the time! And all the time, God is good!" But, as soon as the Israelites came through the Red Sea, they went straight into the wilderness. In the wilderness, they can't find any water. Now, in place of the singing, there is grumbling, fussing and complaining. They even began to long for captivity. Have you ever been there? Everything is going well, and then it all falls apart. It makes me think of Isaiah 54:1, "Sing, O barren woman!" The prophet is telling the people to sing even in their barrenness. To praise God not just for what He's done, but for what He *will* do. And Isaiah goes on to tell the barren people to prepare for what God will do. He tells them to "stretch" and to "enlarge their tent stakes" in preparation for the blessing of God.

So whether you are in want or have plenty, you are still to "sing to the Lord!"

# Engraved

*"I'm absolutely convinced that nothing – nothing living or dead,
angelic or demonic, today or tomorrow, high or low, thinkable or
unthinkable – absolutely nothing can get between us and God's
love because of the way that Jesus our Master has embraced us."*
*– Mary DeMuth, Live Uncaged*

*But Zion said, "The Lord has forsaken me, the Lord has forgotten me."*
*"Can a mother forget the baby at her breast and have no compassion on
the child she has borne? Though she may forget, I will not forget you!*
*See, I have engraved you on the palms of My hands." (Isaiah 49:14)*

In ancient times, it was not uncommon for the name of a master
to be tattooed on his servant. But never was the name of a servant
tattooed on his master. That would mean that the master was devoted
to the servant. In Isaiah 49:14, God says, "I have *engraved* (not tattooed)
you on the palms of My hands." The word "engraved" is a very specific
Hebrew word that means: engraved with a hammer, chisel or a spike. And
centuries later, Jesus appeared to a man named Thomas, who doubted
the Savior's love. And Jesus said, "Look at the palms of My hands. This
is how much I love you." Jesus was forsaken, so that we would *never* be
forsaken.

# Back-To-Back

*"If you live to be 100, I hope I live to be 100 minus
1 day, so I never have to live without you."*
*— Winnie the Pooh*

*A person standing alone can be attacked and defeated, but two
can stand back-to-back and conquer. Three are even better, for
a triple-braided cord is not easily broken. (Ecclesiastes 4:12)*

*Y*ou have an enemy that wants nothing more than to get you alone
and isolated. If he can get you isolated, he will go to any lengths to
convince you that you are the only one going through what you're going
through. He'll try to tell you that you've done something to bring this
trouble upon yourself. He'll whisper that God doesn't care and won't
come to your rescue. Isolation opens you up to major spiritual attack.
Depression almost always follows, with anger not far behind. The enemy
will try to convince you that no one can ever understand what you're
going through, and that you'll be an outcast if you bring it into the light.

It's so important to surround yourself with Godly friends. If you don't
have any, please consider joining a small group, a discipleship class, or
some kind of activity offered at your church. Pray that God would send
you a friend or two, because *"two can stand back-to-back and conquer."*

SEPTEMBER 26

# Go North

*"The Word of God I think of as a straight edge, which shows up our own crookedness. We can't really tell how crooked our thinking is until we line it up with the straight edge of Scripture." – Elisabeth Elliot*

*Then God said, "You've been going around in circles in these hills long enough; go north." (Deuteronomy 2:2)*

I've already told you I love to hike. I've also been known to get lost when I hike. A few years ago, I was hiking in the mountains of West Virginia and determined that my logic made more sense than the directional signs on the hiking trails. Seven hours later, I found myself passing the same signs over and over. I'd been circling the same trails for hours. I had no idea where I was or how to get back to where I started. So I went "north." I made my way to the top where I could see the surrounding area, hoping to see something familiar. Don't we do that in life sometimes? Rather than look at our map or read the signs in God's Word, we use our own logic instead Doing it "our way" inevitably leads to circling around and around, over and over.

Do you feel like you aren't getting anywhere? Are you repeating the same patterns over and over? God says to you today, "You've been going around in circles long enough; go north." North is God and His Word. Go north today, my friend.

## SEPTEMBER 27

# Bye-Bye

*"Some things don't need to be cut back. They
need to be cut off." – Beth Moore*

*Remember ye not the former things, neither consider the things of old,
behold, I will do a new thing, now it shall spring forth. (Isaiah 43:18-19)*

God wants to do something new and fresh in your life, but the condition and requirement for receiving the new is letting go of the old. One of the greatest hindrances to breakthrough is memory. We tend to drag our past into our present and our future. But, God tells us that the only way to get the new is to let go of the old.

When Elijah ascended into the heavens in a chariot of fire, Elisha prepared himself to receive the double portion anointing by stripping himself of his old clothes. To receive the new, you have to take off the old.

Where do you need to see a "new thing" in your life? Is it in your relationships, your finances, or your health? You may need to let go of some old habits to form some new ones. You may need to let go of some old friends to make some new friends. God says to you today, "Forget the past and the old things, I will do a new thing! Just watch and see!"

# Spiritual Eyes To See

*"Great impressions can be made from a distance, but reality can only be tested up close." – Howard Hendricks*

*When Sanballat heard that we Jews had begun rebuilding the wall, He became furious and began to ridicule us. But we prayed to our God and kept men on guard against them day and night. (Nehemiah 4:1,9)*

When you're going through a battle, are you responding with a spiritual response or an emotional response? When the enemy comes to attack, he doesn't play fair. He doesn't care about your feelings. He will come at you in your weakest moment. In trials, it's critical to fix your eyes on spiritual things, not feelings. Emotions make things blurry. But when you see things with spirit eyes, you can discern clearly what's really happening around you.

The enemy tried to taunt, threaten and distract Nehemiah and his people from rebuilding the wall. Instead of reacting based on his feelings, he fixed his eyes on God. He prayed and asked God to protect him.

No matter how things look in the natural, when you call upon the name of the Lord, the enemy gets nervous. You can trust that help is on the way!

# Buckets Of Grace

*"Lord, I crawled across the barrenness to you with my empty cup…If only I had known you better, I'd have come running with a bucket." – Nancy Siegelberg*

*But God's not finished. He's waiting around to be gracious to you. Your time of tears is over. Cry for help and you'll find that it's grace and more grace. (Isaiah 30:18-19)*

Grace is like the waves of the ocean. It never stops - wave after wave. Grace is so simple, yet so vast at the same time. And grace is only available to us through Jesus Christ. God put His love on the line for us by offering Jesus as a sacrifice while we were of no use whatever to him! He doesn't ignore our sin or excuse our sin. Rather, He looks past our sin and He accepts us in spite of it. That's grace and more grace. Rather than telling us to change, He creates the change. We don't clean up so He can accept us. He accepts us and begins cleaning us up. Your sin will never outweigh God's love. Grace tells us to change, and gives us the power to change. Grace is God's love and strength being poured out into your life in just the right place at just the right time. God has enough grace to solve every problem you have, wipe every tear you cry, and answer every question you ask.

"Cry for help and you'll find that it's grace and more grace."

## SEPTEMBER 30

# Good Works

*"You have enough time to do everything God wants you to do. If you haven't enough time, you are doing something that God does not want you to do." – Rowland Croucher*

*For we are God's handiwork, created in Christ Jesus to do good works, which God prepared in advance for us to do. (Ephesians 2:10)*

*W*hen Jesus called His disciples He had two purposes in mind for them. First, they were to have an intimate relationship with Him. And secondly, they were to be sent out into the world in ministry. These are our two purposes as well. But, how do you balance it all? We need to ask the Lord each morning to help us identify the good works that He has planned for us on that particular day. Are there unimportant things that need to be eliminated? Are we allowing for "pauses" each day? At the end of the day, we all have the same twenty-four hours to live our lives. It's in how we live those hours that the real story is told.

What "good work" has God called you to do? Have you tabled it because you feel overwhelmed? Ask the Lord to show what needs to be eliminated in order to make room for more of Him and what He's called you to.

You are His handiwork and He created you for a purpose before you were born!

OCTOBER 1

# Guarding Your Quiet Time

*"Satan does not care how many people read about prayer if only he can keep them from praying." – Paul E. Billheimer*

*And in the morning, rising up a great while before day, He went out into a solitary place, and there prayed. (Mark 1:35)*

*I*f you are reading this, I assume you understand the importance of quiet time with the Lord. When life gets busy, it's really tempting to skip that time. It's critical that we guard our devotional life. Jesus regularly spent time in prayer, especially during periods of intense activity. After a really long day and evening of healing the sick and praying for people, we read that, "Very early in the morning, while it was still dark, Jesus got up, left the house and went off to a solitary place, where He prayed." Jesus prayed often and especially before important decisions, like choosing the disciples, feeding the five thousand. He prayed fervently when facing His arrest in the garden of Gethsemane. He also withdrew from everyone to pray after times of exhausting ministry. The busier He became, the more He prayed. He realized that He needed time with God to get refreshed. Jesus also stayed in the Word of God – so much so that when the devil challenged and attacked Him in the wilderness, He could respond with the Truth.

Are you leaving margin in your day to spend time with the Lord? It's the most important part of your day. Don't let the things on your to-do list and the appointments on your calendar distract you from the refreshing that you so desperately need.

## OCTOBER 2

# Making Assets Of Your Liabilities

*"When fate hands you a lemon, make lemonade."*
*– Dale Carnegie*

*There was a man there. His name was Zacchaeus, the head tax*
*man and quite rich. He wanted desperately to see Jesus, but the*
*crowd was in his way – he was a short man and couldn't see over*
*the crowd. So he ran on ahead and climbed up in a sycamore*
*tree so he could see Jesus when He came by. (Luke 19:2-4)*

Zacchaeus's liability was that he was short. When he heard that Jesus was in town, he wanted a chance to see Him. Jesus would be walking through town on the main street. People were everywhere. But, Zacchaeus knew if he just walked out there, he'd only see the backs of the people in front of him. So, he climbed a sycamore tree. He didn't expect Jesus to notice him. But, of the hundreds of people who lined the streets that day, Jesus chose him to speak to directly. He looked right at him and said, "Zacchaeus, make haste and come down, for today I must stay at your house." He met his Savior face to face that day. It happened because of, not in spite of, his liability.

What is your greatest liability? Whatever it is could turn out to be your greatest asset if it drives you "up a tree" and causes you to see Jesus.

# Push Through

*"Things do not happen. Things are made to happen."*
*– John F. Kennedy*

*But Jesus said, "Someone deliberately touched me, for I felt healing power go out from me." When this woman realized that she could not stay hidden, she began to tremble and fell to her knees in front of him. The whole crowd heard her explain why she had touched him and that she had been immediately healed. "Daughter," He said to her, "your faith has made you well. Go in peace." (Luke 8:46-48)*

*Y*ou are familiar with the story of the woman with the issue of blood. This woman knew, "If I could just get to Jesus…" She had to push through a lot to get to Him. She had to push through people. She had to push through the report of the doctor. She had to push through her financial devastation. She had to push through the rejection of her family and her community. She had to push through her sickness, her pain, her exhaustion, and her weakness. She had to push through her depression. She had to push through the lies of the religious that she was unclean and unworthy. But after twelve years of suffering, she was desperate! "If I could just get to Jesus."

What about you? What gets in your way of getting to Jesus? Maybe you've been hurt. Maybe life has worn you out. Friend, you have to push through and deliberately touch Jesus. He will turn to you and say, "Child, your faith has made you well."

## OCTOBER 4
# Speak Life

*"Words have incredible power. They can make people's*
*hearts soar, or they can make people's hearts sore."*
*– Dr. Mardy Grothe*

*"Go, stand in the temple and speak to the people*
*all the words of this life." (Acts 5:20)*

My oldest daughter was invited for a meal at the home of a friend-of-a-friend. The home was not a Christian home. My daughter called me after and said, "Mom, I have never met kinder people in all my life. They were so generous and so welcoming." It bothered me. How is it even possible that someone in the world can see more love in an unbeliever than in a Christian? I believe as a whole, we have become distracted. The enemy of our faith stays busy keeping us distracted. It's so easy to get distracted with things *about* God, that we take our eyes *off* the Savior. The devil would also love to get your eyes fixed on your problems to distract you from what God has called you to do. We are to get up, chains and all, and go. In Acts 5, *while* the apostles were in prison, the angel of the Lord came to them and told them, "Go! Speak to the people all the words of this life!" In other words, "Go, speak life to the people." It should be *us* speaking life to the world. It should be *us* that are so magnetic that the world is attracted to us and wants what we have.

Today, chains and all, go! Go speak life to those around you!

# Jesus Wept

*"The devil, darkness, and death may swagger and boast, the pangs of life will sting for a while longer, but don't worry; the forces of evil are breathing their last. Not to worry…He's risen!" – Charles R. Swindoll*

*Then, when Mary came where Jesus was, and saw Him, she fell down at His feet, saying to Him, "Lord, if You had been here, my brother would not have died." (John 11:32)*

The definition of resurrect is to restore that which is dead to life, to revive, to resuscitate. When I think of someone being raised from the dead back to life, I think of Lazarus. Word was sent to Jesus that his friend Lazarus was sick. One would have thought that Jesus would have rushed to Lazarus, but it wasn't until he had been in the grave for four days that Jesus arrived. Lazarus' sister Mary was so upset that she fell at Jesus' feet and said, "Lord, if you had been here, my brother would not have died." When Jesus saw her weeping, He was deeply moved and troubled. He cried. If He knew that Lazarus would live again, why would He be so moved? Why would He weep? Because He loved Mary so much, it hurt Him to see her hurt.

Even though Jesus sees how the dead things in your life will be resurrected… Even though Jesus sees that your grave clothes are already falling off… Even though Jesus sees your marriage coming alive again… He loves you so much, that He is "deeply moved in spirit and troubled" for you.

Your dreams are being resurrected even though it may seem that they are dead. But when you weep, Jesus weeps.

☙

## OCTOBER 6

# Prayerless Decisions

*"Prayerlessness is disobedience, for God's command is that men ought always to pray and not faint. To be prayerless is to fail God, for He says, 'Ask of Me.'"* – Leonard Ravenhill

*Now Sarai, Abram's wife, had bore him no children. But she had an Egyptian slave named Hagar; so she said to Abram, "The Lord has kept me from having children. Go, sleep with my slave; perhaps I can build a family through her."*
*(Genesis 16:1-2)*

Have you ever made a decision without praying about it first? Prayerless decisions typically lead to trouble and tragic loss. God had already promised Sarah and Abraham a child. Did He forget His promise? Or did He get busy with other things? Sarah and Abraham decided to take matters into their own hands. And their prayerless decision caused great grief and pain for countless people.

Have you asked God for something and you feel like He's forgotten you? If He's made you a promise, then He will be faithful to keep it. You have to trust His timing. Don't be tempted to take matters into your own hands without praying about it first.

Lord, we thank you for Your promises and for answered prayer. Help us to be patient as we wait.

# Endurance

*"Most people never run far enough on their first wind to
find out they've got a second." – William James*

*…And let us run with endurance the race that
is set before us… (Hebrews 12:1)*

*P*aul talks about the race that all Christians must run. He suggests
that we need endurance to finish this race. He doesn't say, "Let us
run this race with joy." Or, "Let us run this race with peace." Or, "Let us
run this race with hope." He says, "Let us run with endurance." In the
Greek, the word endurance means: "to bear up under." It's the power to
withstand great pain or hardship and the ability or strength to continue
despite fatigue, stress, or adverse conditions. We don't like the word in
our culture. Most people don't want to bear up under anything. Most
want to be delivered *from* everything. But sometimes God says, "I'm
going to take you *through* this. And I'm taking you *through* it so I can
develop the muscles you're going to need to do what I've called you to do."

There's only one way to run this race, and that's with endurance.
I've begged God to take away trials in my life, to make them go away.
But for His glory and for your good and for my good, He chooses to
take us through them.

Run with endurance the race that is set before you!

## OCTOBER 8

# Desperation

*"Mankind at its most desperate is often at its best."*
*– Bob Geldof*

*Be careful then, dear brothers and sisters. Make sure that your own*
*hearts are not evil and unbelieving, turning you away from the living*
*God. You must warn each other every day, while it is still "today,"*
*so that none of you will be deceived by sin and hardened against*
*God. For if we are faithful to the end, trusting God just as firmly as*
*when we first believed, we will share in all that belongs to Christ.*
*(Hebrews 3:12-14)*

Have you ever been a place of desperation? When you knew that if God didn't show up, you would fall flat on your face? I have a few times in my life. In particular, many years ago, when the economy took a dip, my business suffered terribly and I was headed for financial ruin. I was desperate. There were no options. I spent many hours on my knees and on my face crying out to God in desperation. Honestly, I never feel as close to God as when I'm desperate. I think that a lack of desperation for God can be deadly. We definitely don't cry out to Him as we do when we are desperate. We begin to think we are managing on our own. My desperation caused me to pursue God as if my life depended on it. And it did.

I'm ever so thankful for that season, and the other desperate seasons in my life. I've learned that life can take a turn in a matter of moments. I know I can't do it on my own. How about you?

# Pause

*"Take care of the minutes and the hours will take
care of themselves." – Earl of Chesterfield*

*As He went along, He saw a man blind from birth. As long
as it is day, we must do the works of Him Who sent me.
(John 9:1, 4)*

*I*'ve learned through the years to never look at the person in front
of me as less important than the work that I need to get done. It
may be, that *they* are the work that I'm to do. I've learned to "pause" in
the midst of my busy days. In the middle of Jesus' busy ministry, He
didn't let urgent things crowd out the important things. There was no
"tyranny of the urgency." The New Testament is full of accounts where
Jesus "paused" with people. Jesus didn't pause with everyone, and we are
not able to spend time with everyone. We need to pray that God will
show us the people with whom He wants us to pause. The pause could
be for us to learn something from them, or for us to give the touch and
say the words that could transform their lives.

Are you busy? Are you too busy to "pause" when the Holy Spirit
leads you? I hate to think of the opportunities that I've missed because
I was too busy to pause.

Father, show us the works that You have for us. Help us to pause
when it is Your will for us to do so.

# Not Guilty

*"Is God's voice the loudest voice in your life? That's the question. If the answer is no, that's the problem."*
*– Mark Batterson, Whisper: How to Hear the Voice of God*

*For the accuser of our brothers and sisters has been thrown down to earth – the one who accuses them before our God day and night. (Revelation 12:10)*

*H*ave you ever been accused of something you didn't do? Twice in my life I was sued, once by someone I thought was my friend, the other by someone that I was trying to help. Both cases were thrown out, but there really are no words to describe how I felt when I was served papers accusing me of something that didn't happen or wasn't true. You and I both have an enemy, that according to Revelation 12:10, accuses us before God, day and night. I want you to notice *who* he accuses, he accuses "the *brothers and sisters*". Satan doesn't just accuse anyone. *Brother* and *sister* in the Bible are terms that are reserved for people who are born again. The ones that Satan accuses are not the ones who are living like hell. He already has them. The people that he's trying to take down are the brothers and sisters. He loves to come whisper that you're disqualified because you've somehow failed the Lord. But, just like in my personal situation, you can't accuse someone successfully of something they haven't done.

Are you being accused of something by someone you know? Or, is the devil whispering accusations in your ears? Your Father hears these accusations, but He is not surprised by them. He is your Advocate and your Defender.

OCTOBER 11

# Don't Burn Out!

*"If there be anything that can render the soul calm, dissipate its*
*scruples and dispel its fears, sweeten its sufferings by the anointing*
*of love, impart strength to all its actions, and spread abroad the joy*
*of the Holy Spirit in its countenance and words, it is this simple*
*and childlike repose in the arms of God." – S.D. Gordan*

*Then He said to them, "The Sabbath was made for*
*man, not man for the Sabbath." (Mark 2:27)*

Years ago, when my children were still small, I couldn't get out of the
bed. I was depressed. It didn't make any sense to me, I couldn't think
of a reason that I should be depressed. But as I took a personal inventory
of my life, it occurred to me that I had been working non-stop. From
raising my children, taking care of the house, working a full-time job
and serving in ministry, I simply had run out of steam. I had burned
out. The Lord showed me the benefits of Sabbath rest. He created
Sabbath for me! Even Jesus realized the importance of withdrawing to
rest, even in the face of pressing needs. All of us need to rest, relax, and
withdraw. How we spend that time will depend on our own personality.
The important thing is that we take time out altogether from work and
ministry at regular intervals.

Are you enjoying the benefits of Sabbath rest? In order to be your
best at home, on your job, in your ministry, it is crucial to withdraw,
rest, relax and be refreshed.

# Do You Believe This?

*"You never know how much you really believe anything until its truth or falsehood becomes a matter of life and death to you."* – C.S. Lewis

*Jesus said to her, "I am the resurrection and the life. He who believes in Me, though he may die, he shall live. And whoever lives and believes in Me shall never die. Do you believe this?" (John 11:25-26)*

Jesus is insistent on the necessity of faith. Within His inner circle, Jesus never allowed love, affection or admiration to substitute for faith. Though He loved Martha and Mary and their dead brother dearly, Jesus demanded an answer before He restored Lazarus to life. He said, "He who believes in Me will live, even though he dies…" And then He asked the question: "Do you believe this?"

And this is the question for you today. Jesus is deeply moved in His spirit and troubled for what troubles you. But, do you believe that He can raise the dead things in your life? Faith comes before the promise.

Do you believe this?

OCTOBER 13

# Suck It Up, Buttercup!

*"Heroism is endurance for one moment more."*
*– George F. Kennan*

*We gladly suffer, because we know that suffering helps us to endure. And endurance builds character, which gives us a hope that will never disappoint us. (Romans 5:3-4)*

*I*'m guilty. Looking back, I shouldn't have rescued my children as quickly as I did. Instead of rescuing them every time they hit a bump in the road, we need to allow them to endure some things. We have a generation that wants instant promotion and instant success. We don't want anything that requires a bit of pressing in. "I don't like this job, I'll get another one." "This class is too hard, I'm quitting." "I don't like this church, I'll find a new one." Sometimes we *do* need to get out of things. But, sometimes we just need to "Suck it up, buttercup!" Sometimes, we abdicate and we walk out way before God ever means for us to walk out. Then, we blame God that we didn't get to the finish line and fulfill our purpose and destiny. But, it had nothing to do with God. It had everything to do with us – because we refuse to endure.

Are you suffering today? Instead of quitting, ask God what He wants to teach you in the suffering. Suffering helps us to endure. And, endurance builds character, which gives us a hope that will never disappoint us!

## OCTOBER 14

# Dry Bones

*"On with the dance! Let joy be unconfin'd; no sleep till morn, when youth and pleasure meet." – Lord Byron*

*Then He caused me to pass by them all around, and behold, there were very many in the open valley; and indeed they were very dry. "Son of man, these bones are the whole house of Israel. They indeed say, our hope is lost, and we ourselves are cut off!" (Ezekiel 37:2, 11)*

Israel was suffering from spiritual emptiness. Ezekiel was supernaturally taken to an ossuary, where bones would be gathered in Israel before final burial. Ezekiel 37:2 stresses that these bones were *very* dry. Sometimes life can be like that. How do you know if your life is dry? Verse 11 explains what dryness is. Your life is dry if you see no hope. How did the bones get in such a state? In Ezekiel 36:17 we read, "They defiled it by the evil way they lived." In other words, they were doing things their own way and their disobedience had created distance. And this distance from God had created dryness. If you are living with no hope, or every day you wake up to "dryness," it's possible that there is distance between you and God. Dirty = Distance, Clean = Close. In my own life, my driest seasons have been when I've tried doing things my own way.

Distance between you and God can close right now! Invite Him back in! Let Him lead, and it won't be long before those dry bones will be dancing again!

# Remember Who You Serve

*"If our identity is in our work, rather than Christ, success will go to our heads, and failure will go to our hearts."*
*– Tim Keller*

*Whatever you do, work at it with all your heart, as working for the Lord, not for human masters, since you know that you will receive an inheritance from the Lord as a reward. It is the Lord Christ you are serving. (Colossians 3:23-24)*

Working in ministry, I serve many people. And of course, I want to serve them well and I want to meet their expectations of me. But, if I'm not careful, I will forget Who it is that I really serve. The truth is, although usually well meaning, the people around you can have agendas. In Jesus' ministry, everyone had their own agenda for Him. His family wanted to slow Him down, the crowds wanted to make Him King, the zealots wanted Him to lead a revolution, the Pharisees wanted to shut Him up, and the sick wanted Him to heal them. Despite all the pressures, Jesus didn't let demands from others control how He spent His time, nor was He put off by criticism or threats. Jesus was the most comfortable human ever in His own skin. When we face the demands of friends, family, work, or the church, we need to remember Who we are actually serving. Of course, serving Christ will lead us to serve others in His name, yet Jesus is the One who ultimately dictates the terms. His will takes priority and at times this means making choices that those around us may not understand or respect.

Remember Who you serve.

# Turn Your Pain

*"We bereaved are not alone. We belong to the largest company in all the world – the company of those who have known suffering." – Helen Keller*

*Blessed are those who mourn for they will be comforted. (Matthew 5:4)*

There are millions of people in the world right now that are mourning but are not blessed. There are tons of people deeply grieving and they are not blessed. So, is Jesus fibbing in Matthew 5:4? No, He isn't. The Bible goes on to tell us that, "Blessed are those who turn their pain toward God, for their pain will be vindicated, understood, and totally healed. Therefore, producing lasting comfort and peace." Jesus is saying, "Blessed are those who turn their pain toward Me. They will be comforted. They will be healed." God wants to heal our hearts, but only when we turn our hearts toward Him.

Are you mourning? Are you in pain? If you will give it to Jesus, you will be comforted and you will be healed.

Jesus, we turn our pain towards You today. You are our Comforter and our Healer.

# Fingers Crossed

*"When a deep injury is done to us, we never heal*
*until we forgive." – Nelson Mandela*

*But I say to you who hear: Love your enemies, do good*
*to those who hate you, bless those who curse you, and*
*pray for those who spitefully use you. (Luke 6:27)*

I'm not a hateful person, but there are a few people in my life that I've disliked immensely. I had a little torture chamber down in my heart and I would drag them down there regularly and beat the stuffing out of them. I would actually dream about their demise. But the Lord began to deal with me, as He often does. He told me to pray for them. But not just pray for them…to bless them. I said, "No, thank you. Lord, if I pray blessings on them and You actually bless them, I'm going to be really mad." He was very quiet. So, I prayed blessings over them with my fingers crossed. The Lord told me to pray for them every day like I would pray for myself. "But they don't deserve the good stuff I deserve." Ugh. I continued to pray for them daily and to ask blessings on them. Miraculously, after a few weeks of not meaning it, I began to mean it. My heart became softened towards them, and I really meant it when I asked the Lord to bless them. I became free in that moment.

Is there a name you hear that causes your teeth to clench? Who do you need to forgive? Who do you need to begin praying blessings upon? If you want to be free, truly free, take my advice – pray for them until you really mean it.

# The Hurt Whisperer

*"To forgive is to set a prisoner free, only to discover*
*that the prisoner was you." – Lewis B. Smedes*

*Be angry, and do not sin. Do not let the sun go down on your*
*wrath nor give place to the devil." (Ephesians 4:26-27)*

The devil is a hurt whisperer. He uses every pain in your life as an opportunity to plant a thought. The problem with pain is not pain. The problem with pain is the message in the pain. And pain always has a message in it. C.S. Lewis said "Pain is God's megaphone." There's nothing wrong with being angry. But if you go to sleep while you're angry, you give the devil a foothold. If you go to bed with anger, you open the door for the hurt whisperer. Thoughts will race through your mind and most of those thoughts will be from the devil. Most of what we think and believe about other people that we're mad at comes from the enemy. He hates everything good in your life. You can be sure that he'll show up at every betrayal, every disappointment, every failure, every funeral, every bankruptcy, and every courtroom. And he uses those hurts to whisper messages into your soul.

Don't open that door for the enemy when you go to bed tonight. If you need to have a conversation with someone with whom you're angry with, do that! Don't give place to the devil!

OCTOBER 19

# Equipping Others

*"Use your ministry to build people, not people to build your ministry." – Jacquelyn K. Heasley*

*...to equip the saints for the work of ministry, for building up the body of Christ...(Ephesians 4:12)*

When I left home for college and lived on my own for the first time, I didn't know how to cook or a variety of other domestic chores. God love her, but my mother never taught me. We've actually talked about it and she admits that she preferred to do things herself. It takes time to teach someone to do what you do, but it is time well spent. God calls us to equip others to do the work that we do. Not to mention the fact that we can't do everything ourselves. Jesus didn't feel that He had to do everything Himself. He equipped other people to serve as well. He trained them, shared His vision and He delegated. It should always be our goal to multiply what we do by involving others. If there is a choice between doing something ourselves, or teaching someone else to do it, we should always choose to teach someone. The success of a job or ministry should never depend on one person. Passing the baton shouldn't threaten us; it should excite us – because that means God will open up new avenues for us.

What do you do? Do you work or volunteer? Are you in ministry? Are you a mother or father? Who can you equip to do that which you do?

# Consider Your Ways

*"It is not hard to obey when we love the one whom we obey." – Saint Ignatius*

*… But from this day I will bless you. (Haggai 2:19)*

*B*lessings always come with obedience. I don't know why this is such a hard concept to grasp. Well, it is for me, anyway. It was for the people in the book of Haggai as well. As long as they did things their own way, nothing seemed to work out for them. And God told them repeatedly, "Consider your ways." In other words, "Duh. Think about it. Do you not wonder why you don't feel good, the money is gone, there's chaos in your life, and nothing seems to satisfy you? If you honor Me, I'll honor you. Consider your ways. Before you chose to listen to Me, you had holes in your pockets." But I can testify, as could the people in the book of Haggai, from the moment you decide to listen and obey, "From this day I will bless you."

Are you at a place in your life where it seems as if nothing is happening? There's no harvest and it feels like your pockets are empty and your life is in chaos? God says to you, "Consider your ways." The moment you choose to listen and obey, blessings will come.

# Take Your Hands Off The Basket

*"I have learned that faith means trusting in advance what will only make sense in reverse." – Max Lucado*

*… She put the baby in the basket and laid it among the reeds along the bank of the Nile River. (Exodus 2:3)*

It's hard to just let go, isn't it? It's especially difficult when it comes to our children or loved ones. It's hard to believe that anyone could take better care of them than us. That's what Moses' mother had to do. It was one thing to put her baby in the basket…she could have done that all day long. But to actually take her hands *off* the basket and let it float in the alligator infested waters was another thing altogether. But it was in that split second that the whole story changed. She leaned over and put the baby in the water in the little vessel. However, the moment she took her hands off and began to walk away, all the powers of Heaven began to work on behalf of that baby! The moment she took her hands off…

Is there someone or something that you need to take your hands off today? Do you need to put someone or something in the basket, put it in the water and let it go? As long as you hold on, God will let you. But the moment you let go, He will take over.

# Priorities

*"To change your life, you need to change your priorities."*
*– Mark Twain*

*But He said to them, "I must preach the kingdom of God to*
*other cities also, for this is why I was sent." (Luke 4:43)*

Sometimes I get so distracted by the piles of stuff on my desk, unanswered emails, etc. that I forget what my priorities are. For instance, I may have a message from someone who desperately needs counsel or prayer, but I feel like I need to get the work on my desk done first. One of the devil's tactics is to distort our priorities. Jesus teaches us about priorities. After a busy day of healing and casting out demons, people begged Him to stay, but He said, "I must preach the good news of the kingdom of God to the other towns also, because that is why I was sent." Jesus was also choosy with whom He spent His time. Our priorities will be different depending upon the gifts He has given each of us and the situation in which He has placed us in.

Do you ever get distracted? Ask the Lord to remind you what is the most important thing that He wants you to do.

Lord, what is important to you? Help us to prioritize according to Your will and purpose for our lives.

# Just One Touch

*"One touch of Christ is worth a lifetime of struggling."*
*– A.B. Simpson*

*A woman in the crowd had suffered for twelve years with constant bleeding, and she could find no cure. Coming up behind Jesus, she touched the fringe of His robe. Immediately, the bleeding stopped. (Luke 8:43-44)*

How long has it been since you "touched" Jesus. I love the story of the woman with the issue of blood. All it took for her to be made well was just one touch. She had just enough faith to believe that if she could but touch even a thread on His clothes, if she could just touch Him, she would be healed. I wonder if she was hoping He wouldn't notice. But my friend, all of Heaven notices that kind of faith! Maybe, like this woman, your enemy whispers lies in your ear, telling you that you are unclean and unworthy to get anywhere near Jesus. Let me remind you that there is nothing that you've ever done, nor will ever do, that will cause Jesus to love you any less or any more than He does at this very minute, all because of His marvelous and amazing grace. Jesus Christ, the Son of God, the King of Kings, was entirely focused on this one woman, this one outcast. Her loneliness and illness had put all Heaven in a rage, and God sent His Son for her alone at this moment. And that is true for you.

If there is anything that is getting in your way of getting to the feet of Jesus, He wants you to push through it all and run to Him. One touch was all it took for her. She didn't even have to tell Him what she needed. She just needed enough faith to reach out her hand.

OCTOBER 24

# Inquire Of The Lord

*"We pray when there's nothing else we can do, but God*
*wants us to pray before we do anything at all."*
*– Oswald Chambers*

*The Israelites sampled their provisions but did*
*not inquire of the Lord. (Joshua 9:14)*

Joshua and the Israelites made a treaty with the people of Gibeon
without consulting with the Lord. Three days later, they found out
they had been deceived. But they had already sworn an oath before God
and couldn't go back on it. So, because they didn't inquire of the Lord,
they were stuck with these dishonest people forever.

Have you ever regretted not asking God's guidance for an important
decision that ended up going bad? Truth be told, I would say most of
us have had to face the stark reality that a bad decision might have been
avoided if we had only taken time to first pray about it.

Do you have important decisions to make? Inquire of the Lord, even
in the small decisions and He will direct you.

Thank You Lord, that You direct us in decisions, big and small.
Guide us today, Heavenly Father.

# Nothing Can Separate

*"Therefore let us repent and pass from ignorance to knowledge, from foolishness to wisdom, from licentiousness to self-control, from injustice to righteousness, from godlessness to God." – Clement of Alexandria*

*For I am persuaded that neither death nor life, nor angels nor principalities nor powers, nor things present nor things to come, nor height nor depth, nor any other created thing, shall be able to separate us from the love of God which is in Christ Jesus our Lord. (Romans 8:38-39)*

*I*'ve made many mistakes in my life. One of those mistakes was epic. For years, I did everything in my power to cover up that mistake. Even as a Christian, I carried the weight of that sin for longer than I'd like to admit. Jesus didn't put that sin on me to carry. He took it away on the cross. I chose to pick it up every day and carry it on my back. Romans 8:38 tells us, "that neither death nor life, nor angels nor principalities nor powers, nor thing present nor things to come…" The writer says that nothing in your present or your future can separate you, but notice, he never says that things from your past can't separate you. Things from your past won't change God's love for you. But, trust me, things from your past *can* separate you, if you let them. Yet, this isn't because God can't and won't forgive. You see, the writer knew that if you don't get out from under condemnation and guilt, you won't feel worthy to be in God's Presence.

When I finally "came clean" to the Lord and those closest to me, my spiritual posture changed. I was no longer bent over from the weight of it all. *Nothing* can separate you from the love of God!

# What Kind Of People

*"The God who created, names and numbers the stars in the heavens also numbers the hairs of my head. He pays attention to very big things and to very small ones. What matters to me matters to Him, and that changes my life."*
*— Elizabeth Elliot*

*When the Pharisee who had invited Him saw this, he said to himself, "If this man were a prophet, He would know who is touching Him and what kind of woman she is — that she is a sinner." (Luke 7:39)*

God knows what kind of people we are. Thankfully, He doesn't wait until we are perfect to let us touch Him. We'll never be perfect! Have you touched Jesus? Or, are you waiting until you "clean that up", or "get that thing resolved?" Are you paralyzed by your past or by the voices that have been whispering lies in your ears? God loves you exactly where you are, in exactly the condition that you are in. God loves you as you are, not as you should be. None of us are as we should be! You can't explain the love of God. You can't measure the love of God. You can't limit the love of God. You can't comprehend the love of God. He just loves you. He accepts you. And, He knows what kind of person you are.

Reach out and touch Jesus today, dirty fingers and all! He already knows "what kind of person" you are. Still, He loves you all the more!

# High Price For Disobedience

*The one concern of the devil is to keep Christians from praying. He fears
nothing from prayerless studies, prayerless work, and prayerless religion.
He laughs at our toil, mocks at our wisdom, but trembles when we pray."*
*— Samuel Chadwick*

*"Your slave is in your hands," Abram said. "Do with
her whatever you think best." Then Sarai mistreated
Hagar; so she fled from her. (Genesis 16:6)*

I s prayer your steering wheel, or is it the spare tire in your trunk?
You can't live a life doing what you want to do part of the time and
what you think God wants you to do the rest of the time. The works
of the flesh and the works of the Spirit can't live together comfortably.
Prayerlessness, impatience, and disobedience led to Hagar despising
Sarah and Sarah despising Hagar. Sarah blames Abraham and abuses
Hagar. An innocent child gets hurt in the middle of all this. Sarah and
Abraham blamed God for delaying. Instead of consulting with Him, they
took matters into their own hands. No one remembered His promise
to provide a son. It would seem that since they had chosen to go their
own way, God stepped aside to let them live with the consequences of
disobedience.

Is there a decision that needs to be made in your life right now?
Could God be waiting until your ability has ceased so His promise can
be supernatural?

# I'm Weak!

*"The world breaks everyone, and afterward, some are
strong at the broken places." – Ernest Hemingway*

*Three times I pleaded with the Lord to take it away from me.
But He said to me, "My grace is sufficient for you, for My power
is made perfect in weakness." (2 Corinthians 12:8-9)*

Today is my son-in-law's birthday. He is proof that you should never stop praying for your children and their future spouses! His favorite scripture is, "My grace is sufficient for you, for My power is made perfect in weakness." Herman is one of the strongest men I know. But no matter how strong someone appears on the outside; we all have weaknesses. God's power is made perfect in those weaknesses. God has a purpose for your life. Paul knew the worst thing he could do was become arrogant. It was more important to keep Paul humble than it was to make him comfortable, so God allowed the weakness in his life.

Do you feel weak today? Are you under attack? Do you feel inadequate to handle the pressures and the problems? Child of God, your Father says to you, "My grace is sufficient for you." His strength will be made perfect in your weakness.

# It's Not About You

*"What hurts most is that you know your love for God is strong, yet you can't seem to understand what He is trying to work out in your life." – David Wilkerson*

*For I know the plans I have for you," declares the Lord, "plans to prosper you and not to harm you, plans to give you hope and a future." (Jeremiah 29:11)*

Often, when I'm closing a sermon, I will say, "This is not just about you." Of course, it's true that God cares about every single detail in your life. In fact, Jesus said that even the hairs on your head are numbered. We always shout when we read, "For I know the plans I have for you, plans to prosper you and not to harm you, plans to give you hope and a future." But God's plan is not always a "feel good plan." His intent isn't to make you happy all the time. Sometimes His plan will take you places you weren't expecting to go. God's plan for you is not just to benefit you personally. And sometimes He is not quick to remove you from difficult situations. He promises to restore, but it may not be on Tuesday.

Today, you may be in the battle of your life. God wants you to know He has a plan. He wants you to know that as you submit to His plan, He will use you to bless the world around you. The plan is still on during both good times and difficult times.

Will you trust His plan no matter what this day holds? How does God want to use you to be a blessing to others today?

# Choose Your Company

*"Life is partly what we make it, and partly what is made by the friends we choose." – Tennessee Williams*

*Do not be misled: "Bad company corrupts good character." (1 Corinthians 15:33)*

My youngest daughter is probably one of the most loyal people I know. Although I've always admired that (and so many other things) about her, her loyalty has gotten her into some bad situations with "friends" that were not really friends. You can become like those with whom you choose to spend your time. That's why it's so important to surround yourself with wise and Godly friends. Even when Jesus was just a child, He spent His time with the wise. He spent time in the temple asking questions and listening. Find older Christians from whom you can really learn. Ask questions and study their behavior, how they live, their priorities, their strategies, and their prayers. Seek to learn what it is that makes them effective in God's service and emulate it.

As my daughter matures in Christ, she is learning to set necessary boundaries. She is now strategic about the friends with whom she spends her time.

Who are you hanging around? Are they Godly and do they have wisdom? If not, please remember that, "Bad company corrupts good character."

Lord, remove anything and anyone from our lives that may be corrupting our good character.

OCTOBER 31

# Daily Inventory

*"People travel to wonder at the height of mountains, at the*
*huge waves of the sea, at the long courses of rivers, at the*
*vast compass of the ocean, at the circular motion of the stars;*
*and they pass by themselves without wondering."*
*– St. Augustine*

*Let us examine our ways and test them, and let us*
*return to the Lord. (Lamentations 3:40)*

*T*hings pile up. It's like the trash. Most of us have a trash service that comes to pick up our garbage on a regular basis. It's impossible to keep trash from accumulating. But every week, we get to start fresh after the old trash has been taken out. The same goes for our sins. We are human and we have human thoughts and human responses. We need to do a daily inventory and keep our accounts clear. Otherwise, like trash, sins accumulate. It is sin that weakens our witness more than anything else; it consumes our energies and our thoughts and it distracts us from our calling. Things like pride, gluttony, lust, anger, envy, and greed creep in and paralyze and distract us.

Let us examine our ways and test them daily. Let's keep our accounts clear. Let there be nothing between us and our Lord and the calling that He has for each of us.

## NOVEMBER 1

# Bitter Water

*"I have no faith in my faith. My faith is in the faithful God."*
*– Leonard Ravenhill*

*When they came to Marah, they could not drink its*
*water because it was bitter. (Exodus 15:23)*

You've probably lived long enough to know that life can be bitter. We love the good times, but the bitter times, we can do without! Life can become bitter because of financial, family or work situations. What do you do when life becomes bitter? When Moses and Israel were in the desert, they couldn't find water. When they came to Marah, they couldn't drink its water because it was bitter. Have you ever come through a problem and thought you'd found a solution, only to find you have a new problem? When life turns bitter, you need to remember the faithfulness of God. Not long before the Israelites found that life had turned bitter, God had just delivered them from the Egyptians and the Red Sea. When life becomes bitter, and you find yourself at the waters of Marah, you have to look back at your own Red Sea experiences and remember when God made a way out of no way.

When was the last time that God made a way out of no way for you? Thank Him for His faithfulness and trust that He will do it again!

# Remodeling

*"Nothing can stop the man with the right mental attitude from achieving his goal; nothing on earth can help the man with the wrong mental attitude." – Thomas Jefferson*

*For we who are alive are always being given over to death for Jesus' sake, so that His life may also be revealed in our mortal body. (2 Corinthians 4:11)*

Have you ever remodeled a house? Remodeling takes something on the inside, and refigures it so that it's brand new. The process of remodeling can be quite disruptive because in order to remodel, you have to tear the old stuff apart before you can even begin. It's very inconvenient. It can displace you. It can be dusty, dirty and chaotic. But, in order for the new to be revealed, the old must be dismantled. Many of us are looking for a blessing, but we don't want a remodeling. God isn't going to bless you if He can't remodel you. And, in order to remodel you, He has to tear some stuff out, to put some new stuff in.

I have remodeled a home and a business. I have never been so aggravated, frustrated and irritated. But, the beauty and newness of the finished products were well worth the hassle. Jesus is constantly remodeling me. It can be aggravating, frustrating and irritating, but I'm looking more like Him every day!

## NOVEMBER 3

# Accepted

*"Grace is inviting to the unrighteous and threatening
to the self-righteous." – Max Lucado*

*The Word became flesh and made His dwelling among us.
We have seen His glory, the glory of the One and Only, Who
came from the Father, full of grace and truth. (John 1:14)*

In my early twenties, I had a group of friends that got together quite often. We had fun together, but quite honestly, I know they were a bit self-conscious around me. I was the only Christian in the group. Little sarcastic comments were made here and there. I don't recall if I was ever blatantly self-righteous or judgmental. I hope not. Looking back, I wish I'd made more of an effort to be like Jesus. In the Bible, people who were nothing like Jesus actually *liked* Jesus. There weren't simply respectful, they really liked Him. They were comfortable around Him. They invited Him into their homes. They invited their friends over to meet Him. And, Jesus liked people who were nothing like Him. He accepted everyone. That is grace.

Think about the people with whom you spend your time. Are they all like you?

Lord, help us to see the ones that you want us to extend grace to, even if, and especially if, they are nothing like us.

# Can God Really Use Me?

*Many of life's failures are people who did not realize how
close they were to success when they gave up."*
– *Thomas A. Edison*

*"I persecuted the followers of this Way to their death, arresting both
men and women and throwing into prison…" (Acts 22:4)*

*I* have asked God many times, "How can you use someone like me?
You know my past! You know my mistakes! You've seen my sin!" He
always reminds me of Paul. It's tempting to think that he was a super
saint. But, here was a man who was feared and hated by Christians
and did everything in his power to destroy the name of Jesus. Yet, God
reached down in grace and picked this man up from where he was and
used him to literally change the world. We can learn so much from the
story of Paul. When you wonder if God can really use your life, you
need to understand that God has no problem overcoming any of your
obstacles by His power and grace. Your past condition is no obstacle to
God. Your present circumstances are no obstacle to Him. Your personal
characteristics are no obstacle. And, your private concerns are no obstacle
to the Creator of the Universe.

God has never looked for people who fit in or stand out. He always
looks for people who will stand up. God will get the job done in spite of
the earthy vessels He chooses. He then gets double the glory for having
accomplished His perfect plan through imperfect people.

## NOVEMBER 5

# Resist The Enemy

*"Fear defeats more people than any other one thing in the world." – Ralph Waldo Emerson*

*For God has not given us a spirit of fear, but of power and of love and of a sound mind. (2 Timothy 1:7)*

*I* run into so many people who are attacked by fear. Fear is a spirit. It's a tormenting spirit. A tormenting spirit attacks your mind and tries to rob you of peace. It becomes a mental battle. It's a battle to just keep going. A tormenting spirit tries to oppress. Oppress means: "to cause someone to feel distressed, anxious, or uncomfortable". A tormenting spirit's goal is to hinder the children of God from doing what He's called them to do. It can feel like you are in battle after battle after battle. But the Lord wants to remind you that you have power over all the darkness and all the spirits of the enemy. This power comes in the name of Jesus and through the blood of the Lamb!

Do you feel tormented by fear? The Bible says if you will submit to God, and resist the devil, he will pack his bags and run from you! Resist!

Father, we thank you for the authority you give us over tormenting spirits. By the blood of Jesus, the enemy is defeated!

## NOVEMBER 6

# Be Still

*"God is not Who you think He is. God is
Who He says He is." – Anonymous*

*"Be still, and know that I am God..." (Psalm 46:10)*

Be still. How easy is that for you? I have learned to be intentional about shutting down the noise and distractions around me. But it's possible to have total silence and not "be still" with the Lord. Your mind is racing or wandering or both! Whatever is causing your mind to "race," and wherever your mind is wandering off to, can be released to God. The original Hebrew word used for "being still" is "Raphah." It means to stop striving, to cause yourself to let go, to willingly submit to God and His control, and surrender to God.

It's critical in our Christian walk to realize that the more we are deliberately still, the more we hear God's voice. The more we are still, the smaller our issues seem; and the bigger God appears. Psalm 46:10 says, "Be still, and know..." If you want to know Him better, set aside that quiet time, even if it's just a few minutes to "be still" before God.

Father, forgive our busyness. Help us to "be still" in Your presence. You promise in Your Word that if we are still, we will know You more. Thank You that You are Who You say You are.

# Protect Your Pearls

*"Don't waste your time explaining who you are to people who
are committed to misunderstanding you." – LeCrae*

*"Do not give what is holy to the dogs; nor cast your pearls
before swine, lest they trample them under their feet,
and turn and tear you in pieces." (Matthew 7:6)*

*I* love pearls, as does my oldest daughter. Pearls are not easily found. To obtain the richest and most beautiful pearls, a diver must dive again and again and again and again. Then after lifting the shells from the sea floor, he must force open the mouth of each shell and dig through the tough meat of muscle, poking and searching for the tiny white pearl that was formed over a long period of time. The pearls are precious, rare, valuable, and hard to obtain. This is how you should view the things God has done in your life. You can't put a price on what you've learned. Like precious pearls, those life lessons are incalculable in their value because they cost you something. Each time you open the door to those treasures and begin to share them with someone else, you need to remember that you're sharing your pearls with that person. The counsel and advice you're giving may be free to him or her, but it has cost you everything! So if what you're sharing isn't appreciated, *stop giving that person your pearls.*

# A Bad Day

*"Jesus said, "Blessed are the poor in spirit" – contrary to what
we would expect, brokenness is the pathway to blessing! There
are no alternative routes; there are no shortcuts. The very thing
we dread and are tempted to resist is actually the means to God's
greatest blessings in our lives." – Nancy Leigh DeMoss*

*We do not want you to be uninformed, brothers and sisters, about the
troubles we experienced. We were under great pressure, far beyond our
ability to endure, so that we despaired of life itself. (2 Corinthians 1:8)*

*H*ave you ever had a really bad day? Have you ever had a really bad
season? If you are facing something that you don't think that you can
take anymore, then you are a candidate for an amazing breakthrough.
If you feel like you can't take your job, your marriage, or your situation
for one more day...or if you are even despairing of life, you are in a
great place. You are not in a bad place! You are in a perfect place! In 2
Corinthians 1:8, Paul was in a bad situation; so bad, he didn't even want
to live anymore. But in the next verse he says, "Indeed, we felt we had
received the sentence of death. But this happened that we might not
rely on ourselves but on God, Who raises the dead." God will allow you
to go so low that He becomes your only option.

Is He trying to get your attention today? You have to take your eyes
off what you're going through and fix them on the divine purpose for
God allowing you to go through it. He wants you to rely solely on Him.
He will bring life to your situation.

# NOVEMBER 9

# A Wise Woman

*"Nine-tenths of wisdom consists of being wise in time."*
*– Teddy Roosevelt*

*A wise woman called from the city, "Listen! Listen!"*
*(2 Samuel 20:16)*

The Bible has a lot to say about wisdom. It is more precious than gold. We are to seek wisdom. When you imagine wisdom, do you see an aged, silver-haired person? In 2 Samuel 20, we come upon a story of a woman identified only by the name of her city and her description as a "wise woman." The quick version of the story is that Joab is in pursuit of a traitor to the King of Israel. The traitor has hidden himself within the walls of the city of Abel. Joab orders his troops to build ramps to lay siege to the city walls. It's at this point in the story that we meet our unnamed woman. "Then a wise woman called from the city, "Listen! Listen! Tell Joab, 'Come here, that I may speak to you.'" (2 Samuel 20:16) It's a bold move for a woman in that day. Not only does she bravely shout out to the commander of the armies below, but the army responds. They actually stop, and listen. The wise woman first scolds Joab. Then, she offers him the head of the traitor in exchange for a reprieve.

So, wisdom doesn't always look like an aged grandmother reminiscing of days gone by. This wise woman was quick to action, rapid to decide, and even faster to follow through. She was skilled in persuasive conversation, but also endued with incredible courage and impeccable timing. Let us remember to always seek wisdom.

# Encounter

*"Sometimes what makes us insecure and vulnerable becomes the fuel we need to be overachievers. The antidote for a snakebite is made from the poison, and the thing that made you go backward is the same force that will push you forward." – T.D. Jakes*

*The angel of the Lord came and sat down under the oak in Ophrah that belonged to Joash the Abiezrite, where his son Gideon was threshing wheat in a winepress to keep it from the Midianites. When the angel of the Lord appeared to Gideon, he said, "The Lord is with you, mighty warrior. Pardon me, my lord," Gideon replied, "but if the Lord is with us, why has all this happened to us?" (Judges 6:11-13)*

Have the odds ever been against you? Have you ever been afraid? Gideon is known for his cowardice in the Bible. There were two things that contributed to his cowardice: bitterness and timidity. He was bitter with God for not coming through for him. And, to make matters worse, he felt he had nothing to offer to improve his situation. He didn't have the skills and power to turn things around. Bitterness and timidity can only lead to a life full of frustration.

How do we focus on the Lord and not the odds against us? How did this coward hiding in the winepress have a transformation? He had an encounter with God.

Are you hiding in a winepress today, afraid to trust God? Have you been disappointed because you think God has let you down? In the words of the angel of the Lord, "The Lord is with you, mighty warrior."

## NOVEMBER 11

# Your Father Brags About You

*"Some day you will know that a father is much happier in
his children's happiness than in his own. I cannot explain
it to you; it is a feeling in your body that spreads gladness
through you." – Honore de Balzac, Pere Goriot*

*Then the Lord said to Satan, "Have you considered my servant
Job? There is no one on earth like him; he is blameless and
upright, a man who fears God and shuns evil." (Job 1:8)*

*I*'m a bragger. I brag about my children a lot. I am so proud of all
three of them and my son-in-law. I have many flaws, but withholding
praise from my children is not one of them. Accolades were nonexistent
in my childhood, so I made the decision long before I had children that
I would reverse that pattern.

Did you know that your Father in Heaven brags about you? You
have an enemy that accuses you to the Father nonstop, but I imagine
that He just smiles, pulls his wallet out and rolls out pictures of you and
says the same thing He said of Job, *"There is no one on earth like her."*
You may say, "How can He brag on me? After what I've done, is He
not ashamed of me?" When you accepted Jesus Christ as your Lord and
Savior, what *you've done* was completely covered by His blood. When
God looks at you, He sees Jesus.

Right now, right in this moment, your Father is bragging about you.

# Storms

*"I'm thankful for my struggle because without it I wouldn't
have stumbled across my strength." – Alex Elle*

*But the Lord sent out a great wind on the sea, and there was a
mighty tempest on the sea, so that the ship was about to be broken
up... Then the men were exceedingly afraid... And he said to
them, "Pick me up and throw me into the sea...for I know that
this great tempest is because of me." (Jonah 1:4,10,12)*

God will go to any lengths to get His children where He wants them.
He will also go to any lengths to protect them and preserve them
for the calling that is on their lives. Even if that looks like a storm. God
called Jonah to give a life-saving message to a group of people, but Jonah
ran from God and his calling. Jonah bought passage on a ship to get
away. But God sent a bad storm and, later, a large fish.

Have you ever felt like you were living in a storm? Sometimes God
sends a storm in your life to save you from going in the wrong direction.
I can look back and remember devastating seasons in my life. During
them, I would have done anything to get out of them. But now, in
hindsight, I wouldn't exchange them. This is because I can see that they
were instrumental in getting me to where God wanted me to go. We all
lose our way from time to time, but the Sovereignty of God stays on us.

# What Breaks Your Heart?

*"The people who complain most about the suffering in the world usually do the least about the suffering in the world."*
*– David Wilkerson*

*…I asked them concerning the Jews who had escaped, who had survived the captivity, and concerning Jerusalem. And they said to me, "The survivors who are left from the captivity in the province are there in great distress and reproach. The wall of Jerusalem is also broken down, and its gates are burned with fire." So it was, when I heard these words, that I sat down and wept… (Nehemiah 1:2-4)*

When Nehemiah learned that the walls that protected Jerusalem had been destroyed, it broke his heart. And although he was just a cupbearer to the king, he called out to the Lord, prayed and fasted. Then he did something about the problem.

What do you see in society that is broken? What is broken and causes us to constantly complain? For every broken thing in society, there is a godly man or woman that God will raise up to fix it. What breaks your heart? Could it be that God is calling you to be a Nehemiah?

Lord, break our hearts for what breaks yours. Show us what broken things you want us to fix.

# A Rocky Start

*"You weren't an accident. You weren't mass-produced.
You aren't an assembly-line product. You were deliberately
planned, specifically gifted, and lovingly positioned on the
earth by the Master Craftsman." – Max Lucado*

*"Now I say to you that you are Peter (which means 'rock'),
and upon this rock I will build my church, and all the
powers of hell will not conquer it." (Matthew 16:18)*

What could God possibly do with an impulsive, presumptuous, timid, cowardly, self-seeking, slow-to-get-it, conceited, arrogant, big mouth? Apparently, God could and would use someone with these character flaws to be foundational in building the Church. Simon Peter was one of the first followers of Jesus. He was an outspoken disciple and one of Jesus' closest friends, an apostle, and a "pillar" of the church. He was enthusiastic, strong-willed, impulsive, and, at times, brash. He had many strengths, but also many failings. Still, the Lord, Who had chosen him, continued to mold him into exactly who He intended Peter to be. Jesus had given Peter a promise that he would be the "rock" of the church.

Has God given you a promise that has come and gone? Have you since made so many mistakes that you've decided they must have disqualified you? Let Peter's "rocky start" encourage you today. God will complete in you and through you that which He began.

## NOVEMBER 15

# Twelve Springs

*"When I do good, I feel good, and when I do
bad, I feel bad." – Abraham Lincoln*

*Then they came to Elim, where there were twelve springs and seventy
palm trees, and they camped there near the water. (Exodus 15:27)*

Obedience brings blessings. Moses told the Israelites, "If you listen
carefully to the Lord your God and do what is right in His eyes, if
you pay attention to His commands and keep all His decrees, I will not
bring on you any of the diseases I brought on the Egyptians, for I am
the Lord, Who heals you" (Ezekiel 15:26). God would rather heal than
hurt. He wanted to teach them something in the wilderness. He wanted
to teach them not to be like the ones who had no regard for Him or His
Word. So, He said, "I'm going to put you in a situation where all you
have is Me and My Word. And, if you trust Me, you will be healed. I
will deliver you. If you don't trust Me, you'll only see My discipline."
With obedience, the Israelites went from a place of bitter waters to Elim,
"where there were twelve springs and seventy palms."

Obedience always brings blessings.

Father, we submit our will, our lives, our families, our today, and
our tomorrow to You.

# Brokenness

*"God uses broken things. It takes broken soil to produce a crop, broken clouds to give rain, broken grain to give bread, broken bread to give strength. It is the broken alabaster box that gives forth perfume. It is Peter, weeping bitterly, who returns to greater power than ever." – Vance Havner*

*The sacrifices of God are a broken spirit; a broken and contrite heart, O God, You will not despise. (Psalm 51:17)*

Brokenness is the road to breakthrough. What is brokenness? Brokenness is the act of surrendering your will to God's will. To be broken means to say yes to what God wants over what you want. To be broken is a decision to humble yourself and acknowledge your need for help. Brokenness is God stripping you of your self-sufficiency and pride.

My greatest breakthroughs have been the result of my greatest brokenness. God makes it very clear that He responds to those who are humble and contrite of heart.

Do you need a breakthrough today? If you will humble yourself and tell God that you need His help, He will help you.

Lord, forgive us of our self-sufficiency and pride. We can't do this without You.

# It's The Small Things

*"Be faithful in small things because it is in them*
*that your strength lies." – Mother Teresa*

*But Ruth replied, "Don't urge me to leave you or to turn back from*
*you. Where you go I will go, and where you stay I will stay. Your*
*people will be my people and your God my God." (Ruth 1:16)*

There is something to be said for loyalty and for doing the right thing…every day, in every situation. Will loyalty and doing the right thing make headlines? Not usually. Heaven is not looking at the headlines. God is looking for a remnant that will trust Him every day, day-in and day-out.

Ruth chose to be loyal to her mother-in-law although she could have gone out on her own and started over. She remained loyal to her family and she was faithful in small things. Little is much when God is in it! Everyday decisions of life, how you act on your job, how you pay your bills, how you treat your spouse and your children, what you do when no one is looking, how you converse with your best friend, how you respond in conflict…these are the things that God is watching. Sometimes we make life all about the great things that we miss the little things. Loyalty and faithfulness day-in and day-out brought great rewards to Ruth. Better yet, they will bring great rewards to you as well.

# "I Know You"

*"I have called you by name." – God*

*"Before I formed you in the womb I knew you…"*
*(Jeremiah 1:5)*

I am adopted and have recently been contacted by some of my birth family on my father's side. It has been a rollercoaster ride. I've learned some very disturbing things about my heritage, but some wonderful things as well. Growing up, and even into adulthood, I've really struggled with "belonging" and being "known." Through the years, I tried to "belong" and to be "known" in my own efforts, yet time after time, the result was me feeling like I belonged less. Just last week, I had the privilege of meeting my older sister. As I walked down a cobblestone street to meet her at an Italian restaurant for lunch, in the middle of quite a few people, I caught the glance of a beautiful woman looking at me. I'd never met her, but I "knew" her. As we embraced for the first time, the first words she spoke to me were, "I know you."

I believe we all want to be "known." We want it, but because we've been hurt in the past, we keep ourselves from being known. God wants you to know today that He knows you. I know, as sure as the sky is blue, that He orchestrated that moment with my sister. "I know you." He wants to remind you today, "Before I formed you in the womb, I knew you." How marvelous is that?

# Only Believe

*"A believer is never disturbed because other persons do not see the fact which he sees." – Ralph Waldo Emerson*

*Faith is the confidence that what we hope for will actually happen; it gives us assurance about things we cannot see. And it is impossible to please God without faith. Anyone who wants to come to him must believe that God exists and that He rewards those who sincerely seek Him.*
*(Hebrews 11:1, 6)*

There was a man by the name of Jairus, a synagogue ruler, who says to Jesus, "My little daughter is very sick. Please come and place your hands on her, so that she will get well and live." Jesus agreed to go with him, but along the way, was interrupted. During the interruption, some messengers came from Jairus' house and told him that his daughter had already died. Jesus didn't pay them any attention, and told him, "Don't be afraid, only believe."

Faith is the confidence that what we hope for will actually happen. Even if there are things that appear dead in your life, Jesus says to you today, "Don't be afraid, only believe." It's impossible to please God without faith. God will reward you if you sincerely seek Him.

# True Friends

*"A true friend never gets in your way unless you happen to be going down." – Arnold H. Glasgow*

*Some men arrived carrying a paraplegic on a stretcher. They were looking for a way to get into the house and set him before Jesus. When they couldn't find a way in because of the crowd, they went up on the roof, removed some tiles, and let him down in the middle of everyone, right in front of Jesus. Impressed by their bold belief, He said, "Friend, I forgive your sins. (Luke 5:18-20)*

*I*f you were in a desperate situation, and needed help, who would you call? Do you have a friend that would go to any lengths for you? The crippled man in Luke 5 had those kinds of friends. His friends really knew the Lord. They had made up their minds, "We have to get our friend to where Jesus is. He needs a miracle, and we're going to take Him to the One that can do it!" The Bible says they placed him on a mat and they carried him to where Jesus was. But when they got there, there was an obstacle in their path. The crowd was too big. They couldn't get their friend through the door. But they refused to give up. They had bold, audacious faith. So they hoisted their friend up the side of the house, tore the roof off and dropped him down into the presence of the Lord.

You need some friends in your life that will pick you up and not let you stay in a crippled condition.

# Awake, O Sleeper

*"To live is the rarest thing in the world. Most*
*people exist, that is all." – Oscar Wilde*

*But their evil intentions will be exposed when the light*
*shines on them, for the light makes everything visible. This*
*is why it is said, "Awake, O sleeper, rise up from the dead,*
*and Christ will give you light." (Ephesians 5:13-14)*

As believers in Jesus Christ, we are instructed to let our light shine to bring glory to God. It's possible to be morally good but unenlightened. It's possible to be religious yet unanointed. And it's very possible for a good, faithful, and loyal church member to be spiritually asleep. There is a call for all of us in Ephesians, "Awake, O sleeper, rise up from the dead, and Christ will give you light." Your workplace, your community, and your city are full of darkness. You may be the only light they will ever see. The enemy would love nothing more than to lull us to sleep. He does not want you to shine the light on the evil that is running rampant in this world.

Father, forgive us for falling asleep when we should, instead, rise up and shine in the dark world we live in. Let your glory shine through us today.

# Sabbath Rest

*"There is virtue in work and there is virtue in rest.
Use both and overlook neither." – Alan Cohen*

*"This is what the Lord has said: 'Tomorrow is a Sabbath
rest, a holy Sabbath to the Lord.'" (Exodus 16:23)*

The Lord had been providing manna for the children of Israel every day. He told them to gather double on the sixth day so that, on the seventh day, they could rest. Before the sixth day, some of the people gathered more than their daily portion. They thought, "What if we wake up and there's not enough?" So they gathered more, just in case. When they woke up the next morning, it had rotted and there were worms in it. God had promised, "I'll provide for you, just trust Me." When they gathered double on the sixth day, it lasted. No rot. No worms. God was trying to teach them to take a day off. God commands us to take a day of rest. He provided Sabbath for you, not for Him. Many don't trust Him to provide if they obey this commandment. Sabbath rest is also a witness. When the people in your world who are working themselves to death see you take a Sabbath day for rest, and still flourish, they will want to know how you do it.

Are you tired? Will you trust the Lord to provide manna for you on the seventh day? He will provide and you will be refreshed.

# Point Of Contact

*"For each one of us, there is only one thing necessary:
to fulfill our own destiny, according to God's will, to be
what God wants us to be." – Thomas Merton*

*Before they call I will answer; while they are still
speaking I will hear. (Isaiah 65:24)*

*D*id you know that God has already decreed His will for you? And, He decreed it before you ever talked to Him about it. It's sort of like someone making a deposit into your bank account, but telling you that *you* must make the withdrawal. The money is there. But, it could sit there for the rest of your life if there's no withdrawal from it. God has ordered the end from the beginning. The assumption is that you will call on it. When you call on it, that which has already been decreed, He dispenses. Prayer activates the will of God. Prayer doesn't make it happen, it just grabs it because it's already been decreed to happen. Prayer is the mechanism that grabs something out of the invisible realm so that you can see it at work in the visible, physical realm. You pray. God answers. Then, you become the distribution point for His supernatural activity. You are the point of contact and the switch is flipped with prayer.

Heavenly Father, thank you that you have a will and plan for our lives. We call on that, which has already been decreed. We would like to make a withdrawal today!

# Digging Ditches

*"What is my task? First of all, my task is to be pleasing to*
*Christ, to be empty of self and be filled with Himself, to be*
*filled with the Holy Spirit; to be led by the Holy Spirit."*
*– Aimee Semple McPherson*

*And he said, "Thus says the Lord: 'Make this*
*valley full of ditches.'" (2 Kings 3:16)*

God is attracted to empty. God is attracted to need. God told the prophet in 2 Kings, in the middle of his need, to dig a ditch. God told him he wanted him to make the valley full of ditches for when the rain would come. You may not see clouds. You may not see any sign of rain. But you need to dig a ditch anyway. God says, "Come to me with your need and wait for the miraculous. Ask Me for more." We can become so self-sufficient that we have no ditches. Let me let you in on a little secret: the increase never has to stop! It only stops when we stop digging ditches.

The moment you say, "I'm full" or "I don't need anything," I believe God's rain will find someone else who has dug a ditch. And, they will go from glory unto glory and from faith unto faith.

It's time for digging ditches.

# Still Strong

*"There are far, far better things ahead than*
*any we leave behind." – C.S. Lewis*

*"As yet I am as strong this day as on the day that Moses sent me;*
*just as my strength was then, so now is my strength for war, both for*
*going out and for coming in. Now therefore, give me this mountain*
*of which the Lord spoke in that day..." (Joshua 14:11-12)*

In Joshua 14, Caleb was set. He was going to be taken care of. The children of Israel had come into the Promised Land. But, Caleb knew *there was more*. For forty years he kept his mouth shut and settled for "mediocre," even though he could have been in the Promised Land all that time if the people had trusted God rather than believing a negative report. He believed there were more great battles to fight as long as the Lord would be with him. If the Lord said Caleb could drive out the giants in that land when he was forty, then, even at eighty-five, he was still willing to say, "Here I am Lord; use me!" Caleb was a man (an old man) who dared to believe God for mighty things.

You're never too old to work for the Kingdom. As long as you have breath in your body, God is NOT finished with you yet. Just make yourself available!

Lord, here we are! Use us!

# Emptied

*"Do you have a hunger for God? If we don't feel strong desires for the manifestation of the glory of God, it is not because we have drunk deeply and are satisfied. It is because we have nibbled so long at the table of the world. Our soul is stuffed with small things, and there is no room for the great. If we are full of what the world offers, then perhaps a fast might express, or even increase, our soul's appetite for God." – John Piper*

*But He assured them, "I have food to eat of which you know nothing and have no idea... My food is to do the will of Him Who sent Me and to accomplish and completely finish His work." (John 4:32, 34)*

While the disciples wanted to fill their bellies with food, God wanted to fill a city with revival. Some churches have become like that today. We have no room for more. We sit and receive until we are full to our ears. Pews can turn into recliners with our "remote controls" flipping through what we do and don't like in a service. We can become so stuffed that we have no room for more and no passion for Jesus. If the twelve apostles could miss it, you and I are certainly capable of taking for granted the goodness of the Lord. We can easily become so full of ourselves that we must be emptied through fasting and prayer, seeking the Lord in brokenness.

I believe with all of my heart that God is looking for people who will not lose their passion. If you've lost yours, consider a season of prayer and fasting. Get hungry for God again. Let Him rekindle your passion!

## NOVEMBER 27

# Crisis

*"I'm not afraid of the devil. The devil can handle me – he's got judo I never heard of. But he can't handle the One to whom I'm joined; he can't hand the One to whom I'm united; he can't handle the One whose nature dwells in my nature." – A.W. Tozer*

*After this the Moabites and ammonites, and with them some of the Meunites, came against Jehoshaphat for battle. Some men came and told Jehoshaphat, "A great multitude is coming against you from Edom, from beyond the sea; and, behold, they are in Engedi." (2 Chronicles 20:1-2)*

Have you ever been in a crisis? A crisis is when you have so much coming at you at the same time that you can't handle it. Or, you have one thing coming at you, but it's so big, it might as well be a multitude of things. Jehoshaphat was in a crisis. He was being attacked and surrounded on all sides by a multitude of enemies. Crisis can come in many forms. You can be in financial crisis, when the bills are so high and the income is so low that you see no way out of your debt dilemma. Or maybe you're in a relational crisis – a relationship where there seems to be no way to patch up the problems and you see no hope. Perhaps you're in a vocational crisis – you've been laid off or you have a boss that makes your life miserable.

What do you do when you are in crisis? In 2 Chronicles 20:3, Jehoshaphat turned his attention to seek the Lord.

Do you feel like there's no way out? The very first step is to turn your attention to seeking the Lord today.

# Good Verse In A Bad Chapter

*"Blessed are the single-hearted, for they shall enjoy much peace…
If you refuse to be hurried and pressed, if you stay your soul on God,
nothing can keep you from that clearness of spirit, which is life and
peace. In that stillness you know what His will is." – Amy Carmichael*

*This is God's Word on the subject: "As soon as Babylon's seventy
years are up and not a day before, I'll show up and take care of you
as I promised and bring you back home. I know what I'm doing.
I have it all planned out – plans to take care of you, not abandon
you, plans to give you the future you hope for." (Jeremiah 29:11)*

*M*ost of us are familiar with and love Jeremiah 29:11. What you should know is that this great verse is in a bad chapter. Maybe you are coming out of a bad chapter, which is perhaps following another bad chapter. Then, this verse is for you. Because this verse says, "Even if you are in a bad chapter that's part of a bad book, God has plans for you." His plans are for your well-being, and not for your calamity. And, His plans have to do with your tomorrow, not your yesterdays. "To give you a future and to give you a hope." This verse is designed to tell you that in spite of hopelessness, God can turn your yesterdays into better tomorrows. Everything that has led up to this point no longer has to define where you are going.

# Death Is Necessary For Life

*"Any fool can count the seeds in an apple. Only God can count all the apples in one seed." – Robert H. Schuller*

*Unless a seed falls to the ground and dies, it remains only a single seed. But if it dies, it produces many seeds.*
*(John 12:24)*

If you know anything about a seed, then you know that inside a seed is a greater life than you can see just by looking at the seed. When you look at it, all you can see is the outer exterior shape of the shell. The life is inside the seed. You can wash the seed, decorate it, and shine a special light on the seed, but until it's buried, nothing will happen. Anything public you do for the seed will not help any life come forth. Death must occur. When death occurs, the shell gets broken. When the seed gets buried and the shell gets broken, all the good stuff that was held compact on the inside is free to express itself. But, it won't happen until it's buried. Why are some of us walking around, but not really living? We are unwilling to die to ourselves. We don't want God to strip us of the hard shell of our independence, self-sufficiency and pride. But, when we die to ourselves, God can multiply the life that is in us.

Are you *really* living? If not, a death may need to take place. It's not a pretty thing, but it is necessary for abundant life!

# God Likes Lowly Folk

*"God is looking for broken men who have judged themselves in
the light of the cross of Christ. When He wants anything done,
He takes up men who have come to the end of themselves, whose
confidence is not in themselves, but in God." – Harry Ironside*

*For this is what the high and exalted One says – He Who lives forever,
Whose name is holy: "I live in a high and holy place, but also with
the one who is contrite and lowly in spirit, to revive the spirit of
the lowly and to revive the heart of the contrite." (Isaiah 57:15)*

God loves broken people. He tells us that He lives in two places. He
says, "I live high and exalted. But I live also with the lowly and the
contrite." Our high God loves to hang out with the lowly folk. The
word contrition in the Bible had to do with grinding something or
gnashing something. It's like taking a brick and breaking it, chopping
it into pieces, and grinding it into powder. Contrite people are broken
people. Sometimes we think God has not come through for us, but
actually He's waiting for us to rid ourselves of our self-sufficiency and
independence. God wants to grind our pride, independence and self-
sufficiency into powder.

God, we humble ourselves before You. Forgive our pride and bring
us to the end of ourselves.

# But Even If He Does Not

*"Cheer up, Christian! Things are not left to chance: no
blind fate rules the world. God hath purposes, and those
purposes are fulfilled. God hath plans, and those plans are
wise, and never can be dislocated." – Charles Spurgeon*

*If we are thrown into the blazing furnace, the God we serve
is able to deliver us from it, and He will deliver us from your
majesty's hand. But even if He does not..." (Daniel 3:17-18)*

Shadrach, Meshach and Abednego understood the *whole* counsel of
God. We shout with them in Daniel 3:17: "The God we serve is
able to deliver us!" But, we get quiet when we get to the next verse, "But
even if He does not." God certainly may bless you. He may certainly
provide for you financially. He may certainly heal you. But, what are
you going to do if He doesn't? How will you respond if it's not in your
timing? The three Hebrews not only understood the power of God.
They understood the sovereignty of God. They understood that God
makes the final call. He is able. He is sovereign. He must make the final
decision and that's why the Bible says to pray, "if it's Your will, Oh God."
In other words, "I know You can. I believe You will. But, I'm leaving
the final decision to You."

Heavenly Father, You alone are Sovereign. We know You can and
we believe that You will, but even if You do not, we will still love You.
We will still serve only You.

# Wisdom

*"Where fear is present, wisdom cannot be." – Anonymous*

*While they were battering the wall to bring it down, a
wise woman called from the city, "Listen! Listen!"*
*(2 Samuel 20:16)*

Wisdom has nothing to do with age, intellect or education. Wisdom is a gift given from God. There is a nameless woman in 2 Samuel 20 who is referred to as a *"wise woman."* How did she qualify for such a title? Her city was under siege. When no one else did anything about it, in courage she boldly faced the threat and defused the situation, which resulted in an entire city being saved from an attack. She had to make some hard decisions, even having a man beheaded and throwing his head over the city wall. One of the ways she demonstrated wisdom is that she used the Word of God as a weapon. She reminded the commander of the attacking army that he was bound by a Biblical law to offer peace terms to a city before attacking it. She literally "threw the book" at him. She had to be familiar with God's Word to use it as a weapon against her enemy. We can learn so much from this wise woman.

If we want wisdom, first the Bible says we must ask for it above anything else. Secondly, you need to meditate on the Word day and night. When in a crisis, you may not have time to pull out a Bible concordance to look for solutions. And finally, we must pray without ceasing. Waiting until a tragedy to pray doesn't produce wisdom, but an ongoing dialogue with the Holy Spirit will.

DECEMBER 3

# In The Fire

*"I'm not afraid of the devil. He can't handle the
One to whom I'm joined." – A. W. Tozer*

*"Look!" he answered, "I see four men loose, walking in the
midst of the fire; and they are not hurt, and the form of
the fourth is like the Son of God." (Daniel 3:25)*

One way you know that God is God is when He delivers you from the fire. But another way that you know God is God is when He does not deliver you *from* the fire, but instead joins you *in* the fire. In Daniel 3, King Nebuchadnezzar had thrown Shadrach, Meshach and Abednego into the fire. But when the king looked into the fiery furnace, he saw not three, but four men walking around in the midst of the fire. He noted that the fourth man looked like the Son of God. This was miraculous because up until that point, King Nebuchadnezzar was not a believer in the Most High God. God was in the fire with them. And when God is with you in the fire, no harm can come to you. In verse 27, we read, "They noticed that the fire had *no effect* on them." They didn't even smell of smoke. They were in the fire, but it didn't affect them.

Are you in the fire today? Did you lose your job? God is your Provider. Did you receive a bad report from the doctor? God is your Healer. Is your marriage hanging on by a thread? God is your Restorer and Counselor. You may be in the fire. But God is with you in the fire. "And not a hair on their head was singed" (Verse 27).

# Ask, Read, And Pray

*"The chief means for attaining wisdom, and suitable gifts*
*for ministry, are the Holy Scriptures, and prayer."*
— *John Newton*

*The fear of the Lord is the beginning of knowledge, but*
*fools despise wisdom and instruction. (Proverbs 1:7)*

Wisdom is a priceless gift. If you want it, you *have* to acquaint yourself with the Word of God. You can't bypass it. You need to meditate on it day and night. Memorize it! Assimilate it! Digest it! Surround yourself with others who love the Lord and His Word and are wise in His Word. But, most importantly, simply ask God for wisdom. Remember Solomon? God told him He would give him anything he asked for in prayer. He could have asked for riches, a big house, and a fancy car, but he asked for wisdom; and he ended up the richest man of all time. James says, "You have not because you ask not." Ask God for wisdom.

Do you desire wisdom? Here's the formula: Ask for it, read His Word, talk to Him often, and surround yourself with people who do the same.

Lord, thank You for the priceless gift of wisdom.

# Courage

*"One isn't necessarily born with courage, but one is born with potential.*
*Without courage, we cannot practice any other virtue with consistency.*
*We can't be kind, true, merciful, generous, or honest." – Maya Angelou*

*Fear of man will prove to be a snare, but whoever*
*trusts in the Lord is kept safe. (Proverbs 29:25)*

How do you get courage? For me, it's by staying in the Word of God. If the Bible is true, and I know that it is, it tells you and me that we are to be courageous. How? If you really know the One that has your back (your front and your sides, too!), you can walk with a swagger everywhere you go! "But whoever trusts in the Lord is kept safe." No exceptions! Just trust in the Lord! Courage doesn't mean your legs won't tremble and your voice won't shake sometimes. Courage means that you know how this thing is going to turn out. Courage knows that God's Word is your weapon. Courage means that you meditate on His Word so that it flows out of you naturally in any scary situation. Courage means that you talk to the Lord without stopping. You do *nothing* without consulting Him, which means you can make the hard decisions that need to be made.

Do you need some courage today? Get in God's Word! Start with the passages about courage and being courageous. Then face your day with your head up and your shoulders back, knowing Who has your back!

# Hell Has Been Put On Notice

*"Hell doesn't have access to the plans of your future unless
God reveals it to them. But hell can make predictions about
your future based on observation." – Christy Sawyer*

*When all the people heard of Jesus' arrival, they flocked to see Him and
also to see Lazarus, the man Jesus had raised from the dead. Then the
leading priests decided to kill Lazarus, too, <u>for it was because of him</u>
that many of the people had deserted them and believed in Jesus.
(John 12:9-11)*

It takes nothing more than being a born-again, blood-washed believer for the enemy to want to take you out. Living your life for Jesus Christ is enough for all of hell to want to keep you down. The leading priests wanted to kill Lazarus "for it was because of him that many of the people believed in Jesus." Lazarus wasn't even evangelizing! He was just eating dinner. But the second Lazarus got up from that grave, even with the stench of death still on him, Hell was put on notice. Hell will stop at nothing to shut him (and you) up before he has a chance to tell his testimony. But, Christ truly set Lazarus free. In the same way, Christ has set you free. Galatians 5:1 says, "Now make sure that you stay free, and don't get tied up again in slavery…"

Tell your story! Jesus raised you to do just that!

# Never Leave The Table

*"The Bible is very easy to understand. But we Christians are
a bunch of scheming swindlers. We pretend to be unable to
understand it because we know very well that the minute
we understand, we are obliged to act accordingly."*
*– Søren Kierkegaard*

*But God is so rich in mercy, and He loved us so much, that even
though we were dead because of our sins, He gave us life when
He raised Christ from the dead. (It is only by God's grace that
you have been saved!) For He raised us from the dead along
with Christ and seated us with Him in the Heavenly realms
because we are united with Christ Jesus. (Ephesians 2:4-6)*

*Y*ou have a position in Christ, and you have a seat with your name
on a placard at the King's table. This is why the devil hates you so
much… because of your position. The enemy much prefers you to be
flat on your back, laying in your sins. But, now that you are up, you
have a position. You are positioned at the table with the King. Anytime
the enemy wants to come after you, he walks in and sees you at the
table. He says, "Ugh, they're still at the table, let's go back later and try
again." He comes back again and sees you're still at the table. As long as
you are up from the grave and seated at the table, the enemy can't get
to you. When you continue to *feed* off what the King is sharing with
you, eating the Word of God, and being strengthened to do everything
that you've been called to do, you are untouchable.

# From Here To There

*"Getting over a painful experience is much like crossing monkey bars.*
*You have to let go at some point in order to move forward." – C.S Lewis*

*Then Joshua rose early in the morning; and they set out from*
*Acacia Grove and came to the Jordan, he and all the children of*
*Israel, and lodged there before they crossed over. (Joshua 3:1)*

The Israelites have been wandering for some time. They've had some highs and they've had some lows. They've had some victories and they've had some losses. They've seen tragedy and they've seen miracles. But, they suddenly find themselves at a place of transition. God is ready to take them from *here* to *there*. We see them standing on the banks of the Jordan River. It's at the edge of the Jordan where many of us just stop. We have a fear of the unknown…of what we can't control. What we find ourselves doing is simply circling. We're stuck…in a perpetual holding pattern. But there is a Voice calling you and me. This Voice is telling us, "It's time to go from *here* to *there*. It's time to cross over into the Promise I have for you." No day should look the same as yesterday. The scenery for tomorrow should have brand new views.

It's time to cross over – from here to there.

# You're Looking More Like Jesus Every Day

*"Are you ready for a change? Take a look into the mirror of God's Word and see yourself the way God sees you: as a conqueror, an overcomer, a royal priesthood, a holy nation, and His very own possession!" – Jesse Duplantis*

*Now the Lord is Spirit; and where the Spirit of the Lord is, there is liberty. But we all, with unveiled face, beholding as in a mirror the glory of the Lord, are being transformed into the same image from glory to glory, just as by the Spirit of the Lord. (2 Corinthians 3:17-18)*

We all, with unveiled face, beholding as in a mirror the glory of the Lord… Another way to say that is: we are beholding the glory of the Lord, but we wake up and discover it's like looking into a mirror. Why would the writer give us this analogy? He says, "We are being transformed into the same image." It's like a mirror because what we see is what we become. What you look *at* is what you look like. Why do you think the enemy wants you to be introspective? Why do you think he wants you looking inward all the time? Because you only reproduce what you see.

What are you looking at today? What do you see? Keep your eyes fixed on the One Who is transforming you into His image from glory to glory. You're looking more like Jesus every day!

## DECEMBER 10

# "I Need A Little Help Here"

*"An edited testimony helps nobody." – Christy Sawyer*

*"Roll the stone aside," Jesus told them… And the dead man came out,*
*his hands and feet bound in grave clothes, his face wrapped in a head*
*cloth. Jesus told them, "Unwrap him and let him go!" (John 11:39, 43)*

The story of Jesus raising Lazarus from the dead is mind-blowing. I think it's interesting that the Son of God Who created everything, put the stars in the sky, and tells the sea where its boundaries are – raised a dead man, but then told his friends to roll away the stone and to remove the grave clothes. Jesus comes to do what we can't do, but requires us to do what we *can* do. When Jesus raised *you* from the dead, He gave you life, but your grave clothes didn't immediately fall off. Jesus ordered Lazarus' friends to help remove the grave clothes. You never get free by yourself. You need Jesus and you need a church family to help unwrap you. And, you need help rolling the stone aside. It's hard to go back and uncover stuff you've buried.

You know, it is possible to be upright, going to church every week, taking care of your family and your job, and still have grave clothes on. It can be regret, shame, doubt, unforgiveness, bitterness or frustration. God puts people in your life to be the hands of Jesus, to help unwrap those grave clothes. What is still wrapped around you today?

Jesus, would you bring the right friends into our lives to help us remove the grave clothes. In Your Word, You promise that you will replace them with a garment of praise.

## DECEMBER 11

# From Strength To Strength And Faith To Faith

*"Let us move forward with strong and active faith."*
*– Franklin D. Roosevelt*

*As they pass through the Valley of Baca, they make it a spring; the rain also covers it with pools. (Psalm 84:6)*

The Hebrew word Baca means weeping. Have you ever gone through a season of weeping? You may be there now, but you are not meant to stay there. It's just a temporary pit stop. It's necessary, but it's temporary. You stop, by then you are to turn the Valley of Weeping into springs of refreshing. In Psalm 84:7, we read that they go from "strength to strength." God allows you to stop at the Valley of Weeping, but it's part of the process of going from "strength to strength" and "faith to faith." He is going to take you from one dimension of strength to another dimension of strength...from one dimension of faith, to another dimension of faith. From exercising your faith *here,* to exercising your faith over *there.* And, the thing to note about this journey is that it doesn't matter what you see. Your current circumstances may look nothing like His promise to you. James says the testing of our faith produces patience (which literally means spiritual strength), and we are double-minded if we don't expect and believe God to come through. Here's a truth: God will never take you from a place where you have to stand in faith to a place where you no longer need to stand in faith.

The Valley of Weeping was necessary. But, now He calls you to move from there - to move from strength to strength and faith to faith.

DECEMBER 12

# As He Is, So Are We

*"Jesus touched the untouchables of the world.*
*Will you do the same?" – Max Lucado*

*…As He is, so are we in this world. (1 John 4:17)*

"*A*s He is, so are we…" Okay, so how *is* He? He is resurrected. He is ascended. He is glorified. "*As He is, so are we in this world.*" Looking inward and becoming infatuated with gifts and favor shuts that down. But becoming infatuated with the One, the One Who is wonderful, the One Who is all Power…what we see, is what we become. John the writer of 1 John is the same John who laid his head on Jesus' chest at the Last Supper. He's the one that was called, "the one that Jesus loved." John saw Jesus betrayed, and he was the one in Revelation 1 who saw the glorified Jesus. This is the same man who wrote, "As He is, so are we in this world." Jesus went ahead of you. Jesus was raised so you could be raised. Jesus got up so that you could get up. Jesus has already been glorified to empower you to go from glory to glory. You have only one absolute destination, and that is to fully and accurately represent the Lord Jesus "in this world." "*As He is, so are we in this world.*"

Many believe that it will be in Heaven that we will become like Jesus, but Jesus intended us to become like Him right now.

As He is, so are *you*…today…right now.

## DECEMBER 13

# You're Safe

*"The violent winds of suffering and trouble blow us into the Lord's protective hands." – Sadhu Sundar Singh*

*"After we were brought safely through…" (Acts 28:1)*

*H*ave you ever had a bad day? The Apostle Paul goes from one bad day to another bad day, from one bad experience to another bad experience. Amazingly, however, he keeps getting back up. No matter what comes his way or catastrophes he faces, he keeps moving forward. He says, "But one thing I do; forgetting what lies behind and straining forward to what lies ahead, I press on toward the goal." He keeps moving forward, from faith to faith, strength to strength and glory to glory. Bad days will happen. Bad things do happen, even to good people. But, we all have a choice. Your response will determine your results in this life. I can't determine what people may do *to* me or what life will throw at me. But I *can* determine how I respond.

In Acts 28, Paul has been through a deadly storm. He said from the beginning, "The winds are against us." His ship was violently storm-tossed. He and the people on board began to throw things overboard. It was perpetually dark. There was no sun, moon or stars in sight for many days. Paul said, "All hope of our being saved was at last abandoned." The food was gone. Their vessel was torn apart. But, notice, Paul says this, "After we were brought safely through…"

Have you been through a storm? Maybe you felt like it would take you out for good. But, you're here. God has brought you safely through. Just look up. There's land in sight.

# Issues In The Tissues

*"The remarkable thing is, we have a choice every day*
*regarding the attitude we will embrace for that day."*
*– Chuck Swindoll*

*"I call heaven and earth as witnesses today against you, that I have set*
*before you life and death, blessing and cursing; therefore choose life, that*
*both you and your descendants may live…" (Deuteronomy 30:19)*

Our families have the greatest influence on our development, including the development of our patterns of sin. Cycles of behavior and sin can definitely be passed down through families. We inherit many traits and preferences that aren't always a positive influence on ourselves or others. As adults, we often mimic what we saw as children. The enemy says, "Your family is cursed. They've always struggled with that thing. You will struggle with it and so will your children." When you partner with a lie, the lie turns into a belief that turns into a behavior. Then, you continue a cycle or pattern. There are definitely consequences of sin and habits and cycles. But, you have choices. In Deuteronomy 30:19, it says that you can choose between life and death - blessing and cursing.

What are you choosing today? Who are you partnering with in your life? Jesus died and rose for you so that you could live. Partner with Jesus. Partner with the Truth. *"Therefore choose life, that both you and your descendants may live.*

# God Loves A Hungry Heart

*"Because the face of God is so lovely, my brothers and sisters, so beautiful, once you have seen it, nothing else can give you pleasure. It will give insatiable satisfaction of which we will never tire. We shall always be hungry and always have our fill." – Augustine*

*Then Moses said, "Now show me your glory."*
*(Exodus 33:18-23)*

You know, there's something about a hungry heart that Jesus loves. There's something about that cry that comes from deep within us that God loves. It's the cry of David saying: "My heart and my flesh long for You." It's the cry of Peter that says: "Lord, Lord, where else can I go?" It's the words of Moses saying: "Don't send us up from this place. What else will distinguish me and Your people from all the other people on the face of the earth? Show me Your glory." I don't think for one moment that God ever intended to send Moses up without His Presence. In fact, in the verse right before Moses makes that request, God specifically says to him, "I *will* go with you. And I will give you rest." Try to see the heart of Moses in this. His desire for the Presence of the Lord was not some secondary, incidental, or ancillary thing for him. It was the primary heart of everything that he was concerned about. That's why he grabbed hold of that promise and said, "Lord, if Your Presence doesn't go with us, nothing else matters." And there was something about the heart cry of Moses that God loved.

Father, we want You. We just want you. We will not allow our hearts to be satisfied with anything less. The only thing that will satisfy our hearts is Your Presence, Lord. Show us Your Glory!

# I Can Do Nothing Without Him

*"As many have learned and later taught, you don't realize*
*Jesus is all you need until Jesus is all you have."*
*— Tim Keller*

*"…For without Me you can do nothing." (John 15:5)*

Jesus said, "Without Me, you can do nothing." He didn't say, "Without Me, you can't *do* anything." That would be a different claim. You know, the truth is, we *can* do without Him. We can do work without Him. We can do marriage without Him. We can do family without Him. We can do life without Him. We can even do ministry without Him. We can build churches and empires and kingdoms without Him. We can preach and pray and sing without Him. But, at the end of the day, things that are done without Him amount to no more than sandcastles on the beach. Without Jesus, all things amount to nothing.

I believe the Holy Spirit says to us, "I will never send anyone away empty, unless they come full of themselves." God is looking for people whose hearts are so hungry for Him that they're willing to say, "Lord, I want you above everything. If Your Presence isn't there, nothing else matters anyway."

Lord, give us Your Presence! We need You above everything! We want You above everything!

# Elijah's God

*"We may ignore, but we can nowhere evade the presence of God. The world is crowded with Him. He walks everywhere incognito." – C.S. Lewis*

*Elisha picked up the mantle that had fallen off Elijah and went back and stood on the bank of the Jordan.*
*(2 Kings 2:13)*

Elisha made a discovery when he picked up the mantle from Elijah. The mantle was symbolic of the job he was to do and the position that he was to take from his mentor. It was a symbol of authority and promotion. Elisha was taking over Elijah's ministry. But, Elisha hadn't even made it down the mountain before he reached an obstacle that would not bow down to his new title. The Red Sea was in his way and the Red Sea didn't care about his title. It was in this moment when Elisha realized that if he was going to be able to walk in the footsteps of Elijah, he would need more than Elijah's mantle. He would need Elijah's God. So, he lifted that mantle and he struck the water. He cried out words that have rung through history: "Where is the Lord, the God of Elijah?" Titles, positions, promotions, pedigrees and even heritages are wonderful. However, if they become a substitute for God's presence, you have been robbed of the Greater thing. Elisha could have done very well in his life as the leader of Elijah's ministry. He would have had recognition and position, but we would not be reading about him today. We know about Elisha not because he caught Elijah's mantle, but because he found Elijah's God.

# I Won't Let You Go

*"No affliction or temptation, no guilt nor power of sin, no wounded spirit nor terrified conscience, should induce us to despair of help and comfort from God." – Thomas Scott*

*"… Yet I have loved Jacob, but Esau I have hated…" (Malachi 1:2-3)*

It amazes me what God looks for in the people He wants to use. It's very different from what we seek. Jacob was not the kind of character we would think of as a good guy. His name actually means deceiver, and that's exactly what he was. He was a trickster and a crook, but God saw something in Jacob that He loved. God loved that Jacob had carried within him a deep longing, hunger, and yearning his entire life. I doubt he even knew what it was, but he was "hungry" all the time. At first, what he thought he was hungry for was his brother's birthright. But when he defrauded Esau to get it, it still left him empty. Then, he thought what would fill him would be the blessing of his father. But when he got it, he realized that his soul was crying out for something else. Finally, one day he came face-to-face with the Angel of the Lord, and when Jacob grabbed hold of Him, he realized, "this is it!" This is what he'd been searching for his entire life. And that's why He said to the Lord, "I will not let You go." He'd had other blessings. But none of them fulfilled him. He realized, "I just want You." And so he pressed in and took hold of God himself.

That is what God is looking for…hearts that are not satisfied with anything else. Do you find yourself hungry today? Only Jesus will do. Just grab hold and don't let Him go.

DECEMBER 19

# When…Then

*"God won't let you bring your yesterday into your today."*
*– Christy Sawyer*

*"When you see the ark of the covenant of the Lord your God,*
*and the Levites bearing it, then you shall set out…"*
*(Joshua 3:3)*

*W*hen God calls us to move, He always gives us a plan. The Ark of the Covenant was the very Power and Presence of Almighty God. He said to the children of Israel and He says to you today, "You're not going around this thing. I'm going to take you through it, but you aren't to take one step until you see Me." So, the children of Israel waited. They waited for three days; but in the waiting, they prepared themselves. While they waited for God to lead them out and over, they did what *they* could do to get themselves ready. They had to be willing to leave their pasts behind. God won't let you bring your yesterday into your today. He always has something fresh and new for you, and, He's not willing for you to settle for rotten day-old or twenty-year-old bread. While they waited and prepared themselves, they had to get into a posture of obedience. In other words, they had to be *willing* to be led. And so He says, "*When* you see Me, when you hear Me call you out, *then* you need to start moving."

Do you see Him? Do you hear Him calling you? He has something fresh for you today.

DECEMBER 20

# Shake It Off

*"Lives with many aims are like water trickling through innumerable*
*streams, none of which are wide enough or deep enough to float*
*the merest cockleshell of a boat; but a life with one object is like*
*a mighty river flowing between its banks, bearing to the ocean*
*a multitude of ships, and spreading fertility on either side."*
*— Charles Haddon Spurgeon*

*Once safely on shore, we found that the island was called Malta.*
*The islanders showed us unusual kindness. They built a fire and*
*welcomed us all because it was raining and cold. Paul gathered a*
*pile of brushwood and, as he put it on the fire, a viper, driven out*
*by the heat, fastened itself on his hand. When the islanders saw*
*the snake hanging from his hand, they said to each other, "This*
*man must be a murderer; for though he escaped from the sea, the*
*goddess Justice has not allowed him to live." But Paul shook the*
*snake off into the fire and suffered no ill effects. (Acts 28:1-5)*

The closer you get to the things of God, the more the enemy will try to attack you. In Acts 28, Paul has just been through a life-threatening ordeal. He's cold, hungry and tired. But despite his condition, he chooses to serve his people anyway. He begins to gather wood for the fire to keep them warm. While he is serving and as he gets closer to the "fire," a snake fastens itself on his arm. Life is full of "snakes" - distractions, obstacles, and loss that will try to fasten to you to keep you from getting closer to what God has for you. You can either walk through life with "snakes" fastened to you, or you can do as Paul did and "shake the snake off into the fire." And, amazingly so, the Bible says that he "suffered no ill effects."

What is fastened to you today? Offense? Unforgiveness? Frustration? Anger? Do not let the enemy keep you from the fire of God and the promises He has just for you. Today, do as Paul did… SHAKE IT OFF!

# Making Room

*"All the Christmas presents in the world are worth nothing without the presence of Christ." – David Jeremiah*

*...There was no room for Jesus in the Inn. (Luke 2:7)*

There was no room for Jesus. Those are chilling words. Most years, as Christmas approaches, the day we celebrate the birth of the Prince of Peace, my peace is nowhere to be found. For some reason, in past years, I convinced myself that my worth as a mother was measured on how perfect I could make this one holiday. From the gifts, to the stockings, to the elaborate meals, to the atmosphere…in my mind I would be graded according to every perfect (or not) detail. I'll never forget sitting around the table a few years ago with my husband, my three kids and my son-in-law for Christmas Dinner. Everyone was relaxed, comfortable, and enjoying themselves. Meanwhile, I was red-faced and dripping in sweat. I hadn't even showered for lack of time. My arms and hands were marred with oven burns and knife cuts from frantically getting the perfect dinner ready. And we hadn't even gotten to the gifts – gifts purchased not because of thoughtfulness, but to ensure that each kid had the same number of presents under the tree. Where was Jesus in all of it? Nowhere to be found, I'm afraid. I made a decision last year. My family would make room for Jesus. Making room for Him means clearing some "space" …less presents, less elaborate meals, less shopping, less stress and less perfection. This will all be replaced with more time together, more laughter, more love and, most importantly, more remembering our God Who sent His Son to be born of a virgin and to walk among us in preparation for the ultimate gift of His life thirty-three years later.

How about you? Is there room for Jesus in your Christmas season this year? More Jesus, more Peace. Make room for Jesus.

# What's In The Manger?

*"Once in our world, a stable had something in it that*
*was bigger than our whole world." – C.S. Lewis*

*"This will be a sign to you; you will find a baby wrapped*
*in cloths and lying in a manger." (Luke 2:12)*

When Baby Jesus was born, His mom placed Him in a manger. The angels told the shepherds they would find the Messiah lying in a manger. When the shepherds arrived in Bethlehem, they found the baby where the angels said he would be…in a manger. In light of the Christmas story, the manger seems a small and insignificant detail. But, in Luke 2, God thought it important enough to point it out three times. What was a manger used for? It was an eating-place that held food for the animals. What's the point? In Exodus 16 the Israelites were led out of captivity and into the wilderness. They complained about not having food. God gave them manna from heaven, and they complained about that too! In John 6, Jesus fed five thousand people with five loaves of bread and two fish. He tells the crowd: "…it is My Father Who gives you the true bread out of heaven. For the bread of God is that which comes down out of heaven, and gives life to the world… I am the bread of life…" Then, in Matthew 6 Jesus tells us that God knows what we need and even teaches us how to pray. He says, "Give us this day our daily bread…"

So, this Christmas season, as you look at your nativity scene, notice the manger. When Jesus was born and laid in a manger, God sent Manna from Heaven for you and for me. Jesus is our "Manna from Heaven." He is the same person who was later rejected and killed for sins He never committed. But, Jesus arose from the dead! Now, we can go to our manger and eat daily from the Bread of Life.

# Why Am I So Favored?

*"You can never truly enjoy Christmas until you can
look up into the Father's face and tell Him you have
received His Christmas gift." – John R. Rice*

*"Why am I so favored, that the mother of my
Lord should come to me?" (Luke 1:43)*

"Iₜ's the most wonderful time of the year," we hear on the radio. But
for some, today may be far from wonderful. Maybe your life has
been devastated by a tragedy, or you've received a bad doctor's report.
Perhaps you recently lost a loved one, or some other painful event is
causing you to cry out, "Why, God?"

Elizabeth knew devastation. She was aging and childless, and in that
culture she was disgraced. I'm sure she'd given up all hope of becoming a
mother long ago. I wonder if the women in her village talked about her
behind her back, "What do you think she did to make God punish her
this way?" But, God made her a promise and she soon became pregnant.
Months later, her cousin Mary came with even greater news. She was
to become the mother of God's son! Many would have been jealous,
but Elizabeth exclaimed, "Why am I so favored, that the mother of my
Lord should come to me?"

No matter your circumstances, look in awe at Jesus and ask yourself,
"Why should I be so blessed that Jesus has come to save me, fill me, use
me and give me life?" Why are you so favored? Because He loves you.

## DECEMBER 24

# Pondering

*"The Almighty appeared on earth as a helpless human baby, needing to be fed and changed and taught to talk like any other child. The more you think about it, the more staggering it gets. Nothing in fiction is so fantastic as this truth of the Incarnation." – J.I. Packer*

*Mary treasured up all these things and pondered them in her heart. (Luke 2:19)*

Mary had her share of struggles. She had her wedding dress picked out when God stepped into her life and told her that she would give birth to the savior of the world. Despite the complications this would bring to her life, she responded in faith, "I am the Lord's servant… May Your word to me be fulfilled."

Mary's journey took her with her husband to Bethlehem, where she gave birth to Jesus. Shepherds showed up talking about a bright light and a choir of angels and then left shouting praises to God. I can see Mary's brow furrowed as she "pondered" these things, trying to make sense of it all.

Then the wise men showed up with all of their pomp and circumstance. Not long after, Mary and her family narrowly escaped being killed by the king. Only thirty-three short years later she watched Jesus die on a cross. I'm sure, even after that, she was still "pondering" these things. But the Bible calls her "blessed" because she believed what the Lord had said. Amazingly, she had responded in faith and decided to go all in, no matter where God's adventure would take her.

On this Christmas Eve, are you willing to take God at His word, no matter your circumstances? God's love will never let you go.

# Indescribable

*"So God throws open the door of this world – and enters as a baby.*
*As the most vulnerable imaginable. Because He wants unimaginable*
*intimacy with you. What religion ever had a god that wanted such*
*intimacy with us that He came with such vulnerability to us? What*
*God ever came so tender we could touch Him? So fragile that we*
*could break Him? So vulnerable that His bare, beating heart could*
*be hurt? Only the One who loves you to death." – Ann Voskamp*

*Thanks be to God for His indescribable gift! (2 Corinthians 9:15)*

*I* love surprising my kids. I pay attention to them all year long, listening for "clues" as to what would delight them on Christmas morning. It brings me great joy to watch them open a gift that they really wanted but had not expected.

Your Father in Heaven loves to surprise you. He pays attention to you every minute of every day and looks for ways to lavish His gifts on you. He knows the desires of your heart. He put them there! And, it brings Him great joy to watch you "open a gift" that you really wanted but had not expected.

God's give to you today is the most expensive gift you will ever receive - not just His birth, but His death…so that you might have life. His gift to you is not for you to keep just for yourself. Who comes to mind that you could share His love with today? His love can look like a phone call, or a visit, or an invitation. Ask the Lord for open doors to share this indescribable gift in days to come.

Lord, thank you for your gift that is indescribable. Help us to accept your gift and share it.

From my heart to yours, "Merry Christmas!"

# The Day After

*"Christmas isn't a season. It's a feeling." – Edma Ferber*

*Jesus is the same yesterday, today, and forever!*
*(Hebrews 13:8)*

Do you ever have a letdown feeling after Christmas? Dirty dishes are in the sink. Discarded pieces of wrapping paper are on the floor. The Christmas tree looks naked without all the beautifully wrapped presents under it. Friends and family are gone. All the build-up, the planning, and the preparation leading up to the "big event"…and then it's over. Or is it?

What was it like the day after Jesus was born? The angels were gone, the shepherds were back with their sheep, and the wise men were afar off. But, Jesus wasn't gone! And even the day after in our own homes, Jesus is still with you. The Bible promises, "He will never leave you or forsake you."

Maybe you are having the day-after Christmas blues. Maybe you are asking yourself, "Now what?" I challenge you to spend today pondering all the "gifts" He's given you. Spend time thanking Him and worshiping Him. Jesus isn't an event. He doesn't come just one day every year. He's with you today. And let me remind you, "Jesus is the same yesterday, today, and forever."

DECEMBER 27

# Opportunities

*"New year – a new chapter, new verse, or just the same old
story? Ultimately we write it. The choice is ours."*
*– Alex Morritt*

*Be wise in the way you act toward outsiders; make the
most of every opportunity. (Colossians 4:5)*

*D*id you see the movie "Captive" that tells the true story of Ashley
Smith? One day, several years ago, she came home to find a murderer
who was on the run from the police in her apartment. He held her hostage
at gunpoint for several hours. During what must have been the most
terrifying hours of her life, Ashley did something extraordinary; she took
advantage of the opportunity and witnessed to her captor. She cooked
him breakfast, read from Rick Warren's book The Purpose-Driven Life,
and told him about God's plan for his life. She told him about Jesus.
Later, the man gave himself up to the police.

Colossians 4:5 reminds us, "Be wise in the way you act toward
outsiders; make the most of every opportunity." I believe God gives us
opportunities to witness often, but we let them slip away because we are
not wise enough to see them for what they are. Paul says we are "God's
workmanship, created in Christ Jesus to do good works, which God
prepared in advance for us to do." God will place good works before
you in the form of opportunities to share your faith and your story with
people who need to hear it.

As this year closes and you enter the New Year, are you willing to
make the most of every opportunity (no matter how unusual or strange)
that God gives you?

# They're Good Plans

*"What a wonderful thought it is that some of the best days of our lives haven't even happened yet." – Anne Frank*

*"I know the plans I have for you," declares the Lord, "plans to prosper you and not to harm you, plans to give you hope and a future." (Jeremiah 29:11)*

God's plans have always been to prosper His people. He can transform ordinary events and difficult trials into key moments that help His plans to prosper. He is not out to harm us, but the dark moments we experience can be part of the most important lessons to help us grow nearer to Him. You may be ecstatic to see this past year come to a close. It may have been one of the toughest years of your life. But I think it's important to remember that God will use even the toughest of those times for your good and His Glory.

God's ways are not our ways. His thoughts are higher than our thoughts. His ways may be hard to understand, but His ways are all part of the plan that He has for your life.

God, thank You for bringing us safely through this past year. We trust You. And we believe that Your plans for us are good plans, plans to give us a hope and a future.

# Hope For A New Year

*"Hope smiles from the threshold of the year to come,*
*whispering, 'it will be happier.'" – Alfred Lord Tennyson*

*No one who hopes in You will ever be put to shame.*
*(Psalm 25:3)*

*D*ays away from the beginning of a new year, we look forward in hope to a year filled with potential and promise, but there may be some uncertainty as well. As we ponder the year that is coming to an end, most likely we are reminded of the changes that a year can bring – good ones, but also painful ones. What will this New Year bring?

What is your source of hope? Is it your job, your family, the lottery or your horoscope? The Bible tells us that if we put our hope in Jesus Christ, we will never be put to shame. Jesus has all power and glory. In Him we find victory, security and work completed.

May all your hope be in Him in this upcoming year.

Lord, in this uncertain world, we thank you for the comfort, peace and hope that we have because we belong to you.

## DECEMBER 30

# Let Us Run

*"Character is the ability to carry out a good resolution long
after the excitement of the moment has passed."*
*— Cavett Robert*

*Let us run with perseverance the race marked out for us, fixing our
eyes on Jesus, the pioneer and perfecter of faith. (Hebrews 12:1-2)*

*F*aith is a verb. Faith is a spiritual muscle that allows you to take action.
Faith is what will help you persevere even in the middle of difficult
circumstances. Faith is what will hold your hand as you step out with
courage and takes risks in this New Year.

Faith will enable you to see living possibilities where others see only
dead ends. Faith will give you spirit-eyes to see victory where those
around you see defeat. But, Jesus not only wants you to see with eyes
of faith; He wants you to "run" with faith. In other words, act on that
same faith.

"Let us run with perseverance the race marked out for us..." Jesus is
the perfecter of your faith. God is the author of your story. He's already
marked your journey on His map. This past year is not supposed to
look anything like this upcoming year. "Forgetting what is behind..."

Let us run!

# The Best Is Yet To Come

*"Strength shows not only in the ability to persist, but
the ability to start over." – F. Scott Fitzgerald*

*"Everyone brings out the choice wine first and then the
cheaper wine…but you have saved the best till now."*
*(John 2:10)*

The Christmas tree will be taken down soon. All the wrapping paper
has been thrown away. When I distribute the gifts on Christmas
morning, there's always an order in how I do it. I always save the best,
the biggest or the most meaningful until last.

That's how it was at the wedding at Cana. The banquet master didn't
know who had provided the new wine. He just knew that it was better
wine than had been served earlier in the evening. He also knew that this
was unusual. Most hosts serve the best wine first, but at this wedding
the best was served last. This miracle of Jesus suggests something to us
about the Kingdom of God. God always saves the best for last. The
blessings we experience in our life with God, the freedom that comes
with His forgiveness, and His goodness are all just a taste of the new
life God has promised in Jesus.

As the year ends, we look forward in hope, for…

THE BEST IS YET TO COME!

# FINAL THOUGHTS

*M*y friend,

I can call you friend because we've just spent a year together! I pray that Arise, My Love has been a blessing to you. May you never forget that you are loved and chosen. God has a purpose and a plan for your life. Arise and take another step towards the promise He has for you. Stay in His Word, talk to Him and stay connected to the Body of Christ. And, as my River Girls know so well, don't forget that "where the River flows, EVERYTHING will live!"

May the Lord bless you and keep you; may He make His face shine on you and be gracious to you; may the Lord turn His face toward you and give you peace. (Numbers 6:24-26)

Your sister and friend,

Christy Sawyer

Made in the USA
Monee, IL
15 January 2020